220

CW01604832

R. Gilboa studied at Tel-Aviv University and gained a BA in English Literature and History of Art, and an MA in History of Art. She then came to Manchester University for a PhD, her thesis eventually transforming into *Intercourses in the Book of Genesis*. Now working as an architectural designer, she lives in Tel-Aviv.

Collingwood College
South Road
Durham DH1 3LT
Tel. 0191 374 4500

INTERCOURSES IN THE BOOK OF GENESIS

Mythic Motifs in Creator–Created Relationships

R. Gilboa

The Book Guild Ltd
Sussex, England

This book is sold subject to the condition that it shall not, by way of trade or otherwise, be lent, re-sold, hired out, photocopied or held in any retrieval system or otherwise circulated without the publisher's prior consent in any form of binding or cover other than that in which this is published and without a similar condition including this condition being imposed on the subsequent purchaser.

The Book Guild Ltd.
25 High Street,
Lewes, Sussex

First published 1998
© R. Gilboa, 1998

Printed in Great Britain by
Athenaeum Press Ltd, Gateshead

A catalogue record for this book is
available from the British Library

ISBN 1 85776 232 0

To Yarden and Yonathan

CONTENTS

VI. Reading Aids

PREFACE

This book is a simplified version of a Ph.D thesis presented to The University of Manchester; simplified only inasmuch as a fluent reading of text and footnotes is concerned. Otherwise, it retains much of the nature and virtues of an academic research because, to my mind, there is no other way to convey an intricate and complicated subject within *The Book of Genesis*, a book which has been and still is discussed.

The leading concept of this book is the realization that a good research does not terminate discussion by proposing final answers, but rather offers suggestions for further discussion. Therefore, I do not intend this suggested interpretation to be THE final answer to the meaning of some issues in *Genesis*, but rather a possible beginning for a new outlook; one which, I hope, will assert the logical nature of both the text and its philosophical outlook.

I am not presenting here something which is totally new; seeds of my arguments were scattered among various commentaries to which I am greatly indebted, even to those whose opinions I have finally rejected. While picking up ideas, I also added something of my own and 'created', in the *Genesis* sense of the word as I explain it, a new perception. I do hope that the final result will cause others, as it did my son Hed, to say: 'Thanks for releasing *Genesis* from the hold of theology and bringing it back to me'. It was this kind of attitude, shared also by others, which encouraged me to continue in my unconventional approach to its unconventional conclusions.

ACKNOWLEDGEMENTS

I am greatly indebted to the University of Manchester and its Department of Middle Eastern Studies for supporting the research as far as they could: Mr. Leon Yudkin who accepted the somewhat eccentric subject and supervised the first stages of the work, and Prof. Phillip Alexander who corrected and helped in its final stage. Thanks are due also to Dr. M. Weitzman (Department of Hebrew and Jewish Studies, University College, London) for his illuminating final remarks.

Mrs. Rina Refaeli (Hebrew University, Jerusalem) was always handy and cooperative whenever grammatical and linguistic issues arose; Dr. D. Mendels and Mrs. G. Gershfeld contributed their 'innocent eye' and proofread the text.

A note of gratitude is hereby sent to my supportive friends who were happy by the prospect of the publication of this book and landed a helping hand (Y. Padan and Sh. Stempler) or their encouragement P. & A. Mendels. A special note of gratitude to Prof. B. Abrahamson who practically initiated my voyage into *Genesis*.

This book was realized due to the combined efforts of my 'other half' G. Gilboa, Y. & Sh. Greenhouse – each contributing a part in the publishing process, and last but not least – The Book Guild publication team.

ABBREVIATION OF PERIODICAL TITLES

Abr Naharin – Melbourne, Australia.

AOAT – (Alter Orient und Alter Testament), Sonderreihe, Germany.

AJSL – (American Journal of Semitic Languages and Literature), Chicago

AUSS – (Andrews University Seminary Studies), Barrier-Springs, MI.

ASLL – (American Journal of Semitic Languages and Literature), Chicago.

BA – (Biblical Archaeology), Michigan, U.S.A.

Biblical Archaeologist, Philadelphia, PA.

BR – (Biblical Review), Washington, D.C.

BAR – (Biblical Archaeology Review), Chevy-Chase, MD.

Beer Sheba – (Pub. of Ben Gurion University), Beer-Sheba, Israel.

Beit Mikra – Jerusalem.

Biblica – Roma.

BIBIll. – (Biblical Illustrator), Nashville, TN.

BT – (The Bible Translator), Aberdeen, U.K.

BTB – (Biblical Theology Bulletin), New York.

BSa – (Biblioteca Sacra), Dallas, Texas.

Bz – (Biblische Zeitschrift), Paderborn, Germany.

CA – (Current Anthropology), Chicago.

CBQ – (The Catholic Biblical Quarterly) Washington, D.C.

Criticism and Interpretation – (Pub. of Bar-Ilan University), Ramat-Gan, Israel.

CTQ – (Concordia Theological Quarterly), Fort Wayne, IN.

Dor LeDor – Jerusalem.

Hagut Bamikra – Jerusalem

Harvard Theological Review, Cambridge, Mass.

Hebrew Studies – Madison, WI.

Hibbert Journal (The), Edinburgh, U.K.

JAAR – (Journal of the American Academy of Religion), Chico, CA.

JANES – (Journal of Ancient Near East Society of Columbia University), New York

JBL – (Journal of Biblical Literature), Chico, CA.

JETS – (Journal of the Evangelical Theological Seminary), San Diego, CA.

JNSL – (Journal of Northwest Semitic Languages), University of Stellanbosch, South Africa.

JQR – (Jewish Quarterly Review), Merion Station, PA.

JSOT – (Journal for the Study of the Old Testament), Sheffield, U.K.

JSS – (Journal of Semitic Studies), Manchester, U.K.

JTS – (Journal of Theological Studies), Oxford, U.K.

Leshonenu – (*Leshonenu La'am*), Jerusalem

LB – (Linguistica Biblica), Bonn, Germany.

NTT – Nederlands Theologisch Tijdscrift), Wageningen, Nederlands.

OTA – Old Testament Abstracts, Washington, D.C.

Prooftexts – (A Journal of Jewish Literary History), Baltimore.

Religion – London.

Scripture – Scripture Bulletin.

Semeia – Chico, CA.

Shnaton – (*Shnaton Lemikra Uleheker Hamizrah Hakadum*), Jerusalem.

Tarbitz – Jerusalem.

TBT – The Bible Today, Collegeville, MN.

Theological Studies – Baltimore.

TNB – The New Blackfriars, Oxford, U.K.

VT – (Vetus Testamentum), Leiden, The Netherlands.

Supp. VT – (Supplementary to Vetus Testamentum), Leiden.

ZAW – (Zeitschrift für die Alttestamentliche Wissenschraft), Berlin.

TECHNICAL NOTES ON PRESENTATION

1. Notes and footnotes
– the explanatory footnotes are marked by asterisks; they clarify the translation and the eclectic choice made from various options.
– numeral footnotes are purely bibliographical references which do not contribute to the discussion. They are gathered in a separate chapter at the end of the whole discussion.

2. Paragraphs inside the regular margin of the text indicate a clarification of a specific issue.

3. Printing signs
– emphasis within the text is given in italics.
– single inverted commas signify a subject; double inverted commas a quotation. Thus, 'to work' or 'work' are the verb and the act discussed as subjects, whereas "work" is a quotation from a text.
– square parentheses, in general, are the writer's personal comments; round ones a clause within the discussion.
– Hebrew books – title is given in italics; Hebrew periodicals – publications given in italics.

TO THE READER

Naturally, as a text suggesting a different *and secular* understanding of *The Book of Genesis*, this book may appeal to students of Literature, Bible Studies, Hebraic History and – via its conclusions – of Philosophy and Psychology; in short – the Humanities.

On the other hand, and this is what I hope for, it also may become a literary companion to anyone outside academia who is willing to accept *The Book of Genesis* not only as part of the Canon of Scriptures, but as a magnificent pure literary text.

For what I have suggested here is to join me on a literary journey of discoveries; to participate in a voyage of the kind that geographical pioneers undertook whilst being driven by forces which were not always within their control, using basic technical means and, thereby, pursuing an idea. This literary journey started in the same manner: armed with a native speaker's command of Hebrew, a relatively wide knowledge of the Bible, and profound studies of contemporary literature and methods of analysis – I pursued the idea that the ancient text of *Genesis* has more to offer than commonly perceived.

The first drive toward this idea emanated from the impression I had, since my highschool days, of pure logic projected to me by the story of the creation of a world in the first chapter. Then I asked myself if such a logical, almost scientific story (which, surprisingly enough, corresponds to Evolutionist theories of the late 19th Century more than the following Greek, Roman and

Medieval scientific perceptions) may still be considered as "just a legend".

The second drive emanated from my error in analyzing the Biblical term "TIMSHAL-BO" (The Cain Afair) during a lecture I gave in Adelaide, Australia, twenty years ago. The issue is presented in John Steinbeck's *East of Eden*, in the amazing anecdote of three elders of a Chinese clan who, in their Eighties, learn Hebrew and start an inquiry into this very term. Their problem, as is ours even today, is the relationship between Man and Sin: does Man rule Sin, or *vice versa*? And if TIMSHAL-BO was intended as '*capacity* to rule Sin', as some interpreters suggest, then why was this 'capacity' not applied to YIMSHAL-BAH, when stating that Man rules Women?

The third drive emanated after years of reading and rereading *The Book of Genesis*, resulting with the profound conviction that the elements of unity of the text as a whole, are stronger than those which may point to disunity created by an assumed compilation of sources. And if the unity of the text is accepted, then the logic of the first chapter should prevail all along, even into parts which have obvious legendary elements. This unity may indicate a text with a unifying common core to all its parts.

While comparing the Hebrew text to several English translations and reading many interpretations, I found that perceptions of the meaning of text vary and, what is more important, that there are several opinions on the basic factor – WHAT is actually written in it. Illusions about a fair command of Hebrew as sufficient means to approach the text were shattered when I realized that it is not enough, and that the Biblical language suggests more options for interpretation than a superfluous reading assumes. But no interpretation, known to me so far, suggested *a unifying secular logic core* of the kind that I found in the first chapter of *Genesis*.

I decided to take my own journey, not knowing to where it would lead me. I did not attempt to treat all of *Genesis* but rather to look into its main subject-matter: intercourses between God and His created ones – 'Creator–Created Relationships', as the subtitle suggests. The idea I was pursuing in this voyage was: to find a logical unifying core in the explicit and implicit meanings of the stories, that is – in the literary meaning and in the esconced universal element (the mythic motif) of the three stories of the created entities: a world, human beings and a nation.

Armed with technical means of literary analysis, with findings in linguistics and psychology that previous researches provided, I started the slow investigation of every crucial word and sign in the Hebrew text, avoiding literary and conceptual prejudices of any sort.

The parameters of my research are laid down hereafter for the benefit of a diligent reader. However, if one is not willing to enter into the arguments of each parameter, I would suggest to turn to the conclusions (page 27) that summarize the methodological approach of this research.

As suggested on the jacket, this book offers a ground for a different, secular and free reading, of *The Book of Genesis* and of its focal events: *The Garden of Eden, The Battle of the Yabbok* and *The Binding of Isaac*. Moreover, the found nature of creator–created relationships suggest the total liberation of Man, a kind of freedom and responsibility that so far Man is unwilling to take.

Chapter I
INTRODUCTION

A. Presentation of the Topic

Aiming to find WHAT is written in *The Book of Genesis*, and thereby to discover its explicit and implicit meanings, requires some elaboration on the nature of the book and the above engaged terms regarding 'meaning':

From a literary point of view, Genesis is generally regarded as an expression-in-writing in the form of accumulated traditional stories by which the Jewish people perpetuated their history. The terms 'story', 'narrative' and 'account' are preferred because they imply neutrality with regard to genre (terms such as 'legends' or 'myths' are avoided, and the reason will be clarified below).

As traditional stories, Genesis is the equivalent of other traditional stories which depict other peoples' histories[1] and in many respects it presents themes and motifs which can be found in other sagas:

> 'Saga' is "a long narrative..." (O.E.D.). A saga, thus, might have several legends (or as preferred here, several stories). Regarded as saga, some parts of Genesis are often compared to the Babylonian saga of Gilgamesh. In both cases, each saga presents several issues, each of which might be regarded as a story.

When stories of different origins suggest common literary characteristics, philosophical meaning or moral lessons, we assume that they correspond to a human common core which unites different people by the same spiritual need; in other words, if traditional stories of different origins present the same theme, then we can say that this theme is a universal one. The kind of literary expression capable of projecting a universal common core is usually called "myth" or "legend" (O.E.D.). In common use of words, we tend to look at legends as tales concerned essentially with the life, problems and aspirations of ordinary people, whereas myths concern or cross the borderline between men and Gods.[2] The literary borderlines, however, are not clearly defined and the alternative, therefore, is to abandon altogether genre-definition and to conclude that what we are dealing with is simply a narrative.

The narrative's continuous attraction as a long-lived traditional story lies in some quality within its nature — an implicit particular and universal essence which, in this book, is termed "*the mythic motif*" (to be elaborated further on). Some of the stories in Genesis, especially those belonging to the 'creation' category, are considered myths because they have acquired a universal importance, despite the variety of interpretations concerning their meaning or aim.

Multiplicity of interpretations will always arise when the existing ones do not correspond to acute contemporary human needs. The fact that the narrative is there, enables "the fantasy of mankind [to take] over the creative continuation of the mythical events" suggests H. Deutsch;[3] in other words, human imagination then takes over the kernel of the traditional story and, regardless of its original function, meaning or historical context, adapts it — through interpretation, different emphasis or extended legends — to contemporary needs. These mythical stories, thus, are paradigms of the continuing human situation and we, by our subjective interpretation, are involved in them.[4]

With regard to myth-interpretation, two factors have to be taken into consideration when attempting to find the "true" meaning of a literary narrative and thereby its mythic motif:

1) It has to be carried out *on the basis of the literary text examined*, regardless of its assumed origin.

This approach contradicts a popular tendency of the early 20th Century. E.g.: T. Reik[5] looks for the interpretation of the Biblical Fall-Story via some assumed reality of a primordial era, in the dawn of history, which preceded the time of Yaweh's concept, and into the evolutions of its religious ideas. I doubt if all these are relevant to the Genesis narrative because, as it seems to me, his psychoanalitic approach overshadows and ignores given details, the literary work and its possible meanings.

The effort, I believe, should be directed toward discovering the meaning that a subjective writer who "took over the kernel of the myth" is trying to convey. The discussion on a given text, thus, aims to examine how it appeals to or serves the reader and not to trace its roots, evolution or derivation.

2) Whatever is finally suggested as its meaning is bound to be subjective, reflecting the interpreter — his conscious and unconscious prejudices, and his methods — despite an honest attempt at objectivitiy. Subjectivity, therefore, applies also to our intended journey.

The topic of this book, within the above stated limitations, is to look into one issue in Genesis, "creator-created relationships", through three phases narrated in their corresponding chapters: creation of a world (1-2:3), of humankind (2:4-4), and of a nation (various chapters and verses, stated in due course).

Through linguistic findings and literary research, this book aspires to find the mythic motifs in these creation accounts, *as they have come down to us in their present form*, and to see whether the emerging motifs convey a coherent philosophical idea. But what do I mean by "mythic motifs"?

B. The Mythic Motif

The mythic motif was defined (p. 4) as a quality in the nature of a traditional story, commonly regarded as 'myth'; hence my semantic choice of the term "mythic motif" for this quality. *The mythic motif,* therefore, *is an essence in the narrative* and not a literary part of it; that is why it may be found also in other literary genres, and another reason added to the previous ones (p. 4) for altogether abandoning genre-definition.

The above presented perception of the mythic motif requires elaboration about the mythic essence, namely — about the nature of the narrative which has it, and about the process by which to expose this nature. For the discussion on both issues, I would like to address G.S. Kirk's comprehensive presentation in The Nature of Greek Myths,[6] because it surveys opinions on and approaches to myth-investigation since the beginning of this century.

Kirk presents two different approaches to myth-investigation which, in their final conclusions, may be termed as 'the function' and 'the psyche'. The first group presents five theories, all sharing a common trait: they comprehend the nature of the narratives in relation to the circumstances and purpose in which they were told and of the service which they render to the community. The 'functional' aspect of a story, thus, may be: a) nature myths — meteorological and cosmological phenomena (animism, personification, anthropomorphism — all these underline the idea of nature Gods and myths in the physical world;[7] b) aetiological — implying a cause or explanation of something in the real world (myths as a kind of primitive science);[8] c) charters — a set of perceptions or rules for customs, institutions or beliefs;[9] d) spiritual revival — establishing, in some sense, *the creative era*, the element of Golden Age wishfulness;[10] e) ritual — a close association with, or even derivation from, rituals.[11] Kirk argues that while each theory may answer for the nature of some stories, none of them embraces all that is defined as myth.

The second group regards myths as "products of the psyche", meaning: they are held to be primarily concerned with feelings of the individual, where even the objective functions of the 'functional' theories are really secondary to the *psychological needs* of the individual or the society.[12] Three main theories are suggested: a) Aristo's idea of *catharsis*;[13] b) Freud's "wish-fulfilment fantasy";[14] c) Jung's "collective unconscious" as embodied in the archetypes.[15] Kirk's reservations towards this group are the same as towards the first one, namely — while each theory may answer for the nature of some stories, none embraces all that is defined as myth.

Kirk's opinion on the subject of the elusive element within myths, the quality which elicits them and other traditional stories is, that it

> "should be associated not with a special mode of mythical expression but with the overall subject-matter, or even the special circumstances in which they are told" (p. 88).

His appreciation of the psychological trend is reserved for the relations, found by Freud, between dreams and myths, but with a certain reservation:

> "If myths resemble dreams in their dislocation of events, it is not for the kinds of psychological reason envisaged by Freud [the Oedipus Complex, i.e. the sexual drive]. Rather I suggest that the dislocation of everyday life is in itself life-enhancing and liberating" (p. 90).

The complexity of finding an all embracing theory for the nature of myths is evident in Kirk's cited conclusions: he unites, or mixes, their functional (the special circumstances in which they are told; their subject matter), and psychological (the dislocation) facets. While rejecting Freud's explanation of the last one, he comes close to Aristo's idea of the catharsis effect (liberating) as the nature of myths.

The key to the understanding of the full meaning of myths, however, is ensconced within Kirk's confusion: if, according to his conclusion, the complexity of myths is such that, at the end, it is a mixture of the functional and psychological, then the way to understand them should be through untying the complex into its components, a Freudian method which Kirk, apparently, overlooked. Freud suggests[16] that there are two levels which *together* constitute the full meaning of a narrative: *the explicit meaning*, which corresponds to the cultural, social and moral needs of the collective (the functional, in Kirk's survey), and the implicit one, *the hidden meaning* which projects the roots of the human psyche (the psychological, in Kirk's survey).

The explicit meaning which projects the subjective understanding of given collectives at given times, therefore, is a subjective component in the interpretation of myths, whereas the implicit meaning projects the objectivity of basic universal human mental needs, that have not fundamentally altered throughout human existence. C.G. Jung's parallel concept to Freud's 'hidden meaning' is 'the collective unconscious' and he explains that he had chosen the term 'collective' because "it is not individual but universal... it is, in other words, identical in all men and thus constitutes a common psychic substance of a personal nature which is present in every one of us".[17] Being universal, suggests C. Lévi-Strauss, it is also eternal: "it explains the present and the past as well as the future".[18]

Psychological studies suggest several possible meanings for the essence of narratives regarded as myth, usually in accordance with Freudian or Jungian theories mentioned above, and in this research they will be applied regardless of possible disputes in the discipline of psychology, inconsistence with one theory or the other, but in accordance to what seems to correspond to the nature of the text. Suggesting one meaning for a narrative, however, does not exclude the validity or possibility of others, as is the case with the several suggested meanings of the Oedipus myth.[19] As already stated, whatever the suggestion — it merely projects the subjective tendencies of its author.[20]

In order to find the mythic motifs in the narratives in question, our first step — following Freud's advice — will be to look for the explicit meaning of the content, and then to attempt to find its latent implication. Hopefully, it will be a modest contribution to the present state of research of Genesis, an outline of which is hereafter presented.

C. Notes on Previous Research on Genesis

As a start, I am paying a tribute to all the unmentioned sources that were rejected for various reasons, but indirectly helped me to consolidate my arguments. Respect is due also to sources that directly helped me in this journey, by adding to or confronting my arguments; they are hereby elaborated upon:

Commentaries and interpretations of the Bible go back to the first translation from Hebrew, the Septuagint, in the 1st century B.C. However, as an *academic* discipline in the modern sense of the word, the starting point may be taken as that of comparative analysis. The first work which corresponds to this category is J. Bryant, A New System of Analysis of Ancient Mythology contradicted later by C. Bradlaugh, Genesis: Its Authorship and Authenticity.[21] The discipline reached the phase with which we are concerned by the establishment of "Higher Criticism" with J. Wellhausen's Geschichte Israels (Marburg, 1878).[22] A further academic attempt to find the true meaning and nature of Biblical myths, those of Genesis in particular, developed when Anthropology discovered their universality,[23] "Comparative Mythology" exposed the common social-psychological root[24] and

Psychology applied its interpretational methods in order to explain their nature.[25]

The extensive data up to the present time makes it a virtually impossible task to relate to all aspects of the findings on Genesis and, for the purposes of this research, some self-imposed limitations on available material are in order. The findings of Biblical research, therefore, are considered on the basis of the following limitations:

1) The main body of sources used are books and articles of the last twenty years, and several earlier ones, interesting for the way in which they illuminate issues under discussion;[26] dissertations from all parts of the world, deposited with the National Library in Jerusalem, have also been consulted.

2) The reference commentaries, summarising the opinions and trends of interpretations of the last century which will be referred to, are: J. Skinner, Critical and Exegetical Commentary On Genesis,[27] [hereafter — Skinner] which gives a full account of research from the late nineteenth century until 1930, and also includes Rabbinical sources; mainly the extensive work of C. Westermann, Genesis 1-11 and Genesis 12-36,[28] [hereafter — Westermann, in the English translation] which has a presentation of previous ideas and a summary of German research up to 1974. The third reference book of this category is E.A. Speiser, Genesis [The Anchor Bible; hereafter — Speiser].[29] Unfortunately I was not able to relate to two recommended interpretations of Genesis: due to language limitations — A. Shöckel's and, because this book was ready to be printed — to the very recent R. Alter's.

The common denominator of the books mentioned above and most of the sources cited favourably in them, is their adherence to Wellhausen's Documentary Hypothesis.[39] Their approach, for all their modifications of Wellhausen's original assumptions, supposes that Genesis is a compilation of several sources/documents written by different authors:

> From the four authors suggested by Wellhausen (J, E, P, D), there have emerged several sub-divisions and combinations (J_1, J_2, P_1...R, etc. The last suggestion, R, seems to close a circle with the traditional view, inasmuch as it regards the book to be the work of one author — a redactor, identified by the Swedish commentator I. Engnell[31] who marked him R^{jep}.

For the convenience of our discussion only, and acknowledging its vast generality, this group of interpreters will be referred to henceforth as "The European School".

A different category in this school, developed during the Eighties and mainly in America, focuses its attention to literary theories on *form* structural and post structural. As I am interested in *meaning*, only conclusions that add to our repository of meaning were included. The same applies to findings in Feminist Interpretation.[32]

3) The Hebrew commentators U.D. Cassuto, The Book of Genesis (a commentary on),[33] (which includes Rabbinical sources and presents views held until 1943; hereafter — Cassuto), and Y.M. Emmanueli, The Book of Genesis,[33] (which relates also to interpretations published in Hebrew until 1976; hereafter — Emmanueli),[34] reject the Documentary Hypothesis and regard the book as a product of one author. For the convenience of our discussion only, and acknowledging its vast generality, this group of interpreters will be referred to henceforth as "The Jerusalem School".

In this book I mention these two main schools but, as stressed above, this is a generalizing division which stresses only the problem of author v. authors/documents (acknowledging that there are others[35]). These definitions and divisions might be misleading: not all European Scholars adhere to the Documentary Hypothesis (and even among them there are several schools of interpretation), as not all Israeli scholars reject it. The tag "Jerusalem" (not to be confused with the Hebrew University!) is convenient because of its traditional connotation which ascribes Genesis (and the Pentateuch) to an author; "European" — because the opposite opinion developed there.

The European School tends to look upon the creation stories as legends,[36] and attempts to interpret them in accordance with what it believes to be the "Sitz im Leben" of the contemporary literary workshop responsible for the text in question, where the four groups of authors' workshops (chronologically) are:

> J — the Jehowist, around 8th century B.C.; E — the Elohist, 7th century B.C.; D — Deuteronomist, 620 B.C., the period of King Josiah; P — the Priestly, 6th century B.C., the second Judean exile period.[37]

The Jerusalem School tends to emphasize the historical aspects and the moral implications of the stories in what may be labelled "Biblical personalized monotheistic perception"; thus Cassuto's common expression is "the Pentateuch speaks...rejects...means" as if he is dealing with a single entity's conception, beliefs or values. The same attitude is evident in Buber's writings,[38] but he expands the scope of 'personality' to the whole Bible — "the Bible speaks..." etc.

Neither school seems to pay much attention to the implicit meanings of the narratives — to their mythic motifs. Therefore, in this book, and it will be my contribution to the research of Genesis, I intend to look into this somewhat neglected field of research on the part of both schools. I will follow the Jerusalem School inasmuch as its perception of "one author" is concerned (and the reasons why will be clarified later on), but free of the school's heavy religious-moral emphasis. The European School's findings will be included only inasmuch as secular objective methods and findings of literary analysis are concerned.

The intended research is on a book; the voyage is through a text. But what is this text?

D. The Book and Its Author

The aforementioned two Schools present different opinions about the text — its authorship and antiquity. The European School regards Genesis as a relatively late patchwork (around 700 up to 500 B.C.) combining several sources and authors. The historical events and scientific data were regarded as legends projecting the authors' intentions and serving the spiritual purposes of the workshop which had composed the text in question. However, in the wake of archaeological discoveries which, in many cases, were found to correspond to written data in the Bible,[39] the European School began to take archaeology into consideration and now pays greater respect to historical and scientific references[40] in the text.

The Jerusalem School, on the other hand, retains the Jewish tradition that Genesis is the work of a single author belonging, at the latest, to the early Kingdom years (1000 B.C.)[41] and some still regard it, on grounds of sociological probability, as Moses' work (around 1300 B.C.).[42] The events described are regarded as historical and as reflecting a true panorama of the period.[43]

The dispute in the field of historical criticism on the origins of Genesis is outside the scope of this research which aims at a literary analysis of the current text. However, a choice of an historical standpoint is imperative because it constitutes the starting point of literary comparison: if the views of the European School are envisaged as the nature of Genesis, then any incoherency, doubling of passages, changes in style or what seems to be a lack of continuity, may be attributed to or justified as an outcome of editorial work; comparisons with contemporary literature may encompass the ancient period until the late 5th century B.C. If the alternative views of the Jerusalem School — of one author of an ancient era — are taken, then all the intricate (so called) deficiencies mentioned above, have to be solved and interpreted through the text (assuming that an author is conscious of what he is doing). In this case, comparisons with contemporary literature, preferably, would be mainly with the Sumerian and Egyptian. (The popular source is J.B. Pritchard, Ancient Near Eastern texts Relating to the Old Testament; hereafter — ANET. Other sources consulted — Note 44). The Babylonian texts, such as the famous "Enuma Elis", the Babylonian epic of Gilgamesh, or the flood story of Atrahasis,[45] despite traces of Sumerian origins, are relatively late to the extent that a suggestion of Hebrew influence might be in order:

> Most common comparisons to Biblical data are with neo-Assyrian (900-700 B.C.) and neo-Babylonian (700-400 B.C.) material, ruling out older Near Eastern sources.[46] Even if one rejects the Mosaic period as the date of composition and assumes that it belongs to the early period of the Kingdom (1000 B.C.), then the expansion of Kings David and Solomon could mean that Hebraic influence was felt in the vicinity of the Euphrates.[47]

The main claim against the supposed antiquity of the Genesis narratives (as it emanates from several articles) is that they are less elaborate, demythologized versions of their predecessors. But, as R.A. Kitchen points out, the rule is that simple accounts or traditions may give rise to elaborate legends, not vice versa; therefore, "it is more likely that we have the original report in Genesis (whatever form this might have taken until writing was used) from which all others derived".[48]

The Canaanite myths are irrelevant, in spite of linguistic and structural similarities between Genesis and Ugaritic literature, because ultimately their subject-matter differs immensely from Genesis.[49]

For the purposes of *a standpoint of literary analysis*, I prefer the more intricate alternative, and choose to cope with the textual difficulties rather than justify or explain them as an outcome of "documents". My research, therefore, is based on the assumption that *one author in an ancient era is responsible for the basic perception of the unvowelled book*[50] (as can be seen in the scrolls in synagogues), and I have chosen to limit literary comparisons to Sumerian and ancient Egyptian compositions.

But the complexity of the literary nature of the text requires further clarification: the text examined is not the unvowelled one but the current vocalized one; Aharon ben Moshe ben Asher who (around the 10th century A.D.,[51] following oral and written tradition of its reading) added the vowels and gave it THE final form we now use, had a great influence on its content. Because vowels determine the ultimate linguistic forms of a text otherwise open to several possible meanings: the well known dispute about the first words of Genesis results from a possible vowelling of the verb BARA בָּרָא as BeRO בְּרֹא (discussed in the second chapter of this book). The time gap between the first stage where, as stated above, "one author of an ancient era is responsible for the basic perception of the unvowelled book" and the last stage where the voweller, the last authority, is responsible for the finality and the character of each minute detail, leaves us with an unclear perception: who is the author? Therefore, and for the purpose of the analysis of the current text, J.P. Fokkelman's definition of the accumulated editorial line of 'Him' as "*the narrator, or the creative writer, responsible for the final version of the text*"[52] reflects the approach used here, whenever the general title "author" is mentioned. It is immaterial whether there was an original author or a redactor who used whatever sources were available, and by 1300 B.C. there was a great body of traditional stories and their versions from which to borrow. If a narrative deals with 'creation', it is bound to find parallels or correlations with one or more accounts of the same subject-matter. Admitting, or even proving, a possible influence of other cultures on the Biblical narratives does not diminish the creativity and originality expressed by the Biblical author, even as an editor of earlier drafts who adds intentional changes.[53] I agree with A.R. Millard who suggests that one should be careful with automatic allusions of sources to the Biblical text because "when all is said, parallels prove nothing".[54]

The text's originality is expressed by that element which distinguishes mechanical copying from creative borrowing and, as I hope to show in due course, that element (added to a different cultural perception which the text projects) is what makes Genesis a conceptual book which far transcends its sources.

This stated attitude prevents us from relating to 'author's intentions' in the text we analyse and leaves us with 'what the text projects'. The relevant question, therefore, is not 'who is the author' but rather 'what kind of *Culture* the text projects', meaning — what is *the attitude of a mind* at work *which determined the* philosophical *values* expressed in the text (the cultural aspect is discussed further on p. 25). "A mind at work", whoever's mind, is an individual mind; and as philosophy (as a discipline) did not exist in ancient Hebraic life, we may assume that what emerges from the text is only *a personal philosophy* — a personal perception of values and attitudes. Jewish philosophy as a discipline, or rather philosophical movements among Jews, began about the 2nd century B.C.[55] In any case, Genesis cannot be regarded as philosophy in the academic sense of the term, because as W.F. Albright suggests: "There is no technical philosophy, or anything approaching it, anywhere in the Old Testament".[56] Any philosophy developed later on, claiming to be grounded in the text, is but its beholder's interpretation and does not necessarily reflect the cultural attitude of the author of the current Genesis.

And the current Genesis is the text that we intend to examine in order to find a coherent philosophical attitude conveyed in it. The actual text is the traditional Hebrew one based on the Leningrad Manuscript, the common Bible in its Massoretic form, regardless of other versions.[57]

The leading translation chosen is that of the poetic King James [K.J.], as modified and modernized in Y. Leeser's The Holy Bible [L].[58] This translation influenced the spelling of Hebrew names in this book and it was constantly compared with the Revised Standard Version [R.V.] and The Anchor Bible [Speiser].

Biblical verses are rendered here in such a way as to convey, as far as possible, the Hebrew syntax and thereby the original stress of certain words, rather than insisting on the use of idiomatic English.[59] Whenever one of the above sources is used it is indicated as such; when the need was felt, an alternative translation was offered, and no source indicated.

Having stated parameters of our topic, of the explicit and implicit (mythic) meanings that we intend to find, of the author and the text — we now have to discuss the method by which this voyage into Genesis is going to be conducted.

E. Aspects in Methodology

Introduction

In this part I deal with approaches and literary means to be implemented during our voyage into the text; it is not on methodology *per se* but, eventually a method of a kind is formulated.

There are several methods of literary analysis of Biblical texts,[60] but as none of them in particular will be engaged in this research, their characterization and the dispute about the validity of each method[61] is redundant and beyond the scope of this book. The general public is often confused by literary methods that have become a science in itself, with its specific jargon, where minute differences excuse the definition of a separate new "ism". For those intrested in the validity and shortcomings of each method, I would highly recommend M. Weiss' discussion in his introduction to The Bible From Within.[62] Weiss presents a comprehensive panorama of literary methods and I fully agree with his reservations, having nothing meaningful to add. At the most, I combine different approaches in order to achieve better understanding of the text[63] and eventually reach Weiss' suggestion of "A Total Interpretation". At the end of the day, what matters is the result — the insight we gain from interpretation.

The 'method' chosen for this research resulted from Genesis chief problem: unlike a literary analysis of almost any narrative where the text is indisputable but interpretation is debatable, the dispute about a Genesis narrative starts with the mere written text, due to the archaic and ambiguous language. The first step, therefore, is to determine WHAT is written in the narrative and then to analyze it.

The intended starting point is — clarification of words and their possible meanings, suggested also by R. Alter.[64] It is followed by relating the word and its chosen meaning to its contextual juxtaposition within the sentence and the passage. The assumption is that an analysis of a part has to be related to and compared with what appears in the text as a whole. Therefore, an inquiry into words and idioms and a comparison with other places in Genesis, is often needed in order to understand the text in question. This process, in some of its parts, resembles a detective plot where the reader has to look for and accumulate hints before deriving a conclusion. It may sound difficult, but I hope to be able to convey the sense of discovery that I felt while undergoing this process.

I avoid classifying the suggested approach as a specific known method (or to form a personal "ism") because, as said before, I intend to engage whatever methodical device that might help to clarify and illuminate problems. As a result of this, no two chapters in this research are the same and each one has its own subtle characteristics, justified by the nature of the narrative.

A more acute point, however, is to clarify the complexity of the general outlook of the intended voyage, i.e. — the philosophical basis and aspects on which it stands. In spite of an attempt to objectivity, the approach presented here is bound to be regulated by personal feelings and cultural prejudices. Therefore, elaboration on my philosophical approach and its aspects — literary, religious and cultural — are in order:

The Literary Aspect

A fundamental point that needs to be made, is that if we assume the text of Genesis to be the work of a single author, even if he is a mere story collector or final redactor, that author deserves the credit of being looked upon as someone who is conscious of what he is doing. This is a strange statement hardly ever referred today to a contemporary author. But such is not the case toward the author of Genesis:

> Remarks of a philosophical nature, such as: "the Biblical writer repeats the Babylonian formulation, *perhaps without full awareness* of the theological implications" (Speiser, 13, emphasis added) are out of place, the more so when Speiser adds afterwards that "at all events, the text should be allowed to speak for itself". If the text speaking for itself shows no consideration for theological implications, one may assume that the writer had no theological considerations.
>
> Less respectful is an approach stating "that the writer of Genesis *probably did not completely comprehend the ideas embodied in the words he used*", enabling the interpreter not to be "restricted by the *limited insights* which he [the Genesis author] had."[65]

Another kind of remark concerns the literary merits of the writing, when it does not withhold expectations: “while the author of Genesis tells us how the world was created, taking the trouble of giving all kinds of details, *he seems to have forgotten* the time element”.[66] Well, if the author does not relate to time elements, then the reasons as to why, should be sought within the text and not be regarded as mere forgetfulness.

The cornerstone of this research is that the author of Genesis was conscious of what he was doing. He is as aware as we are, of possible duplications, incongruous linguistic expressions, a lack of subject-matter continuity and incoherent paragraphs which spoil the literary wholeness. Therefore, whatever literary incoherence seems to exist in the text, *as it stands*, has to be solved within its own frame; shortcomings are mainly those of the interpreter and rarely those of a conscious author. Elimination of the notion of “documents” forces one to pay greater attention to the final stage of the text — to punctuation, vowels, compounds; in short — to every linguistic detail and printed mark in the text. This approach is suggested by N. Leibowitz, a great and well known Israeli Biblical scholar,[67] who ascribes it to the Rabbinical tradition of Rashi, Rambam, Rashban and others, and praises their seriousness toward the written word, “every word... not only the big ones, but to their juxtaposition, syntax, repetitions... to all that is said, *and unsaid*” (a free translation, underlined in the original). I do not accept her last unemphasized words which I have put in italics; they epitomize the Drashic tendency (the free interpretation) of the sources she cites. For the purpose of this paper and its line of thought — “all that is said”, suffices.

It is customary, and logically justified, to compare words and paragraphs of different books of the Bible in order to clarify meanings or difficult passages, and almost all commentators do so. Although a comparison between Genesis and Ezekiel and other books[68] might be an interesting literary exercise, still, one has to be careful before deriving definite meanings in words, conclusions on cultural attitudes (this happens when a "biblical theology", into which all parts of the Bible fall, is assumed[69]) or dates.[70] I intend carefully to apply comparisons with other books only when the Genesis text and its vocabulary do not provide an answer to a linguistic problem.

My brief comment on Methodology, referring the reader to Weiss' discussion on the subject, may be repeated in regard to genre.[71] But as recent researches, to a large extent, are devoted to 'form' (including genre-form) and, naturally, do not provide a satisfactory arguments of its redundancy, there is room for a brief comment:

It is impossible to define a literary genre for Genesis due to the diversity in the composition as a whole, as well as that of each account. It has already been argued that any genre-definition is immaterial (p. 4), and since the book preceded academic literary definitions, *it is of little importance for the understanding of the text* whether it does or does not correspond to any of them. A different opinion is expressed by G.W. Coats, who divides the book into genre-pieces while, at the same time, admitting that the technical terminology, whose terms have been drawn from fields of literature outside the O.T. applies only with a limited degree of accuracy. Moreover, any a priori classification determines the interpreter's attitude because, as Coats suggests: "It makes some difference in how we read a piece of writing, if we know in advance [its genre]. Precisely this is what creates a prejudice in advance and leads to misleading and misinterpretation afterwards".[72] Coats, as might be deduced, is torn between his literary habit of classification, and his realization that in the case of the Bible it is of no importance or, perhaps better said, dangerous.[73]

In respect to my reservations of 'genre', I would like to conclude by citing N. Frye's comment: "two conceptions of genre, however, are obviously fallacious... one is the pseudo-platonic conception of genres as existing prior to and independently of creation... the other is that pseudo-biological conception of them as evolving species..."[74]

A dubious outcome of genre-definition emanated from relating to Genesis as folk tales: the founder of this approach is H. Gunkel,[75] and it resulted by followers regarding the book as "folklore" and the era as "primitive".[76] This kind of genre-relationship developed into comparisons with the Grimm Stories, which invited an evaluation as to whether Genesis corresponds to a similar pattern; and when it did not — the Biblical text was assumed to be corrupt![77]

To sum up the literary aspect of the suggested method for our voyage, I would like to stress again that the aim of this paper is to find the meaning of the narrative which will lead us to a better understanding of its mythic motifs. The literary qualities of the book were extensively discussed by many;[78] elaboration of artistic merits will be discussed only when it serves to clarify content.

The Religious Aspect

This is a very complicated aspect because most of us regard Genesis as part of the "Holy Bible". A different approach is presented here.

Genesis, I suggest, cannot be regarded as scripture, *if scripture is understood as a separate entity of religious literature*, for the simple reason that the word 'religion' does not exist in Hebrew of the period:

> A misleading Hebrew word is 'דָת — DAT': the origin is probably Persian and in the Bible it appears only in the book of Ezra.[79] But 'DAT' means 'law', and the epithet 'אדם דתי — ADAM DATI' describes one who observes the laws. Those

laws (of a later period than the pre-exilic era, let alone the assumed Genesis era) concern aspects of everyday life as well as ritual ceremonies, but for the layman they have very little to do with philosophy or religion. A Jew can believe in God and yet not observe those laws or, what's even more confusing, to observe the laws and pay little consideration to 'belief'. Therefore, the concept of scripture (religious texts) is alien not only to the language but also to its cultural core.

It is not easy to understand that even today Judaism is not a religion in the common sense of the word ("a *system of faith* and worship", as suggested by Westermann[80]). The contemporary system of faith in what is today regarded as Judaism, "The Articles of Faith", was laid down by Maimonides (14th century), and the question of belonging to Judaism only comes up if one's behaviour contradicts them; 'belief' thus is a personal attitude between these borders, and is not equivalent to 'religion'. More so in Biblical times — there is very little in Genesis to point to a system of Faith. Although later generations canonized the text, it does not contradict the fact that it existed as a narrative long before the canon and did not serve as "Holy Writ". The amazing phenomenon in this respect is the total silence of the prophets regarding *The Book of Genesis* or to its data. Thus, when Jeremiah wants to evoke the ancient notion of adherence to God, he recalls the wanderings in the desert (2:2):

> "I remember unto thee... thy going after me in the wilderness" [Leeser]

and not what later on and until today, in canonized Genesis, is regarded as the epitome of faith — The Binding of Isaac.

If, therefore, 'religion' as "a system of faith and worship" can be only partly applied to Judaism even today, the concept of 'scripture' was hardly the case when Genesis was written. Moreover, the word KADOSH (קדש) and its use for holy texts ("KITVEY KODESH — כתבי קדש") do not convey the Christian notion of "Holy" which, as R. Otto suggests, is to stand for "this element of isolation, this 'extra'... *above and beyond* the meaning of goodness (Numinous)".[81] This is not the case with the Hebrew 'Holy':

> KADOSH is "designated or dedicated for, or distinguished from".[82] 'To be holy' then, is to be set apart; in spoken language it is also used in a secular sense. Thus, Bible books are 'distinguished', or 'set apart' from other books; people and God, the Bible tells us, both are holy (Lev., 19:1):
>
> "...ye shall be holy, for I your God am holy".
>
> This practical *and relative* concept of KADOSH has been observed by the great Jewish philosopher B. Spinoza (1632-1676), the first to apply secular attitudes to Biblical research. Spinoza stated that words have meaning in accordance with their usage: 'Kadosh and Divine' are valid as long as people relate to it with respect; but if they are to 'set apart' a criminal act, the previous Kadosh-thing is desecrated".[83]

Therefore, Genesis as literature, for the purpose of this research, stands for the text free of whatever religious connotations that later eras and cultures added or applied in order to satisfy their cultural needs. Any attempt to discover what the text meant when it was first written, therefore, has very little to do with how it functioned when it was first recognized as authoritative or as a part of the ritual of reading it, at the beginning of each year, as part of the reading of the Pentateuch.[84] And the same applies for theology. It is rejected because, as Westermann noted, the biblical primeval story "has given very little attention to talk about human civilization, and even less to its theological significance."[85]

This secular attitude implies that a literary approach to Genesis does not differ from that toward Shakespeare. God, for the purposes of this research, is but a persona in the text and there is no room to assume for him, a priori, qualities or motives that are not written into the very body of the text. Thus, regarding the creator as immaculate, omnipotent, omniscient, etc. is a supposition that has to find its grounds *in the text* and not assumed in advance.

The forthcoming discussion will argue this issue.

The Cultural Aspect

"Culture", for the purpose of this thesis, was defined (p. 16) as "an attitude of mind which determines values", and I am greatly indebted to R.H. Wilenski[86] for it. As there are more than 164 definitions for the concept,[87] the above stated choice requires justification.

> The term 'culture', in the humanistic, social and anthropological studies, is almost regularly confused with, or understood as, encompassing various manifestations of 'civilization'. Thus, no proper distinction between the two is suggested in (what is termed as) its classical definition:
>
> > "Culture *or* Civilization, taken in its wide ethnographic sense, is that complex whole which includes knowlege, belief, art, moral, law, custom, and any other capabilities and habits, acquired by Man as members of society".[88]
>
> Another facet of this unclarity is evident in the inclusion of physical, spiritual and abstract notions in this or other definitions; e.g. —
>
> > "Culture may be defined as behaviour particular to *Homo Sapiens* together with material objects used as an integral part of this behaviour..."[89]
>
> The anthropologist F. Boas was aware of this confusion, and pointed out that it is customary to describe culture as material culture, social relations, art and religion; on the other hand, *ethical attitudes* and rational activities have been hardly touched upon.[90] His approach of differentiating between 'civilization' and 'culture' is today an anthropological trend which terms it "Society and Culture".[91]

I chose to follow Boas' line, and recognize the distinction between the abstract (culture) and the material/social (civilization) because it befits the history and nature of the Jewish people who, once upon a time, wrote the text under discussion:

While one may be able to discuss Jewish culture or even Hebraic-Biblical culture, there is no such entity as Jewish or Hebraic civilization. Social aspects of the civilization of the Jewish people throughout their estimated history of 4000 years did not differ from the people amongst whom they lived, while their ethical attitude of mind which determined different values, created a different culture; 'culture', therefore, is the factor that binds them, and people in general, together[92]

The definition chosen, *an attitude of mind which determines values*, is the most condensed phrasing found, which projects Boas' approach. Boas says the same, as can be seen by the words emphasized, but uses more words:

> "'Culture' may be defined as the *totality of the mental* and physical reactions and activities that characterize the *behavious* of the individuals composing a social group..."[93] (emphasis added).

To what extent does the Biblical culture as expressed in Genesis differ from our own? The philosophical tradition usually regarded the development of civilization and culture as a straight line moving from a primitive state toward the more advanced one.[94] While this outlook has been rejected inasmuch as social or artistic manifestations are concerned,[95] it seems still to prevail vis-à-vis the Bible. The interpreters of earlier periods are considered more familiar with what is sometimes viewed as 'the primitive' cultural outlook of Biblical times,[96] merely because they lived in, technically, less advanced civilizations which were chronologically closer to Biblical times; if one omits the tag of "primitive" — this is mainly a traditional Jewish attitude.[97]

This research adopts the contemporary outlook which regards the development of culture and civilization as the movement of a pendulum; it acknowledges *repetitive modes of thinking* (reached by a state of mental crisis[98]) *that result in a similar state of social affairs*. Therefore, an interpretaton given in European, Byzantine or Islamic cultural environments, bound by religious restrictions of the early Middle ages (and both Jewish and Christian exegesis and hermeneutics developed from that time onwards), does not necessarily elucidate, better than we do, a state of mind which prevailed almost two thousand years earlier. On the other hand, an interpretation given by an unprejudiced mind of the 20th century, (according to the concept of the pendulum-movement of historical development), may be culturally closer to what I regard as the autocratic mind of the author of Genesis. F. Boas says on this issue: "The fewer the number of *traditional elements* that enter into our reasoning, and the clearer we endeavour to be in regard to the hypothetical part of our reasoning, the more logical will be our conclusions"[99] (emphasis, mine). We may continue with Fromm's note: "Perhaps, paradoxically enough, one of the oldest books of Western culture can be understood best by those who are least fettered by tradition and most aware of the radical nature of the process of liberation going on at the present time"[100] and may conclude in Irwin's: "For rooted and moulded in the centuries of the ancient East, Israel yet far transcended them and attained a world of thinking and of concepts much like our own".[101] The Genesis author seems to be of that high standing to be able to create, in the midst of a given set of cultural attitudes toward the phenomenon of creation and in spite of them, an individualistic and unique cultural saga of his own.

F. The Methodological Approach

The above discussed attitudes present a self-imposed method of interpretation, hereby summarized:

The principal topic in each chapter is the nature of the Creator-Created relationship. Through this topic I hope to reach at the explicit meanings of the creation stories and ultimately at their implicit mythic motifs.

The philosophical basis of the intended voyage is in accordance with the following perceptions, already discussed at length:

1. The Genesis text analyzed is the current traditional manuscript.

2. The text, for the purpose of a literary analysis, is regarded as having been written by an "author" who, as stated on p. 20, is responsible for the final version of the text. The findings of the research, therefore, relate to 'what is expressed' in the current form of the text, assuming its unity.

3. The text is to be examined as a secular narrative, free of prejudices about its assumed literary nature or religious orientation. God, therefore, is but a literary persona in it.

4. The analysis of the protagonists and their acts is carried out with no prejudices about an assumed cultural 'Sitz im Leben'.

5. The mythic motifs found are those suggested by known psychological trends; there is no intention to digress into psychological debates.

6. All the suggested interpretations on the above stated perceptions have to be supported by and grounded in *the text and the text alone*.[102]

The research is presented in the following stages:

1. The discussion of the creation accounts will be carried out in three chapters, a chapter for each, according to their chronological order.

2. Each creation account will start with a summary of the narrative and followed by an analysis of key words in the text. As there is no intention to plunge into philology (see appendix, p. 241), the discussion of words will be limited to a choice from among possible meanings, relevant to the issue in question,

examined within the frame of their syntactical content, and related to the paragraph as a whole. When the Genesis text does not offer a linguistic solution, and only then, other Biblical books will be consulted. A brief explanation for this process is given in aesterics in the text-body.

The constant companions for this semantic choice are Mendelkern's *Concordancia* (hereafter — Concordancia);[103] for the Hebrew reader — Steinberg's Hebrew *Bible Dictionary* (hereafter — Bible Dic. This work was preferred above more recent ones because it is the most established dictionary in Hebrew. Its grammatical approach may be somewhat anachronistic (it suggests also two-consonant roots) but, in comparison with other dictionaries, including English ones, it seems to provide a wider range of linguistic possibilities. For the English reader: Hebrew and English Lexicon of the Old Testament (hereafter Eng. Dic.).[104]

Bergsträsser's comprehensive *Hebrew Grammar*;[105] the Hebrew translation (by M. Ben Asher) which I use is the textbook of the Linguistic Dept. in the The Hebrew University of Jerusalem. As stated in its German title, it updates the work of Kautzsh on W. Gesenius' (which was transl. into English by A.A. Cowley in 1910, and is still in common use). These comprehensive works expand the linguistic scope of the research beyond the self-imposed boundaries of Genesis and, indirectly, tie it to the whole Bible.

3. The concluding chapter will look at the findings of all the creation accounts in order to find whether their meanings and mythic motifs convey a coherent philosophical idea.

Well — these are the parameters to guide us in our journey to which *we must take* a Bible-companion. I do hope that my readers will have an enjoyable time and fruitful research and, like me, will find a new perception of the nature of "Creator-Created Relationships". I would be most grateful if I am to receive your response and comments, in writing, or to "e-mail: dian@netvision.net.il".

Chapter II
CREATION of a WORLD

A. Introduction

Most literary approaches to the creation story in *The Book of Genesis* classify it as a record, and the question whether it is an historically true scientific record is irrelevant for the purposes of a literary analysis.

I agree with E.K.V. Pearce who says: "A person could write a book on a non-scientific subject, and yet give evidence of a background knowledge of science".[1] And indeed, while comparisons are made between elements in Mesopotamian and Biblical accounts of creation whose affinity is indisputable, their scientific nature tends to be forgotten.[2]

As an historical record or, better said, as a record which its author believed to be of an historical nature,[3] it is said to be written in a prosaic style that eschews the personal and emotional, in which the wording is minimized to the point of austerity. Nevertheless, this style was recognized by all as implying a sense of grandeur and drama.

While accepting the evaluations of the literary impact of the text, there may be doubts which require elaboration on a) the basic assumptions about its literary nature and b) eschewing the personal and emotional.

a) The ancient scrolls texts were written unvowelled and unpunctuated and, in order to economize on space, they were arranged in sequence of consecutive unversified phrases — as prose. The same literary printing form, and for the same reason of space-economy, continued at a later period when the Biblical text was divided into sentences*, not necessarily of clear or constant metric composition, but still — enabling a poetic presentation of shorter, rhyming or rhythmical lines. The prosaic presentation is still used in contemporary Bibles where the Jewish tradition of of punctuation, TE'AMIM** (employed also as singing notes), could suggest a different division of lines. A fluent reading of sentences laid down in the conventional form usually conveys the misleading sense of prose. This is how modern Hebrew readers read it and, in spite of the singing, the same applies to what is read in synagogues; in most parts of the text it sounds as sung prose rather than sung poetry. And that is how chapter 1 in Genesis was translated into foreign languages, even into the relatively poetic King James version.

> The question of style is raised already by *Skinner*.[4] For him, poetry is imagination, intensity of emotion and elevation of language, and in those respects the stories "do not even rise to the level of impassioned prose". H. Gunkel likewise, states that "Genesis is prose".[5]
>
> The confusion about the stylistic and generic nature of the chapter of creation, as I sum it up, corresponds to W.F. Albright's conclusion that it is "a special category of its own, which originally has been poetic in nature..."[6]

A celebrated attempt to use the TE'AMIM in order to find the literary qualities in Genesis is that of Cassuto where, within

* Verse (O.E.D.) is a metrical composition in poetry, but also a numbered subdivision of a Bible chapter. In order not to confuse the two — "sentences" has been used here.

** Altogether there are 26 signs, more than those in modern use. But customary signs as colon, semicolon, question mark etc. are not part of TE'AMIM, and their place in the sentence is deduced by the content [as done by Speiser in Genesis, the Anchor Bible].
See: J. Blau, A Grammar of Biblical Hebrew, 19-21. For a brief account, see: *Emmanueli*, 33-36; a table of TE'AMIM: Ibid., 36.

the prose, he exposed poetic elements extending beyond the apparent alliteration deriving from repetitive words or similar sounds of vowels at the end of sentences. Cassuto mainly considered the three major TE'AMIM but, as may be seen, they are unsystematically applied in what seems to be his intentional grouping of short lines and orderly phrases.[7] His method does not always result in a constant and clear rhyming or metric system,[8] but nevertheless it brings out *the poetic nature* of Genesis.

Regarded as poetry, the quotations in this book, as well as the suggested translation of the Hebrew text, pay systematic consideration to TE'AMIM,* and present the verses with attention to what should have been the traditional layout, and thereby

* The signs to be considered *and marked* in this research:

The main ones ("Caesars", in Hebrew), placed under the word, are: a sign which indicates a complete sentence — a stroke which appears under the last word of the sentence and thus is the equivalent of a full stop; a sign which breaks the sentence into its main parts — an inverted 'Y' which appears under the last word of the part (probably equal to a semicolon). In verses cited in this paper, the presence of the Caesars indicate new lines.

Within the parts of each line, there are three phases of pauses (in Hebrew: "Kings", "Deputies" and "Lieutenants", in order of their respective lengths) of which only the two degrees of the "Kings" are considered: the three first signs above the relevant word [the common xxx, less common xxx, xxx] indicating larger pauses, expressed in the cited verses by a space gap between it and the next word; and two shorter and frequent pauses [xxx, xxx] rendered as a comma.

This self-imposed attitude, to a large extent, correlates with the "families" suggested by D. Weil & D. Cohen ("Progress in Deductive Research On the Original Performances of Tiberian Accents", 12), only it takes in consideration one mark of the third "family". The other phases of shorter and shorter pauses are ignored because they cannot be rendered into a modern method of punctuation.

analyzing them; this, at the expense of shorter or more modular poetic phrases.

b) Regarded as poetry, the Genesis story of creation tacitly projects also the personal and the emotional, even when it is in the technical presentation where everything is measured to a point of austerity. Poetry, I suggest, always reflects the personal and emotional, even when the author is unknown or, as suggested for the case of Genesis, the last in the line of authors who contributed to the formation of the current text. *The final product of poetry, regardless of its genesis, is ultimately a reflection of an individual state of mind and its philosophy.* An attempt to find the meaning of the poetical narrative of creation, therefore, has to regard it as the product of an individual mind that, whether it does or does not conceal personal feelings, *it reflects personal involvement and perspectives.* Among those perspectives one may point to cultural influences which are projected through motifs, around which the author composed a very individual narrative and, quite often contradicting in essence, that of the borrowed material.[9]

B. The Narrative

The narrative is literally conveyed by an omniscient author. As he was not present at the actual time of creation, he tells what he knows of the creator's acts. It is usually taken to be a story of an omnipotent creator whose actions in a span of time resulted in a spatial state of affairs.

The text (1-2:4) tells of a creation by presenting a sequence of tasks performed within a cycle of seven periods, where physical acts are performed only in six. The seventh period contradicts the others by being a restful one and is juxtaposed at the end of the sequence, thereby becoming the climax of the narrative.[10] The number seven, its uses in the narration of the event and its details, is another literary device which emphasizes the narrative's poetic nature.[11]

The chronological order of the created objects, each in its period, is known: light; firmament and seas; land and sky, flora; heavenly bodies; creatures of sea and sky; land creatures and humanity. As it stands, this sequence may present a scientific order of evolution as it was understood at the time,[12] but a literary attitude implying a meaningful harmonic order is also suggested:[13] pairs of periods in which the second contextually corresponds to the nature of the ground laid down in the first period:

1) light	2) firmament and seas	3) land & sky, flora
{	{	{
4) heavenly bodies	5) water & sky creatures	6) land creatures.

The presentation of tasks performed proceeds in accordance with a basic structure: introduction of the object to be created, statement of the actual act that takes place, naming, explanation of the intended function of the created items and the idiomatic expression of satisfaction.[14] This outline is not applied systematically to every task, but has variations which stress different characteristics of the works and their nature.

C. Word Analysis

Introduction

Before approaching the stage of interpreting the text, there has to be a coherent and *common* understanding of what is written in it — what words and idioms mean. Hence the necessity of an analytical introduction to clarify linguistic problems characteristic of, and relevant to, this chapter (for the methodological approach, see Chapter I, pp 27-29.). This method, in my research as a whole, results in a divided discussion on words: first they are dealt with only in their linguistic aspects and their possible meanings; then they are discussed in their context in the verses, where they perform and contribute to the content. Thus, בָּרָא is first examined in word-analysis for its meanings in general, and then discussed as it functions in the verses. The literary analysis of this book, therefore, moves 'from the parts to the whole'. It presents a different approach to the one suggested by Fokkelman who says: "we should *first* investigate the kind of interaction between prose and poetry... from the whole to the parts: a structural approach" (emphasis added).[15] An important clarification of three fundamental issues, valid throughout the research, is in order at this stage:

a) The most characteristic feature of Biblical Hebrew is the use of the letter Waw which precedes conjugated verbs: *the waw+verb precedes the noun in the sentence.* It is called וָו הַהִפּוּךְ — Waw Inversive, because it indicates an opposite tense to that of the conjugated form.[16] This Waw is the most common stylistic feature of the Biblical syntax, but more often it has linguistic meanings other than 'and',[17] and the tenses it indicates are determined by its juxtaposition and the patterns created by its successive use.

b) *Waw attached to a noun and followed by a conjugated verb* is interpreted in two ways:[18]

1. as a stylistic feature which emphasizes the noun, usually by juxtaposing it at the head of a sentence;

2. as a grammatical form intended to indicate the past perfect, thus describing events which occured *prior* to the one told.

The choice of an alternative, therefore, determines the interpretation of the order of events in a paragraph.

c) Biblical Hebrew, unlike modern Hebrew or other modern languages, is complicated because it is a concrete language lacking explicit expressions for abstract all-embracing concepts: it was already pointed out that 'holy' and 'religion' in their transcendental meaning did not exist, and their equivalent Hebrew terms imply a sort of 'distinction' and a very concrete set of 'rules', respectively. Other relevant concepts such as 'Time' and 'Space', discussed below, have in the Bible a non-abstract, concrete meaning: the non-spatial conception of time follows simultaneously a temporal conception of space; words connoting all-embracing space or time are entirely lacking.[19] This Biblical approach of relating to the concrete, to the practical and relevant in life, should make one alert whenever one is inclined to connote words in Genesis with a broader meaning than that pertaining to practical subjects, and this problem is manifested at the very beginning of the Bible — the first story of creation.

Time

The very first word in Genesis indicates a certain mode of time. It is usually translated "In the beginning",[20] but the particle 'the' is not part of the Hebrew text; the person who vocalized the word saw fit to give it an indefinite sense of time and not the sense of the all-embracing transcendental occurrence: בְּראשִׁית — Be'RESHIT, not בָּראשִׁית — Ba'RESHIT,. Assuming that the voweller was conscious of what he was doing, and this is the approach stressed again and again in this paper,[21] one cannot apply a cosmic interpretation to a text which avoids the cosmic. Therefore when the text states: "בְּראשית ברא אלהים", it means to say only what is written: "in *a beginning* God created...".[22] The problems of whether there were other beginnings or when was THE beginning (a question scientifically yet unsolved) are irrelevant for the story, and the practical text, by the very words used, seems to avoid unsolvable problems by relating only to an undefined time and a beginning that concern it.

The next ambiguous expression regarding Time is יום — YOM. In idiomatic use it means a period of 24 hours, usually deduced from the phrase:

וַיְהִי־עֶרֶב וַיְהִי־בֹקֶר יוֹם אֶחָד

(1:5b) And it was evening and it was morning, one day,*

The common interpretation is based on the deduction that God acted in light, and then came evening (in which he supposedly did not act), followed by the next morning which together form a 24-hour day. This logical deduction is based on the assumption that creation occurred according to known physical phenomena of Time, but neither the assumption nor its deduction are stated clearly in the text. On the contrary — the previous verse states 'day' as an expression of a physical state of light:

וַיִּקְרָא אֱלֹהִים לָאוֹר יוֹם...

(1:5a) And God called the light Day...

'YOM', thus, is also a light-period and there is no indication of how long it continued in terms of hours: after the light comes evening followed by morning [presumably, swallowed in between, is the dark called 'night' (1:5b), but this is not stated]. What is described as "and there was evening, and there was morning", therefore, is a literary use of realistic terms which do not necessarily correspond to time reality; it is but an idiomatic expression for recurring periods, regardless of actual Time.[24]

'Yom' understood as 'a period' and not as a 24 hours' cycle, enables one to comprehend the expression of 1:5b cited above as a literary idiom, and the same pattern of the creation "days" can be understood as undefined periods.[25] This suggested interpretation offers the text a more logical essence which will be elaborated in the forthcoming discussion on meanings.

* "יום אחד" is translated in all the English versions used here as "the first day", but the text does not say the equivalent of first — רִאשׁוֹן. The text's use of the cardinal number 'one' — one day, as suggested in this paper's translation, is because the ordinal form 'first' denotes a place in a series which, at this point in the text, does not exist. Only after the next period is there a 'second' day.[23]

The Earth אֶרֶץ

'ארץ — Eretz' means literally the opposite of sky[26], and the verse states clearly that at a beginning the two opposites were created. It is not the story of the whole universe, not only because the word universe has no Hebrew equivalent[27] but also because that would imply an all-embracing space which apparently was not a concrete enough concept for the author to deal with. The story thus tells about one definite and relevant world which includes its earth on which we stand and its sky (rendered by the letter-particle 'the' which makes it definite, known to us — הַשמים והָארץ — Ha'SHAMAIM Ve'HaARETZ) and they, regardless of other possible earths and skies[28] are the center of this very story — not the center, in the metaphysical sense, of all creation. 'Eretz', however, has many subtle uses and they will be discussed when the verses concerned are presented.

To Create .ב.ר.א

The Hebrew root '.ב.ר.א BARA — to create' is used only in reference to God, and this is an undisputed linguistic fact to which commentators agree. Skinner points to an added fact, that no other ancient language has a verb designating acts which refer only to the deity.[29] The verb was given the disputable meaning of 'creatio ex nihilo', probably because according to a much later monotheistic perception of the deity, He is the only one who can create something out of nothing. But Steinberg's *Bible Dictionary* suggests for this root a more concrete meaning: origination of things, i.e.: conceiving a new spiritual or material state of affairs by transformation.[30] Which meaning regarding the acts of God — creatio ex nihilo, physical or perceptual origination — should apply, is determined by the context in which it appears, and text of Genesis provides us with a clue:

The creation event, in an acknowledged poetical convention,

is introduced and concluded (1:1, 2:3) with the same verb BARA which therefore has the same meaning in both cases. In 2:3, the last Hebrew verse includes both the conjugated verb BARA followed by the infinitive לַעֲשׂוֹת — La'ASOT (to make); this is a grammatical pattern in which the main physical act comes second.* The first verb in BARA La'ASOT, therefore, cannot be an actual act but rather a non-physical one, a conjugated verb which connotes intention and serves as an auxiliary to the main act of 'making'.[31] The structure of the whole paragraph points at the same direction:

(2:1)	Thus were finished the heaven and the earth, and all their host,	
(2a)	And God assessed** on the *seventh day*	his *work*, which he *had made*;
(2b)	and he ceased on the *seventh day*	from all his *work*, which he *had made*.
(3a)	And God blessed the *seventh day*	and distinguished it; ***
(3b)	because thereon he ceased from all his *work*	which God BARA *to make*.

* The grammatical pattern of verb + infinitive, in which the main part of the component is the infinitive, is called in Hebrew: נשוא מורחב (see: H. Dahan, The Paths of Language, II, 7). The verb is either an intention-verb (to wish to, to ask for, etc.) or a verb of physical act which, in such a combination, connotes an intention. The Biblical ברא לעשות — BARA La'ASOT is the same pattern as contemporary עמד ללכת — AMAD La'LEHET; a Genesis example: "הולך למות" — HOLEH La'MUT (25; 35).

Parallels in English: he is going to make it easier for you; I stand to lose a great deal.

** The rendering of "assessed" (in 2:2a) is argued later on, where the Sabbath is discussed (p. 57-58).

*** As a result of the discussion of the word Kadosh (p. 24), I hesitate to use Leeser's "sanctified"; it is correct only inasmuch as it conveys the sense of 'set apart'. A wrong translation, thus, is "and made it holy" (B. Vawter, On Genesis: A New Reading, 62).

The poetic structure of the suggested translation brings out, in the first part of the sentences, the accentuation on the seventh day, in the second part — the act of 'to make'. "BARA", as can be seen, is swallowed at the very climax of the narrative. The structure and the syntax of the poetry, thus, deny the great importance bestowed upon the verb BARA, justifies its auxilliary function and asserts its interpretation as 'originate/conceive' while excluding the connotation of creatio ex nihilo.[32] The same meaning of this verb, as said before, should be applied to the first opening verse — as a non-physical act. The rendering of the verses is suggested as:

(1:1) In a beginning, God *conceived*...

(2:3b) ...for on it he ceased from all the work which God had *conceived* to make.[33]

The above analysis of the expressions of Time and Earth, and the meaning of the verb BARA, give us a starting point to look into the text where they operate. We are now journeying into the very text where the creator "creates".

D. The Omnipotent Creator

1. Introduction

Judging from the more elaborated myths of creation, it seems that the mere existence of wars between gods for acquiring a monopoly over the world[34] denies them *omnipotence in the monotheistic sense*, which means: the supreme omniscient power that precedes everything, and is bound by no one or by any natural phenomenon.[35] In most mythologies the gods are presented as mighty; but this, I suggest, is not equivalent to omnipotence. 'Mighty' is related to and circumscribed by natural phenomena even when the results dwell on the morbid or the unnatural;

omnipotence, as emphasized before, is autonomous. Omnipotence will be regarded in this research as the highest degree of power, beyond the reach or understanding of human capacity, whereas mightiness — as a more limited capacity, its attainability and understanding as being to a certain degree within the scope of human wish-fulfilment [Faust and this type of legend].

The author does not claim either omnipotence or mightiness for his protagonist. The answer to the question 'what kind of creator is described in Genesis' assuming that he is not invested with a priori qualities,[36] has to be drawn *from the nature of his acts*; (the nature of his products is irrelevant for this discussion, and although we shall have occasion to present them, they are not to be discussed). We will follow the acts in order to understand what kind of a creator the author of Genesis chose to present.

2. The Acts of Creativity

The author, as discussed beforehand concerning A beginning, avoids the problem of THE beginning and states the existence of A God-creator. The powers of this God are directed toward a very specific creation:

(1:1)	At a beginning, God conceived	בְּרֵאשִׁית בָּרָא אֱלֹהִים
	The sky, and the earth.	אֵת הַשָּׁמַיִם וְאֵת הָאָרֶץ
(1:2)	And the earth, had been...[37]	וְהָאָרֶץ הָיְתָה...

Unlike the above suggested division, in King James and the Revised Version the phrasing is that of a continuous sentence: "In The Beginning God created the Heaven and the Earth.", thus indicating that the phrase is considered as *an independent prosaic verse* and regarded as a general title which the forthcoming verses are to elucidate. The following verse 2, in their reading, is a new issue; its subject, the earth, is emphasized and juxtaposed at the head of the verse.[38]

A different reading is suggested by Rashi, turning the verb BARA into a construct noun בראשית בריאת — Be'RESHIT BRIAT,[39] thus making the first phrase into a temporal clause; this attitude results two alternatives:

1) Ibn Ezra relates it as a clause of verse 2, thus rendering the interpretation as: "at the beginning of creation of the sky and the earth, the earth was formless and void"[40]; it means that at first, chaos has been created.

2) Rashi relates the temporal clause to the third verse, and many modern interpreters follow him by regarding verse 1 as the protasis (the clause in conditional sentence that contains the condition), verse 2 as the subordinate clause containing the perfect (והארץ היתה — and the earth has been) and verse three as the apodosis which concludes "ויאמר אלהים" — and God said.[41] The reading of the three verses, thus, may be rendered as: When God began to create the sky and the earth — the earth being then without form and void — God said: let there be light!

Usually, the use of tenses in Hebrew is left to the writer's discretion[42], namely: the author could have expressed the first alternative by the pattern: בראשית בְּרֹא... ותהי הארץ or היתה הארץ and the second one as והארץ תהו ובהו omitting the verb.[43] But both alternatives, as well as the suggested English rendering of the clauses (e.g. The Anchor Bible) disregard one of the main traits of Hebrew syntax — the preference it gives to paratactic (coordinate) constructions over hypotactic (subordinate) ones,[44] as the structure of 1-3 presented in the text demonstrates, and as it has been rendered in my suggested translation.

The alternatives mentioned above show that, grammatically, there is no decisive answer to what is written in 1:1-3, and the fact that the Genesis text allows for several interpretations of verse's syntax, requires an examination of content rather than adhering, as Rashi does, to a grammatical formula: he systematically interprets the waw attached to a noun, in a context of actions presented in Ve'YQTL, as indicating the *past perfect*.[45] The implication of Rashi's clause, therefore, is that the earth *has already been* in a state of chaos prior, not at the time, to God's acts.[46]

Rashi's argument for turning the verb BARA into the noun BRI'AT and the interpretational trend which regards it as BRO do not appeal to me because what they eventually amount to is — to indicate a vowelling mistake. The attitude of this research, as repeatedly stated, is that the voweller was conscious of what he was doing, and that the text should be interpreted as it is presented. In my above rendering of verse 2 as: "the earth had been" I follow Rashi's notion about the tenses, but the justification for this attitude as well as the comprehension of the first three verses depend on, and will be found in, the literary premises of the text as a whole.

The content of verses 1:1-2, whatever their grammatical interpretation, offers two alternatives for the nature of God's act; not on types of creation[47] but rather on equivalent literary material relevant to the Genesis account:

A) If 1:1 is regarded as a general title or as a temporal clause of verse 2, then in the event of creation God originated a world out of nothing, 'creatio ex nihilo', where the first created object is characterized by a primordial disorder (v. 2). In this case he is omnipotent in the monotheistic sense because he preceded everything and created something out of nothing of his own volition, although the messy state of affairs raises the question of whether such omnipotence could not have put things in order straight away. A "created chaos" is perhaps contradiction, but this is what the text seens to indicate.[48]

The equivalent Egyptian story from Memphis[49] seems to support the creatio ex nihilo concept: the first god-creators Ptah-Nun and Ptah-Naunet "came into being as the heart and they came into being as the tongue" (the mind/will and the speech, respectively) in the form of Atum who practically "created himself" (Atum = totality). Thus, the primordial factors are not matter but abstract entities which preceded everything existing and which afterwards, together, formed one totality. This totality, in the complementary theory of Heliopolis, could be called matter: Nun (the water of chaos). But as the matter-word Nun is already included in the names of the creator Ptah, the Egyptian concept of the abstract creator seems to be somehow connected with a more tangible medium of matter.

B) If 1:1 is regarded as the protasis of verse 3, or if verse 2 is a remark on earth's state prior to God's acts, then disorder of the elements is a given primordial state, and God's acts are manifested by the order and growth that follow, starting by the command "let there be light". In this instance God is still powerful and creative but his unique power of origination is limited by the primordial matter at his disposal.

The Sumerian concept (around 3000 B.C.) is not available directly in Sumerian texts, unless the Akkadian ones are accepted as reflecting the ancient Mesopotamian tradition. But as the Akkadian texts available to us are, at the earliest, only from 1000 B.C.,[50] this is a late enough date for other cultural influences to have been assimilated into the Mesopotamian tradition (this point is argued in the previous chapter; p. 14). The beginning in the Akkadian "Enuma Elish" stems from two primordial factors — Apsu and Tiamat — who begot the gods; the Mespotamian answer to the state of the beginning, therefore, is that a hylic matter existed, out of which the gods and everything else were created.

The hypotheses — creatio ex nihilo v. hylic matter — are, even today, a subject of scientific debate. Adherence to one or the other trend is a question of fashion or, better said, a matter of perception of the deity, because at the same period different perceptions dictate different attitudes. A theological attempt to reconcile between creatio ex nihilo and the reduction of verse 1 to a secondary stipulation of the following verse is made by Eichrodt, who suggests that "the narrator is moved to reflection not by what preceded the divine creator, but by the fact that nothing but the autonomous decree of the transcendant God determined the form of creation. That the creatio ex nihilo thereby enters the picture is incontestable".[51] The conclusion of our journey regarding the question of God's omnipotence in the primordial state, as said before, will be presented at the end, following a presentation on and discussion of the full panorama of God's acts. But beforehand the linguistic nature of the acts has to be clarified:

If BARA is part of a title conveying a non-physical act (p. 43), then the first action-verb the text uses is "to be — היה" stated in the imperative form: "let there be...". This idiomatic form is followed by two patterns of its results:

a) "and so it was", where the text does not indicate any other kind of action. This pattern, "Let there be... and so it was", when it is not followed by an explanation of the actions, may be regarded the only one that expresses God's omnipotence in the monotheistic sense of the concept of creatio ex nihilo — God commanded and *it came into being*.

b) the suggestion "let there be" is followed by another action which specifies the kind of creation performed; the nature of the act is determined by the verb engaged.

The other verbs engaged are 'ב.ר.א.' — BARA and 'ע.ש.ה.' — ASA (and 'י.צ.ר.' — YATZAR in chapter 2) usually translated in the Eng. Dic. as 'to create', 'to make' and 'to form', respectively. There are two approaches to these three verbs:

a) as synonyms — all indicating physical actions[52]. If such is the case, then their juxtaposition is a mere case of literary variant which bears no weight on meanings. This is the approach taken by almost all commentators.

b) as different words, each having its independent meaning. If such is the case, then their juxtaposition is not a mere coincidence but has an important weight on meaning. This is the approach taken in this research, because the above discussion on the compound BARA La'ASOT distinguished BARA from the other two, identifying it as a *non-physical action* reserved only to God.

'To make — ASA', on the other hand, is a physical action which in Biblical language may be used about and by anyone; in relation to God, it means "to prepare and activate from what there is, in order to fulfil a function"[53], i.e., *creatio ex creato.* The subtleties of the three verbs are better recognized when engaged in one verse where, as in the compound above, each has to have its meaning — *Isaiah*, 43:7:

כֹּל הַנִּקְרָא בִשְׁמִי וְלִכְבוֹדִי בְּרָאתִיו
יְצַרְתִּיו אַף־עֲשִׂיתִיו׃

All that bears my name   and [whom] I have created for my glory;
I have formed, also made it.*

The verse cannot possibly mean that the three verbs are the same kind of action thrice repeated: "also" in the second part indicates that "formed" is not equal to "made". If the third distinction about BARA is applied, the subtleties of the three verbs in this verse convey the idea:

> "for my glory I have conceived it (BARA); I gave it a form (YATZAR) and [from existing elements] made (ASA) it to fulfil a function."

The above clarification of verbs denoting actions will direct the forthcoming examination of God's acts.

* Leeser's translation has another solution for the difficulty in rendering the pronouns and the sense that the singular is plural:

"Every one that is called by my name, and whom I have created for my glory;
whom I have formed; yea, whom I have made".

The main difference with the rendering suggested in this research, however, is the interpretation of AF: Leeser's "yea" creates an equilibrium in the second part of the verse, thus 'form' is a synonym of 'made'. My interpretation renders it, as its usual function in Biblical text, as "also" (see: <u>*Concordancia*</u>, 134), thus emphasizing that another act is performed.

3. The Acts of the Periods

The first act performed is the creation of light, and the author uses the first pattern with the verb 'to be' (v. 3): "Let there be... and there was...". The act, the text thus tells us, is performed by giving a command and there is no explanation as to its intended function, nor of how it was actually executed. Moreover — light is not mentioned among the elements of the possible primordial state of affairs (v. 2) and, therefore, the text as it stands implies that it is a *creatio ex nihilo*.

In the act of the first period the protagonist God is the omnipotent creator in the monotheistic sense because, as discussed above — a mere expression of his will brings things forth into being.

The second act is expressed by the second pattern with the verb 'to be', in which God expresses a wish "let there be a firmament...". But it is followed by an explanation on how it came into being: not by a mere expression of will, but by God's physical act (v. 7: "And God made...") of 'making' a product to its intended function. This implies that God was acting as a mere technician, using existing elements (perhaps of the primordial state) processing his creation, and in light of our definitions — it can not be creatio ex nihilo. Moreover, God does not accomplish his task in the schematic span of a period: the literary expression of satisfaction which indicates it — "and God saw... that it was good" — is missing at the end of the second period but appears when the task is accomplished in the third period (v. 10). In the creation of the firmament, the text tells us, God's act is restricted by the existing elements and by the span of time. Arguments about the discrepancy between the number of tasks and periods[54] seem to result from an ungrounded assumption that, like a children's story made easier to comprehend, the story of creation should have followed a simplistic pattern of one task per period. As the author must have been aware of the simplistic pattern, the lack of it should make one alert to its meaning: God does not make a world in a flash, as he does not complete his task in the second period.

In the act of the second period the protagonist God is bound by two factors and thus is not omnipotent in the monotheistic sense of the word.

The third period witnesses the accomplishment of the previous task which concerns the final stages of the earth and the sky (v. 9) and the accomplishment of another one — the flora (12). In the accomplishment of the second task God is only the activating force that commands the elements to perform by themselves: "Let the waters... be gathered", and the elements respond — as indicated by "and it was so" [Leeser] (v. 9). The same applies to the third act performed: the elements are asked to fulfil the potential ensconced within them: there is a command to the land to act — (v. 11): "Let the earth bring forth..." — and the land responds (v. 12): "And the earth brought forth...". Although the idomatic expression " and it was so" appears in both cases, it does not stand by itself, as in the case of light, but is followed by the acts of the elements.

In the third period the protagonist God is only initiating the actions which are performed by others, and there is no room to regard his act as omnipotence but rather as mightiness — he commands the elements of nature.

The narrative of the fourth period follows the pattern of verbs used in the second and tells of God the technician who, first, suggests the heavenly bodies 'to be' (v. 14), and then 'makes' them (v. 16) and fixes their place in order to fulfil their function. As said before, 'making' is the completion of a process and it implies use of elements that existed beforehand; the making of the heavenly bodies, therefore, is not a creatio ex nihilo.

In the act of the fourth period the protagonist God is a mere technician bound by existing elements; he is not omnipotent in the monotheistic sense.

The fifth period witnesses the first living creatures which came into being — sea and air creatures. The text has the verb 'ב.ר.א. — to create' (v. 21) "and God created...", and as suggested in the analysis of this verb, it implies that sea and air creatures were originated by God,[55] but a problem arises when the preceding verbs are analyzed:

The English versions commonly used to translate "יִשְׁרְצוּ המים" as "Let the waters bring forth" [Leeser; K.J.; R.V.], thus giving the Hebrew conjugated form a transitive meaning which implies that the elements are ordered to perform. But this is a faulty translation because the Hebrew conjugated form suggests *a future state of affairs* in a designated place (waters) and not an action to be performed: יִשְׁרְצוּ - YISHRETZU not יַשְׁרִיצוּ - YASHRITZU. Speiser's translation for the Anchor Bible restores the intransitive meaning of YISHRETZU by using the verb 'to teem': "Let the waters teem" [Speiser].[56] The following form BARA used after God's expressed wish for a certain state of affairs, indicates that God originated new kinds of species (living creatures); it does not elaborate on how the creation has been executed, because a non-physical verb is engaged. Do the expression of will, using verbs which are synonymous to the command "let there be", and the lack of physical action point to a creatio ex nihilo?

Not necessarily. According to the perimeter stated in the linguistic discussion of the verbs, the literary pattern that implies this omnipotence in this case is missing: the text does not say that God expressed a wish, *and it was so*, but suggests a divine intervention, be it a non-physical one — BARA, after expressing the will. This different pattern, I suggest, may indicate that the creation of living creatures required a special origination but the execution (which is omitted) did not differ, in essence, from the 'making' of other creations *because the text elaborates and specifies their intended function* (to make — ASA, has been defined as "to prepare and activate from what there is, *in order to fulfil a function*", p. 49). This conclusion may become apparent when the nature of all the works is estimated.

The sixth period has two acts of which the first does not imply creatio ex nihilo: the earth is commanded to perform and to produce the earth-creatures — (v. 24): "Let the earth bring forth..." — and afterwards God intervenes in the earth's performance and 'makes', (v. 25): "And God made..." that is: God completes the process of creating the creatures for their functions. In the second act the text — as in the case of air and sea creatures — uses the verb 'to create' regarding humankind (v. 27). And as before, concerning those creatures, it means 'to originate'. This conclusion is justified not only by the interpretation suggested for the verb BARA, but also by the preceding idiomatic expression where the protagonist does not express a wish by "let there be..." or commands the elements; He is suggesting "let us *make*... נעשה" (v. 26) which, as suggested for this verb regarding God's acts, indicates creatio ex creato and a mechanical completion of a process toward its function (in this case, to rule). The literary pattern of placing of the verb 'to create' (v. 27) after the suggestion 'to make' (v. 26) does not alter the meaning of the perimeter stated, because BARA does not stand alone in this very context; the change of pattern may point and even accentuate an origination of a new unprecedented concept of a Godlike form, totally different from the other creatures 'made' or 'originated' beforehand. The creation of human beings, therefore, is not a creatio ex nihilo, and a further discussion on humans is due in the next chapter.

In the act of the sixth period the protagonist God is an originator and a maker; but as he is "making" from existing elements, he is not omnipotent in the monotheistic sense.

4. Conclusion: God's Acts of Creativity

An accumulation of all the acts and their natures in the six periods, after which the world and everything in it came into being, presents the following exposition of the protagonist God and his powers:

a) Only the very first act in the first period bears the undeniable mark of omnipotence in the monotheistic sense — God creates something out of nothing, where his mere expression of will brings forth things into being. The first act, therefore, is "creation by word", and as such it parallels the Egyptian cosmogony:

> In the "Book of the Dead of Nesi-Khounsu" (a priestess of Amon, 1000 B.C.) the hymn to God resembles the Genesis concept: "the one, one who hath made everything which had come to existence since primeval times when the world was created. God *who made the heavens and the earth* by his will (or heart)".[57]

b) The mere fact that God did not accomplish his task in the second period limits God's powers to possible achievements within a span of time; this definitely is not omnipotence in the monotheistic sense.

c) All the acts until the fourth period are those of "making" or commanding the existing elements to perform by themselves. These acts, therefore, are "creation by action" and a mixture of patterns using three kinds of actions: origination — conceiving a new idea, a mechanical accomplishment of 'making' from existing elements, and commanding the elements to act or produce; in this sense, the acts of these periods parallel the Mesopotamian cosmogony:

> In the story "The Worm and the Toothache", the introductory

lines describe the creation of heaven as God's act, whereas the following elements result from each other.[58]

d) In the fifth and sixth periods, where living creatures come into being, the 'BARA' is designated for sea and air creatures as well as for humans. The intricate use of the verbs regarding the creatures is noteworthy: sea and air creatures are 'originated' (1:21); earth creatures are 'made' (1:25). This subtlety seems to point to a concept of evolution, i.e., sea and air creatures were first to appear and therefore it required origination of a new form of life, whereas the land creatures evolved.

The verb 'BARA' in both cases is engaged in different patterns than the one of the first act, where an obvious sense of omnipotence is indicated: in both cases there is no imperative result of "and it was so" as in the case of the light. The presence of both BARA and "to make" in the case of humans, denies their creation the possibility of creatio ex nihilo while justifying the alternative meaning of 'to originate'. The implication on the nature of creation of sea and air creatures, I suggest, should be regarded in the same light: the already specified different pattern and the deduction from the spirit of the presentation of creation as a whole (discussed in the next paragraph) suggest that they also are creatio ex creato.

e) God's acts are described in an evident line of decreasing use of His powers: from the obvious omnipotence of the creation of light to a maker using existing elements whose last product, humankind, is originated and made in order to undertake His responsibilities. God plans and makes humankind in order to transfer to him the rule over the world — to "have dominion over" [K.J.], or "subject" [Speiser], all the creatures (1:26, 28). The protagonist God, as it comes out of the text, is slowly developed in a clear direction of becoming a secondary persona in the following chapters of the book. The view expressed regarding the creation of sea and air creatures, thus, gains a textual support: it is juxtaposed within a line of creation, should be regarded as a part of this general line and therefore interpreted in accordance with the overall spirit of the text. This literary outline which describes the decrease in God's involvement, is highlighted at the very end of the creation phenomenon when the shifting of authority occurs.

E. The Meanings of the Story

1. The Explicit Meaning

The discussion on God's acts enables us to gain a new outlook on the subject of creation and, deduced from it, a new perception of God:

'Creation' in the narrative was not performed straight away by the omnipotent command "let there be" resulting in "...and it was" but by a long process. The text, thus, does not project miraculous acts carried out by an omnipotent protagonist, because everything performed is logically perceived and does not contradict an understanding of nature. The uniqueness of the narrative in Genesis, however, is the restricted attention devoted to chaos. While mythologies seem to emphasize it, to dwell on its nature and to include in it morbid details,[59] the Genesis narrative mentions briefly only *the physical state of its elements* TOHU VAVOHU and avoids any implication of morbidity or unnatural phenomena (1:2):

וְהָאָ֗רֶץ הָיְתָ֥ה תֹ֙הוּ֙ וָבֹ֔הוּ   וְחֹ֖שֶׁךְ עַל־פְּנֵ֣י תְה֑וֹם
וְר֣וּחַ אֱלֹהִ֔ים   מְרַחֶ֖פֶת עַל־פְּנֵ֥י הַמָּֽיִם

And earth, had been a formless waste — and darkness, over the surface of the abyss

and an awesome wind — sweeping, over the water.*

* For the linguistic approach of the whole verse — see Appendix.

This kind of presentation proclaims the demythologizing of the event while, at the same time, stating clearly that Creation is God's act.

The protagonist God is one who acts logically within the boundaries of given elements and time. The perception suggested for the question of God's omnipotence in the primordial state and the interpretation of the first three verses is thereby clear: there is a hylic matter at God's disposal, and the three verses should be rendered as they are presented in the Hebrew text — as paratactic constructions of three independent sentences, where verse 2 is a stylistic intrusion of past perfect (as will be seen further on, a common feature in Genesis style). Cassuto's interpretation of verse 1 as a title (p. 44), therefore, is rejected on linguistic grounds and literary reading. God's supremacy and unique achievement (by comparison to human perception and deeds) are expressed by originating new unprecedented creations (indicated by God's special verb BARA). Despite his mightiness, He is presented with humanlike limitations, because the tasks are not always fulfilled by the end of a period. Moreover — at the climax of the narrative, where all details of creation combine to one wholeness, the creator, like any human worker, takes a period of rest, Sabbath, between the creation of the macro (presented by the author as first chapter) and further works in the micro (presented in his second continuing chapter — assuming the unity of the text in which all the chapters are in chronological order). The question "what kind of rest it was" illuminates further on God's human traits:

The verb ש.ב.ת. (from which the Sabbath derives) has two interpretations: "rested" and "ceased".[60] The question "what is the conceptual meaning of the Sabbath" may be deduced by solving another textual problem: if after the sixth day God finished his acts, as stated in 2:1a, then why in 1b does the author state that this is done on the seventh day?[61]

> Westermann regards verse 1 as a title or a concluding piece on creation, whereas its interpretation/elaboration is stated in verses 2-3. The vowels, however, may suggest for 2:1 "to complete — כ.ל.ה." but for 2a "כ.י.ל. — to evaluate/assess"[62]. This suggestion is similar, is essence, to Speiser's "inspect and approve" for the verb, and by accepting it we gain a new outlook on the problem.

The seventh day is regarded as a day of rest, but the text clearly states that it is a rest *only as long as physical acts are concerned* ["...ceased... from all his *work* which he had made"]. Verses 2b-3a also state that God "ceased" and "blessed" — both are mental acts. Therefore, the first act after the statement that everything had been created (2a), should be regarded also as a mental one. The actions of the seventh period, thus, gain a logical continuity: when creation was completed (כ.ל.ה.), God evaluated what He had done (כ.י.ל), ceased/rested (ש.ב.ת.) and blessed (ב.ר.כ.) that 'day' in which He found that nothing more had to be done towards accomplishing the task He had set for himself to do (אשר־ברא אלהים לעשות...).

What emerges from the literary presentation of God's acts and his rest is a very practical protagonist who can be comprehended in terms of natural phenomena; He is not a transcendental entity. But this being said, a quandary arises: God acts in accordance with human perception of natural phenomena and thus He is 'part of this world'; yet, He is the one who creates natural phenomena and thus is above or beyond it, namely — transcendental. The philosophical manipulation of each possibility is beyond the scope of this book, and the context of this comment has to be taken in light of the methodological approach used here, i.e.: only Genesis is discussed, and the author of its basic perception is assumed to be of an ancient era. Therefore, claiming that the persona God in Genesis is not transcendental does not contradict later developments of Biblical perception which regard Him as such. What is relevant for the discussion is the common denominator — God, whether 'of' or 'above' this world, serves in this text as a factor which explains the world, and the literary description employs natural-physical expressions and not transcendental ones.[63] The practical language regarding God corresponds to the text's practical sense: the world was preconceived before the physical acts started (1:1, 2:3b), the acts and their products evolved logically, and after six periods of works done — it was evaluated.

Logic prevails all along, and logic contradicts chaos as well as miracles such as creatio ex nihilo. The logical touch, I suggest, characterizes the explicit meaning of the Biblical account of creation, in which the protagonist, like similar protagonists, serves the social universal need by epitomizing ***the explicit wish of the collective to establish a certain order and meaning within the chaos***. The peak of human touch within this logical presentation is ***the transference of authority to God's look-alike creatures***.

2. The Implicit Meaning — The Mythic Motif

The above discussion of the explicit meaning emphasized two issues: the elimination of the chaotic through logic and order, and the transference of authority;[64] the first issue is the core of the Genesis narrative, whereas the motif of passing-on of authority is its climax. Both issues point to their two universal hidden meanings, referred here as mythic motifs:

a) Almost every known mythology presents wars among gods and a chaotic state of affairs until the victorious side wins and establishes logic and order. Genesis is void of a morbid fascination with chaos to which other mythologies succumb, but it corresponds to their universal common core, apparent in the savage mind as well as in the most sophisticated one,[65] which craves for order. Each form of government or social organization is an expression for this craving and, thus, the mere existence of human life within society is attached to or dependent of order.

The longing for order, therefore, is a mythic motif in creation narratives regardless of culture, civilization and era.

b) Having control of one's own world is an ancient motif expressed also in contemporary myths: the myths of Faust and don Quixote, although dealing with other issues, present the desire for control; so, to a certain extent, does the Oedipus saga. As it is hardly ever attained, any literary expression on the subject is but a wish-fulfilment of the psychological need to control one's world. This universal urge is termed "the instinct to master", a term suggested by Freud[66] whose relevant researches deal with phenomena-development since infancy. Application of definitions from this sphere to the general condition of humankind, to universal patterns of behaviour and thought, is possible because infancy itself is a universal state of affairs regardless of culture or era. Regarding the "instinct to master" as the second mythic motif of the creation story, therefore, is within the boundaries stated in the discussion of the mythic: it is a universal motif. However, I find it necessary to rename it because in psychology it is interpreted as "a non-sexual instinct which only fuses with sexuality secondarily, and the aim of which is *to dominate the object by force*".[67] The last words which I have emphasized seem to limit its validity to relations between people whilst allowing an intrusion of the sexual urge; in both cases, it has very little room, if any, in the creation of a physical world. Dominion, however, may be acquired also by psychological influence such as expression of an idea. As this seems to be the case with the creation story we elaborated upon, the second mythic motif's chosen name is ***The Desire For Authority***.

Chapter III
CREATION of HUMANS

A. Introduction

Unlike the short and clearly structured first narrative of a single issue — the creation of "sky and earth", in the 'creation of humans' the text presents various issues which have inspired several interpretations of subject matter,[1] theories about structure[2] and comparisons with its contemporary mythologies.[3] It is customary to commence a discussion of literary merits by presenting the text's subject matter and its structure, as has been done in the previous chapter. But structure and subject-matter, as well as other literary technicalities, are ultimately determined by a generally accepted reading of the text. The preliminary stage of our discussion, at this stage, is to establish what is actually written.

The approach to the text, aside from the problem of suggesting a suitable translation, will follow the method used in the previous chapter, i.e., an analysis of key words and discussion of the main theme — creator-created relationships. The overall exposition of the text, its subject matter and the narratives, the literary analysis and the suggested interpretation, will be presented in the last part of the discussion.

B. The Two Narratives

The book of Genesis, as it is usually understood, seems to provide two accounts of the creation of humankind: a short one in 1:26-27 in which the proposal to create is presented and the act of creation performed, and a more elaborated one in chapter 2 in which there is no preceding proposal but rather a picturesque description of creation, substance and process, in verses 7-8, 18, 21-22.

These two accounts are usually thought of as a description of the same event, and the obvious literary and contextual differences are put down to the respective school of interpretation. The European School regards each account as belonging to a different source and hence the differences in details, but interpreters do not always agree as to who wrote which part:

e.g.: Speiser — P: 1-2:4a, J: 2:4b-5:2.
Skinner — P: 1-2:4a, J^e: 2:4b-3:19, 23,
J^j: 3:20-22, 24, 4:17-25.

The Jerusalem School regards the first account as a general statement of creation, after which comes an elaborated account of the same event, both accounts belonging to the same author.[4]

As the 'one book — one author' assumption constitutes the cornerstone of the literary analysis of this research, the differences between the two accounts have to be settled within the given text. The answer provided by the European School does not resolve the differences, but rather accentuates them. The argument of the Jerusalem School which explains the differences by declaring the first account as appealing to logic and the second to emotions[5] has to be rejected, because it does not resolve the differences but rather justifies them on subjective, interpretational grounds. Also unacceptable is the School's interpretation of the two events as a general statement (1:27) preceding its full description in chapter 2. A similar claim, regarding the interpretation of the first verse in the narrative of the creation of a world, has been argued and rejected (p. 57), and the claim that it is being employed systematically[6] also in this case is, therefore, questionable.

It is imperative, then, to look for an interpretation based on literary elements within the text, which, like our interpretation of the first verses of the book, imply *a continuity of text and content*

— movement forward, not expanding circles. The difference between the accounts, as I shall try to establish, should be looked upon as reflecting *two different events* which, like other chapters of the whole book, are *literally arranged in chronological order*; the task will be to find a unifying core between these two different stories. This, I believe, is the right approach to the book because, whatever the point of departure — theme, plot, etc. — "the means that create concord are so powerful that they override the aspects of discord" as Fokkelman suggests.[7]

The first account of the creation of humans (1:27), as we have seen, is an integral part of the account of creation, but only a part of it and not necessarily its highlight. Although verse 1:27 has a distinct poetic style, the creation of man is but a part among the creation of other elements. The notion of 'Crown of Creation' is a subjective interpretation by human beings; from the textual point of view, the four verses devoted to them (26-29) do not indicate a greater importance than the five (14-18) devoted to the luminaries. It is placed logically, as we have pointed out in the previous chapter, towards the end of the story and after the creation of the living things which they are to subdue. But the fact that the Sabbath, also distinguished by a poetic style, concludes the whole account, shifts the attention away from humankind and makes the Sabbath the highlight of the event.

The creation of man, in this first account, takes place in the sixth period of seven chronological spans of time, with no reference to a particular space; the periods, thus, are the literary structural units while the created elements are mere details in them. The unmistakable protagonist of this account is a god who, in creating the elements, acts within the limits of the periods.

The second account is set right at the beginning of the Eden story. The creation of the human being and what happens to him constitute the main event of the narrative, while the setting for the creation — given at the very beginning of the account — serves as an introduction: climatic conditions and geographical boundaries of a specific place (2:5-6, 8-15). In this account Time and its span play no role, whereas Space is an important factor. The correct identification of this space[8] seems to me irrelevant for the purpose of literary analysis; it suffices to conclude that the stories refer to two different events, precisely because in one of them a space is specified.[9]

Although God as the creator is the protagonist of the introductory part of the second story and the active persona in the formation of a human being, the narrative shifts its weight to the created. It is done gradually: first the author gives him the prerogative of naming (2:19), and after the creation of woman he sets God as a bystander to the main event that takes part in the setting. God's role at the conclusion of the account is a more active one but, as will be discussed, not assertive enough to re-acquire the role of the main protagonist.

The second account is contextually concluded at the end of chapter 2. But as the chapters are an artificial division (a late 13th century division made by Christian scholars),[10] the discussion below has to have regard for what the author saw as the ending of his account. This way the text reference expands up to chapter 5:2, where the end is marked by the literary phrase "these are the generations of..." as it is done at the end of the first account of creation (2:4).[11] The story of human beings, therefore, is more than the narrative of their mere creation.

The above presentation of some obvious differences between the accounts is only the first step in the attempt to assert that they tell about different issues: the first is a description of a general phenomenon of the creation of humankind whereas the second is about a particular case. Let us now take the second step.

C. Word-Analysis

Introduction

The primary difficulty of comprehending the nature of each account and the differences between them, at this stage, lies in the necessity of making a linguistic distinction between Biblical terms, i.e., to determine when a Biblical expression indicates the concrete and the particular, and when it aims to convey the general. Studies assume the concept of 'a Biblical language'[12] about which I have expressed my reservations (p. 21). My argument against this approach and the meanings automatically applied as a result of such a notion is that according to life-experience, a living language does not retain, forever unchanged, all the meanings of its vocabulary: contemporary English and Middle English are hardly 500 years apart, yet the latter requires a special glossary to be understood. From Abraham to Moses it is the same span of time, and Moses to Ezekiel — almost 700 years. The challenge, as we pointed out, is to solve linguistic obscurities mainly within the framework of the text or, at the most, within the framework of Genesis.

In the second account we have to deal, as we did in the previous discussion, with concepts of Time and Space, and to add a linguistic distinction between 'man', 'human beings' and 'humankind'. The word analysis that follows is but a brief encounter with the fundamental meanings of words. As in the previous chapter, word analysis is the starting point for reading into the text. Further clarifications of meanings and concepts will eventually emerge from the discussion of the relevant issues.

Time

The subtlety of the word "יום" [hereafter - YOM], which in the account of the creation of the world was interpreted in this book as 'period' (p. 40), suggests for the second account further possible meanings. The complexity is evident already in the first verse of the second account (2:4): this verse connects the accounts and is usually considered as consisting of two parts: the first (4a) is regarded as concluding the previous passage and the last part (4b) as opening the next contextual chapter:*

(2:4) אֵלֶּה תוֹלְדוֹת הַשָּׁמַיִם וְהָאָרֶץ בְּהִבָּרְאָם
בְּיוֹם עֲשׂוֹת יהוה אֱלֹהִים אֶרֶץ וְשָׁמָיִם

(2:4a) These are the generations of the sky and the earth, when they were created;

(4b) at the time, that God Yhwh made, earth and sky.

The K.J. translation of BeYOM as "in *the* day" suggests a very definite span of time — a day. This translation sets the following description of events into a 24 hour period in which all creation supposedly occurs and thereby contradicts the seven-period creation account (also named "day") which preceded it. It is unlikely for an author to contradict all he had said in his first chapter by the opening sentence of a new one. The same reservation holds for the order of the creation of the elements in both accounts:

chapter 1 — light, sky, earth, flora, luminaries, sea and sky creatures, fauna and humans.

chapter 2 — earth, humans, trees, animals.

A coherent interpretation of YOM, therefore, has to be sought.

Speiser's "at the time" used in the above translation of the verse [as well as Westermann's "when"], settles the contradiction of seven periods v. one: YOM, in the first account is 'a period', a certain although undefined span of time, whereas in the second

* Cassuto seems to be the only one who regards the two parts of verse 2:4 as one unit (*Cassuto*, 62-64). Contra: Skinner, 54, note 4^{b}-7. Westermann and Speiser join the divisional opinion by a straightforward presentation of each part in a different account.

it points to an elusive, relative, time. My above suggested translation of verse 4 follows Speiser's, and may be understood as differentiating between the time span of the first event of the "generations of the sky and the earth" in the first chapter, and the forthcoming event which occurred in a different sphere of time;* the juxtaposition of the events one after the other leaves room to assume, following the constant literary layout of the whole book, that the second event took place afterwards, at an undisclosed period.

Space

'ארץ — earth' [hereafter — ERETZ], in the account of the creation of a world, presented the possibility of being both what we regard as the planet earth and the physical element opposed to sky, the solid material which constitutes it. In the second account its subtlety offers more possibilities: land (a morphological background), ground (the substance) and, later on, area (and the same subtleties, as The Bible Dic tells as, are valid for ADAMA). The proper terms are underlined hereafter whenever they stand for the Hebrew ERETZ in verses 4-6:**

(2:4a) These are the generations of the sky and the earth, when they were created;

(4b) at the time that God Yhwh made, earth and sky.

(5a) And every shrub of the field, has not been yet on the land and
every herb of the field, has not yet been sprouted;

* This point is not made by Speiser who, adhering to the Documentary Hypothesis, regards the accounts as belonging to different sources which narrate the same event. However, the fact that Speiser gives a different meaning to the expression of the time factor, may be regarded as a tacit interpretation that the events are different occurrences.

** For a different division of lines, presenting a different poetic structure, see: *Cassuto*, 62, 64. This subject has been discussed in p. 44, note 37.

(5b) for God Yhwh has not caused it to rain upon the land, and
man was not there to till, the soil.

(6a) And a flow, would well up from the ground

(6b) and water, the surface of the soil.*

The main difference, and the crucial one, between the above translation and others is the use of "land" instead of "earth"; the first expression denotes locality whereas the second denotes the general entity which today we refer to as "the planet". As the word ERETZ was translated automatically into the generalizing expression "earth", the obvious conclusion for the interpreter of all ages was to apply a general meaning to the passage. Thus, the "ERETZ" of the first account of creation was perceived as being the same as the "ERETZ" of the second; hence the accepted attitude toward the stories, either as two different "documents" of the same event, or as one being a general account of the creation of the world and the other its detailed elaboration.

The interpretation suggested in this paper of "land" as denoting locality, is based on the text's very description of the morphological conditions of *a specific area*, depicted in geographical details in verses 2:9-14. The locality implied by these verses has to be regarded as an integral part of the narrative which also includes details of climatic conditions in verses 5-6. To suggest that the author regarded the morphological conditions of this specific area (usually identified as Mesopotamia) as typical of the whole world is an insult to his intelligence; even animals know that areas differ, and the fact that they choose to live in one does not exclude their knowledge of others. There is no room, therefore, to suppose that if the author described a specific area,

* The structure of the sentences follows the Hebrew pattern; the translation of the whole paragraph takes into consideration both Speiser's and Leeser's vocabulary, and uses whichever I regarded to be more suitable.

he was ignorant of the existence of others, or that he regarded some specific morphological conditions as being universal.

> A suggestion that the Mesopotamian perception of space is limited to what is described on a discovered tablet (No. 92687, in The British Museum),[13] takes a narrow view on Mesopotamian perception. To state such a generalizing conclusion on abstract perception, based solely on a casual find representing part of a map, is to attribute to the piece more substance than it deserves. When humans appeared on the surface of this planet, earth's morphology had already been shaped in various forms and climatic conditions. Animals are aware of these differences and adapt themselves to them. Why attribute to the ancient cartographer a blindness that nature denied to animals?

Hence, in the view presented here, what was considered as two accounts of the same event should be looked upon as two stages: the first describing the phenomenon of the creation of a world and the second being a story of occurrences in one specific area, regardless of what might have happened in others. Almost every mythology, in a similar manner to the Biblical account, accentuates some locality: a mountain, such as the Olympus of Greek mythology; a river, such as the Sumerian legend of Enki and Ninhursag.[14] However, reading these stories does not leave one with the feeling that their narratives project a limited perception of space, of the kind usually applied to the Biblical one. In most cases, these narratives describe what is believed to be the abode of specific Gods, but they are not regarded as the only existing places.

Humankind — Human Beings — Man

The title suggests three manifestations of the one Biblical expression "Adam": the species, the generalizing plural and the individualizing singular, respectively (אנושות, אנשים, איש).[15] The distinction between the general and particular is crucial, because

Adam, which in the Eden story is an individual, signifies also humanity in the first account, as can be deduced from God's proposal:

(1:26) וַיֹּאמֶר אֱלֹהִים נַעֲשֶׂה אָדָם בְּצַלְמֵנוּ כִּדְמוּתֵנוּ
וְיִרְדּוּ...

(1:26) And God said let us make Adam in our image, after our likeness;
And they shall have dominion over..." [L]

Adam, as indicated by the plural pronoun "they" (26b), may be regarded as an equivalent expression for either humankind or human beings. In English, the former is "it" and the latter "they"[16] but, by the text's use of plural preposition (in Hebrew), "Adam" means "human beings",[17] and the correct rendering and reading of the verse should be:

(1:26) ..."Let us make human beings in our image, after our likeness;
And they shall have dominion...

After the creation has been performed, the author alters the meaning of "Adam" by the use of the pronoun "it": "the Adam", in 1:27, may stand for "humankind"; and since this is an important paragraph in regard to content, every commentator has his reading of its poetics.[18] Here is mine:

(1:27) And God Created humankind in his image in the image of God, created he it;
Male and female, created he them.
(28) And he blessed them...

Humankind and human beings, as indicated in both verses, include males and females, and the blessing that follows their creation is given to their plurality and to both sexes. A comparison with other creatures is here in order: they are regarded as a multitude and, accordingly, should be 'adam' — because there is nothing in the narrative to suggest "Adam" as a single pair.[19]

The overall linguistic complexity of the word 'Adam' is revealed in the verses concluding the second account:

(5:1) זֶה סֵפֶר תּוֹלְדֹת אָדָם
בְּיוֹם בְּרֹא אֱלֹהִים אָדָם בִּדְמוּת אֱלֹהִים עָשָׂה אֹתוֹ
(5:2) זָכָר וּנְקֵבָה בְּרָאָם
וַיְבָרֶךְ אֹתָם וַיִּקְרָא אֶת־שְׁמָם אָדָם בְּיוֹם הִבָּרְאָם
(5:3) וַיְחִי אָדָם...

(5:1a) This is a book [on] the generations, of Adam;
(1b) When God had created Humankind in God's image, created he it.
(2a) Male and female, created he them;
(2b) And blessed he them, and called their name Adam when they were created.
(3) And Adam lived...

The above translation suggests three usages of the word: in 5:1a Adam is the individual whose story, in accordance with the customary phrasing, has been previously told;[20] in 5:1b, as derived from the pronoun 'it', "Adam" means humankind; in 5:2b it is the generic name given to human beings (as derived from the use of the plural "them", "their", "they"). In the following verse (5:3) the text returns to tell of the individual Adam's life span and his descendants: "And Adam lived...". How, in this context, are we to relate to the plural and general Adam of the intervening verses 5:1b-2 between the singular Adam of 5:1a and in verse 3?

These intervening verses serve as a reminder of the previous created species of which singular Adam is a part; the text clearly points to this interpretation by wording 5:1b-2a in a similar structure and words as in 1:26. From a literary point of view, therefore, 5:1b-2 is a flashback to the individual Adam's origins, a stylistic intrusion of the kind already discussed about verse 1:2 — paratactic construction of sentences where, as a common literary device in the Bible, some indicated past events.[21] In verse 1:2, the grammatical feature is the Waw attached to a noun, whereas in 5:1b it is achieved by an explicit temporal clause at the beginning. Hence "had created" in my rendering of verse 5:1b.

Now, we have a suggested interpretation for the text's use of the word "Adam" and its perception of time and space.

In the coming chapter, let us follow our findings of word-analysis at work.

D. The Creator and the Created

1. Introduction

In the first account of its creation, as proposed by God, humankind was brought into the world in order to have dominion over it (1:19). This preconditioned vocation, as suggested in the conclusion of the earlier discussion of the creation of a world, can be seen as manifesting God's abdication of authority. The exact meaning of 'dominion' may be open to several interpretations, but 'governing' the land and the sea creatures in the sense of power of organizing the world as a rational ruler, cannot be one of them:

> The plain meaning of ReDU - רדו is 'subdue', but the question arises as to what it means here. Westermann suggests a non-literal meaning, as in 1:16 — the sun rules over the day and the moon over the night.[22] But the author does not use the same verb, and 'MeSHOL מְשֹׁל — to rule' of 1:16 is not the same as ReDU — subdue; the non-literal meaning, thus, is no explanation to what is stated as Man's vocation.
>
> Another unclear notion is expressed in studies looking for a philosophical meaning,[23] most of whom foresaw a possible vegetarian existence of humanity: Cassuto is aware that there is no explicit banning on meat prior to the flood, where its consumption is explicitly mentioned (9:3), but he suggests that "*probably* the intention of the Torah is that Man should avoid eating meat".[24] "Probably" does not suffice, if one takes into account other places in the text

which allow a divergent opinion. And although Cassuto is aware of these places, he seems to bend his interpretation to suit his philosophy. Implausible, too, is the application of contemporary ecological notions such as: "to have dominion = seeing to their survival",[25] because exploitation of nature was hardly the case in human history until the 20th century; 'survival', on the other hand, has always been a human fight against nature.

As a matter of fact, animals are in a constant struggle with man who aspires to use them for his needs; man does not *govern* them — he eats them and manufactures products from them [the leather clothing that God provided to humans (3:21) can be regarded as an example of how *the author understands the notion of dominion* and accentuates it by ascribing it to God]. The authority over animals given to humans, I suggest, has to be understood as providing man with one source of food, while the flora provide another. This statement seems to contradict many commentators who, citing 9:3-7, deduce from it that if no explicit mention of eating meat has been given beforehand, then it was forbidden. 9:3 is thus grossly misunderstood: it is not a "concession" given but rather an elaboration on the issue of blood (9:4). Man is given all the kinds of seed-bearing plants and seed-bearing fruit trees on earth (1:29), but this verse is not exhaustive: there is no use of such victuals as milk, honey, etc. The provisions for other creatures is also not exhaustive: the ones which grow wild in the field are intended for animals (1:30), but nothing is mentioned for the birds or for sea creatures. Yet, no interpretation of this omission has suggested a prohibition on seed-bearing plants for birds, whilst applying it to 1:29 as a prohibition on meat! The specification of the kinds of flora for humans seem to me to be intentional because they do not grow wild in the field but *require cultivation*. Man's authority and vocation, therefore, are determined by his food, which imply corresponding occupations in agriculture, shepherding and hunting. Anthropology regards hunting as the first human occupation, in both the Old and New World, in the final stages of the Pleistocene period (around 10,000 B.C.).[26] Agriculture appears in the Levant and Iraq (that is: the Fertile Crescent) around 9500 B.C.; by 7000 B.C. agriculture had become the primary subsistence in the Levant, and by the same time domesticated animals and sheep appear.[27]

The concept presented in the second account is different: God "formed" a human being in order to work and guard a special garden which he planted in specific geographical boundaries, with its own climatic conditions (2:8-14). In other words, humankind of the first account was autonomous and with a universal vocation and, thus, not limited by geographical boundaries; that of the second account was destined for servitude in a particular place (2:15). This, I believe, is the most crucial facet of the differences between the accounts which so far suggests that in their subject matter they are totally independent of each other.

The first account, as argued all along, is that of a world whereas the second is a story of some locality which does not exclude the existence of other geographical localities or human beings. The author of Genesis seems to point, further on, to this possibility in three textual references:

— Adam is destined to "guard" the garden, and that can be understood as guarding it from outsiders;*

* Skinner, 66: "The question from what the garden had to be protected is one that should not be pressed"; and my response is "why not?" Is it because it shatters the neat convention of Adam being the first and only one to be created? And if this convention can be so easily shattered by the author's use of the word 'guard', is not this convention questionable?

Speiser translates לְשָׁמְרָהּ as "tend it" which amounts to *a synonym* for "to work it — לעבדה" and Westermann suggests "watch over it"; both commentaries choose to address certain possibilities of the verb ש.מ.ר.

— Cain is afraid that "Every one that findeth me will slay me" (4:15), thus pointing to the existence of other human beings;*

— the mention of Cain's wife (4:17) also points to other humans, unless Cain and Abel married their own sisters. As the notion of 'one single couple who begot humanity' is common to the traditional view, a class of interpretation bordering on sexual perversion, which does not correspond to Hebraic Biblical conventions, was bound to emerge; e.g.: "Cain's choices between several modalities of sexual behaviour" and a suggestion that the murder by Cain "has a homosexual implication since his brother Abel was killed to get a wife which had to be Cain's sister, thereby incestuous relations are implied too".**

---

whilst disregarding the obvious one that functions *against* an intruder, i.e., against other human beings.

But this problematic expression is not an isolated instance, and the accumulation of all instances presented in the discussion indicates that there are grounds for contradicting the conventional view.

* Skinner suggests that in "this part of the narrative, Kayin is no longer a personal but a collective name"; but the problematic words כל מֹצְאִי he interprets as "the act [in the future] might be repeated many times on members of the tribe Kain" (Skinner, 110). This, I suggest, is not plausible: the "members of the tribe" are not yet in "this part of the narrative" as they are due to be born much later; the blood vengeance can easily be prevented by Cain's avoidance of procreation.

Cassuto interprets the problematic words as referring to the immediate family and their descendants (*Cassuto*, 151); but this interpretation brings us to the next issue (in the discussion).

** e.g.: Luc De Ves comments (note 28). Rashi, in his attempt to conform to the traditional concept, tries to solve this problem by suggesting that the threefold ET in the text signifies an extension of the scope of the text, teaching that a twin sister was born with Cain, and that with Abel two were born. But "extension of the scope" based on similar speculation, may point also to the author's avoidance of naming Adam's wife (4:25) as indicating, as the legend tells, the creation of another woman who begot

The words and sentences of the textual references cited above were problematic to interpreters who claimed that the accounts are those of the same event. It required a twist of the logical meaning of straightforward words in order to come to terms with an impossible reality where one couple creates humankind. From a literary point of view, the text and the remarks mentioned do not correspond to this kind of imposed interpretation which seems to be based solely on ideological and theological speculations. The alternative approach suggested in this book, which sees the accounts as belonging to two separate events, compels us to look for the realistic elements within the accounts: the fact that it describes the story of an individual in part of the world, does not imply that he is regarded as the only existing human being. We shall return to our conclusion about the overall concept of the text as deduced from the above cited verses, but it suffices here to point out that it corresponds to our previous conclusion on the subject of the creation of a world which does not exclude the existence or creation of others. The text, I suggest, conveys less pretensions to universal knowledge than its interpreters would like to credit it with, and its author narrates only the issue which interests him.

In the second, more detailed account, the text is engaged, not in a mere creation (as in the first one) but rather in the personality and events of one specific creature. The forthcoming discussion of the accounts of 'the creation of humans' will follow the text's interest by the shift in protagonists which occurs: Creator, Created, and the relationship established between them.

Seth, and thereby Seth's descendants make a less incestuous relationship possible within the family and they do not carry the burden of Eve's sin. Both speculations might serve an interpreter's intentions, but neither is explicitly *stated in the text* and, thus, are rejected.

2. The Creator — Acts of Creation

a) The first account (1:26-7)

In the discussion of the acts performed by the creator in the sixth period, it was argued that humans, as well as sea and air creatures, were 'originated' and thus made from existing elements (p. 55). The text mentions earth as the origin of fauna (1:24), but there is no indication of the element of which humans are made. Instead, there is an elaborate treatment of form (the translation follows my suggestion on p. 72):

(1:26a) וַיֹּאמֶר אֱלֹהִים   נַעֲשֶׂה אָדָם בְּצַלְמֵנוּ כִּדְמוּתֵנוּ

(1:27) וַיִּבְרָא אֱלֹהִים אֶת־הָאָדָם בְּצַלְמוֹ   בְּצֶלֶם אֱלֹהִים בָּרָא אֹתוֹ

זָכָר וּנְקֵבָה בָּרָא אֹתָם

(1:26a) And God said   let us make human beings in our image, after our likeness;

(27) And God created humankind in his image   in the image of God, created he it;

Male and female, created he them.

The above verses suggest two factors: Humanity, from its beginning, was made up of males and females, and the form of humanity is דמות and צֶלֶם — the image and likeness of God:

> A similar point can be found in an Egyptian source: "He made the breezes of life (or the life-giving air) for their nostrils. They are images (or likeness) of Him, who came forth from his member."[30] These lines are a scribe's work from the 19th dynasty (1500-1000 B.C.) which allows for speculation on Hebrew influence of the Israelite exiles (around 1300 B.C.) on the motifs of God's image, on origins from a member and on life-giving air. But the original composition is probably almost two thousand years earlier; if so, the Egyptian concept probably influenced the Biblical one.

There seems to be unanimous agreement of the concepts 'male and female', but there are several opinions as to what the author means by "us", the implications on the entity of God, and what can be understood as His image.

The problematic word in the verses is the plural "us" of verse 26: does it mean that the author conceives the deity as plurality? Does it imply a heavenly court? Is it an idiomatic expression implying hastiness or deliberation? Or perhaps a figure of speech?*

There is a linguistic contradiction between the suggestion of the deity in the plural form and the action carried out in the singular — בצלמנו v. בצלמו. But as the pattern in all seven periods of creation is that of a singular deity, there is no reason to suggest a different concept for a part of the sixth.[31] God, thus, is not conceived as a plurality by the monotheistics, unless the plural designation means that God embraces and encompasses everything and thereby he is plural. (The word אֱלֹהִים — ELOHIM denotes plurality, and in this sense it is similar to מַיִם — water).

A heavenly court is a pagan concept, and the Hebrew *legends* referring to angels and cherubs are relatively very late by comparison to the text in question.[32] However, the first chapters of Genesis provide two cases where a possibility for deities may be detected: a) the "cherubim" of the garden (3:24) and b) "bnei-elohim" (6:1-4):

a) Cherubim, in the later books of the Bible (Ezekiel and Psalms), acquire a supernatural connotation, but in earlier books (Exodus and Kings 1) they are mentioned among the ornamental

* Speiser regards the employment of the plural נעשה, where no other divine is mentioned as a *grammatical issue* with no direct bearing on meaning (Speiser, 7); while avoiding the discussion on what the grammatical issue is, he appears to be indirectly suggesting it as a figure of speech.

elements of the temple — cherubim, palm-branches; in Solomon's palace, among other natural animals — lions, oxen. As may be deduced from these books, cherubim were probably a kind of yet unidentified winged creatures but not necessarily unnatural. Interpretation as to their nature in Genesis has to lean on the earlier books rather than on the later one (Ezekiel) which seems to be inspired by characteristic images of winged humans in later Mesopotamian art that contradict the strict prohibition of the second commandment. The picturesque notion, so common to Western civilization, of angels and cherubim being winged deities in human form, I suggest, is out of place in a monotheistic text where all traces of gods' wars, angels and other deities, so typical of other mythologies, were totally eliminated by a monotheistic author in his account of the creation of the world.[33]

b) An assumption of the existence of "sons of God" does not comply with the rational logic that characterizes Genesis, or with the fundamental Hebraic belief that we all are 'sons of God', from which stems the later Jewish rejection of one special 'son of God'. The Hebrew construct form "God's-X" can be either possessive ("of/from God") or adjectival ("divine, awesome, outstanding" — see rendering of רוּח אֱלֹהִים on p. 56). In this light, I suggest, "BNEI ELOHIM" may be interpreted as a linguistic expression denoting "unusual beings".[34]

"Let us make" as a figure of speech denoting hastiness[35] may be rejected on the grounds that it does not comply with the narrative's style regarding all other elements in the account of creation. Everything is created in accordance with the needs of a given phase of time. Whatever reasons suggested for this hastiness,[36] they are mere interpretational assumptions not grounded in any explicit indication on the part of the text.

"Let us make" as a figure of speech and as a form of the 'royal plural' seems to be the correct explanation. Westermann claims that the royal-plural does not occur in Hebrew and he points to its only one Biblical occurrence in Aramaic (Ezra, 4:18); to me, however, by its context this very sentence in Ezra seems to refer *to the court* rather than to a person.

The argument which I wish to emphasize concerns *the context in which the plural figure of speech appears* rather than its linguistic frequency in the language; the following discussion will attempt to substantiate the suggested interpretation of royal plural:

The text's juxtaposition of a plural and a singular form for the deity, both in the same context, is a pattern also found in regard with the form of God: (1:26) בְּצַלְמֵנוּ and (27) בְּצַלְמוֹ. But the question still remains — *a 'royal plural' for what reason?* If we observe how the plural form designating the deity is used in Genesis, we may notice that it is employed in those cases where the creator is compared to, in conflict with or confronted by the created one; in other words, *when God's stature as a ruler is stressed*:

a) Comparison applies when the author relates that humankind is created in God's image (1:26), in a context where His authority is handed over to them;

b) Conflict occurs when a worried God fearing for his status says (3:22) that Adam is "like one of us כְּאַחַד מִמֶּנּוּ";

c) Confrontation occurs when God sabotages the attempt of humans to build the sky-reaching tower (11:7), when they disregard His command to fill up the earth;

In all these cases the plural pronoun is a figure of speech in a comment which, I suggest, is intended to lend emphasis to the superiority of the creator over the creatures *similar to Him;* in all these cases, God's actions that follow are expressed in the singular form.

The first similarity presented in the first account of creation is that of form, defined by two expressions — image and likeness.[37]

This combination of terms occurs twice, when God proposes creating humankind and when Adam procreates Seth:

...in our image,	after our likeness	(1:26)	כדמותנו	בצלמנו
...in his likeness,	after his image	(5:3)	כצלמו	בדמותו

The text presents a chiastic relation between the nouns but keeps the same prepositional terms, thus indicating that they are interchangeable.[38] The same idea is conveyed when each noun is engaged separately: in the first account (1:27) only "image צֶלֶם" is used when the act of creation is performed; in the concluding sentence of the second account (5:1) only "likeness דְמוּת". As the two verses convey the same idea, צֶלֶם and דְמוּת are one and the same. The literary use of those two expressions in their successive order of presentation seems to form an interesting pattern and not mere vacillation:

1:26	1:27	5:1	5:3
(Image, likeness),	image,	likeness,	(likeness, image).

The opening combination (1:26) gives way to a separate use of expressions that follows its very order: "image" in 1:27 is followed by "likeness" (5:1). The last combination (5:3) starts with the "likeness" used in the preceding narrative and thereby creates a chiasm with the opening one. This literary pattern is another factor that may point to the unity of the whole text.

However much later interpretations attempted to distinguish between the two terms for theological purposes of distinction between God and humans, their linguistic use indicates that whatever subtle difference in meanings there is, the text expresses that very anthropomorphic perception — that humans were conceived as having the physical likeness of God. As this is a crucial issue for the monotheistic, I present a brief literary discussion:

> Westermann suggests that at an earlier stage of the tradition, 'Image' could have intended a physical likeness... that when

Gen. 1:26 talks of the image and likeness, it envisages the whole person and not just the corporeal or the spiritual side only, he fears that "such would be too gross an anthropomorphism for [the author] P himself".[39]

But the fear, or avoidance, of anthropomorphism is a late concept; *the fact that it is found in the Bible*, as well as in other ancient Middle Eastern cultures[40] *puts P's authorship in question rather than the anthropomorphism of* Genesis.

Anthropomorphism can be avoided only by explaining 'image' and 'likeness' as abstract rather than physical qualities: "likeness establishes a similarity between the creative act of God and the procreative act of man, whereas 'image' makes man the plenipotentiary of God on earth" says R. Hirshberger.[41] But, I suggest, bringing in abstract notions is speculative interpretation which, in the example cited above, neither the text nor the linguistic use of the words necessarily confirm.

Rejection of anthropomorphism is expressed also by A. Ahuvyah who equates "knowing good and bad" and "the image of God", and thus attempts to refute any possibility of physical connection between God's image and human form.[42] But "knowing good and bad" is *an added* quality to the similarity in form and, therefore, Ahuvyah's suggestion does not solve the issue.

Y. Koler substantiates his reservations by suggesting a comma after (27): בצלם, אלהים ברא and thereby interpreting the verse: "in an intended image, God created it". It could have been a good proposition, had verse 27 stood by itself; but the manipulation with the comma clashes with the clear "In OUR image, after our likeness" of verse 26.

Emmanueli states the heart of the matter for orthodox thinking, saying that it is "*unthinkable* that the author had thought of form-connection between creator and created, that he imagined God in human form",[44] (emphasis added).

But why not? Anthropomorphism was so common that it makes sense to apply it also to Genesis.

The question of sexuality, at this point, is unavoidable. Human beings are male and female and they are made in the image of God; is the One-God androgynous? External sources to the Bible present a long tradition of historical references to the androgynousness of both Gods and Man, and the same notion is found in Jewish traditional interpretations.[46] How much of these notions may be applied to demythologizing Genesis? The gender of God is still open to speculation, but this issue has no bearing on Creator-Created relationships; therefore, it will not be discussed.

The narrative of the first account of the creation of humankind does not mention the elements from which it is created; it just states its form. The supplementary details are given in the second account discussed below.

b) The second account (2:7, 21-22)

(2:7) וַיִּיצֶר יהוה אֱלֹהִים אֶת־הָאָדָם עָפָר מִן־הָאֲדָמָה וַיִּפַּח בְּאַפָּיו נִשְׁמַת חַיִּים
וַיְהִי הָאָדָם לְנֶפֶשׁ חַיָּה׃

(2:7) And Yhwh God had formed the Adam, dust from the ground
and blew into their nostrils, the breath of life;
And the Adam became, a living being.*

* Comments on the translation:

a) The common tense of all commentators is the regular past 'god formed'; this thesis suggests the past perfect 'had formed', as will be substantiated below.

b) In "dust from the אדמה", "ground" was chosen as the proper meaning among the possible ones of אדמה (discussion, p. 80, note 7). The biblical idiom "עפר מן האדמה" indicates that matter is taken *from* somewhere; matter taken from matter is less logical, and hence the translation suggested: "dust from the ground" (or land, in its morphological sense). [cont.→]

This is a complicated verse, not only because it admits several alternative interpretations, but because its position after the account of the general creation suggests that this is another creation of human beings followed by that of other beings (2:19). As already stated, the creation of humans in the first account reports only about form; the second one, although using the verb 'to form' deals with matter (dust from the ground), with particularities of the creative act and, more important, has a separate account for the formation of each sex. As humankind (males and females) already has been reported to have been created, the question of how to comprehend Adam in the second account and what kind of creation is taking place becomes acute — it is the most important question arising from this text. A comparison of the wording regarding the act and the product may provide an answer:

a) The act — as argued before, the existence of created beings does not necessarily exclude the possibility of another *phase* of origination; this argument is justified at this very juncture of the text, by the introduction of a new verb for God's further actions: to form י.צ.ר. This verb adds another dimension to the chain of acts already discussed (p. 47) to create or to originate / ב.ר.א. and to make / ע.ש.ה. To form / י.צ.ר. (as was previously explained) is considered as rounding off that which the act of creation started; to make / ע.ש.ה. is to bring the created to the stage where it is able to fulfil its function. Therefore, when the author presented the creation of all elements in his first account, he engaged the verb "to make" followed by an explicit statement of the element's

---

c) As most translations regard this verse as referring to a singular Adam, the common translation of אַפָּיו is "his nostrils". But אפיו is a *plural form* of אַף — nose [his nose — אפו], and this is one of many cases where an "illogical" singular may be used, preceding pronominal suffix in the plural with nouns denoting limbs of the body; e.g. Gen., 43:15 "in *their* hands" (J. Blau, A Grammar of Biblical Hebrew, Remark, p. 98).

intended function. To form, on the other hand, suggests a different step from a mere creation; whatever this step actually implies, and one possible explanation will be suggested further on, it definitely is not creation anew.*

b) The product — in the first account God proposes the creation of "Adam אדם" (1:26) and the act of creation is that of "the Adam האדם". We have argued that "Adam = human beings" and "the Adam = humankind" (p. 72) and, therefore, the proposal refers to a creature in general whereas the act performed created a new species which included the two sexes. The same order of wording appears in the second account: at first it is mentioned that there is no "Adam" to work the land (2:5), and the following act of forming is that of "the Adam" (2:7). If we adhere to the suggested interpretation on the first account, then the text should read as:

(2:5b) ...and no human beings were there to cultivate, the soil.

(2:7a) And Yhwh God had formed humankind, dust from the ground
and blew into their nostrils, the breath of life

(:7b) And humankind became, a living entity.

Interpreting this verse in the general sense, as opposed to the more commonly accepted individual sense, raises the question of its juxtaposition: if the plurality is indeed what is meant, the author should have placed it after verse 1:27, thus describing at once humankind and its likeness, and the process of its creation. Had he done so, i.e., remove verse 2:7 and the further mention of Adam in verse 8b from the account, the narrative would have gained in continuity of subject matter: verses 5-6 describe ecological conditions of a certain area and verses 8-14 the area

* B. Jacob (Genesis, 15) is aware of this difference and explains it on similar linguistic grounds: "It has been claimed that the following chapter [2] contains a second story of creation. This is not conclusive, as it would be a story of creation in which nothing is created [referring to the omission of the verb BARA]... They [the animals and human] are "formed" and a garden is "planted".

and the garden in it; verses 15-17 convey a logical continuation of the garden into which Adam is introduced. But the author seems to complicate the narrative's possible continuity by scattering the subject 'Adam' among the verses as if out of context:

(7) And Yhwh God formed humankind (האדם)...
...And humankind (האדם) became a living entity.

(8) And Yhwh God planted a garden in Eden, from the east;
And put there the Adam (האדם), whom he had formed.

(15) And Yhwh God took, the Adam (האדם);
And put him in the garden of Eden to till it, and to guard it. [L]

(16) And Yhwh God commanded the Adam (האדם), saying
Of every tree of the garden, you may eat. [L]

The introduction of the subject 'Adam' in advance and in such scattered fashion, before the text actually deals with him as an individual in verse 16, is commonly regarded as a literary device which creates expectation. Furthermore, somewhere between verse 7 which, as interpreted above, talks about plural Adam, and verse 16 in which the singular Adam is evident, the narrative takes a turn — it moves from the plural to the singular.

There can be no room to suggest that until the occurrences in the garden, the narrative still talks of plural Adam; stating that it is dealing with *a husband and wife* suggests that "the Adam" in that particular place is an individual:

(2:25) And they were both naked, the Adam and his wife;
And were not ashamed. [K.J.]

The questions that the suggested interpretation of 2:7 as humankind raises are twofold: why did the author regard it necessary to recall the plurality of the earlier creation, and where and how does the transition from a plural to a singular Adam occur in the narrative?

In the first account the author explicitly distinguished between humans and other beings: the former are the only ones mentioned by their sexes and, moreover, they are made in the image of God. In verse 2:7, on the other hand, the author points out the fact that, in spite of their Godly image, human beings are basically another kind of animal; they also are autochthonous as well as נפש חיה — a living being (1:21).[47] Hence, I suggest, verse 2:7 is a clause in which the previous events of creation are elaborated (the same literary device has been employed regarding the state of the earth (1:2) and will be employed further on in 5:3). It is *purposely placed* before the verse stating that God planted in that land a garden, in which he puts a human being (2:8) that he previously formed (7), *because it is part of a context in which a confrontation between God and humans is to take place*, and in which the lines of demarcation and distinction between Godlike humans and the deity are to be permanently established. The mention of human origins as being from the earth and their essence as living beings like other animals, I suggest, is a clever irony directed at human aspirations, later on, resulting from their Godlike image told about in the first account.

The tangled transition from plural to singular Adam derives, no doubt, from the various possible uses of the expression "Adam", and they seem to create a pattern of what may be called — 'narrowing the subject'. As previously discussed, in verse 7 Adam is plural; in 16 — singular. The transition, therefore, has to be sought in verses 8 and 15.

Verse 15 may provide a leading clue, because it has a parallel verse that indicates the opposite notion through the use of the same vocabulary, involving the verb "to take":

(2:15) And Yhwh <u>took</u>, the Adam;
and placed him in the garden of Eden to till it, and to guard it.

(3:23) And Yhwh God sent him, from the garden of Eden;
to till the land from where he was <u>taken</u>.

Similar vocabulary is used to describe two opposing acts — placing Adam in the garden (2:15) and sending him out of it

(3:23). The purpose of both acts is the same — to till the land. The verb 'to take' has in these verses two verbal modes — active and passive: God takes Adam (15) but the verse does not state where from, and Adam is sent away from the garden "*to the land* from where he was taken" אֲשֶׁר לֻקַּח מִשָּׁם (3:23) [שָׁם: as both Bible Dictionaries tell us, is a different *locality* in which he originally lived], and he is sent there to live — to till that land.[48] Verse 3:23 does not say "to till the ADAMA from which he was formed", which would have automatically implied ADAMA as the material element. When the text indicates the original element of which Adam was made, or his end as the same element, it repeats the vocabulary (ground, dust) employed in Adam's creation (2:7, cited above, p. 85):

(3:19) ... עַד שׁוּבְךָ אֶל־הָאֲדָמָה כִּי מִמֶּנָּה לֻקָּחְתָּ
כִּי־עָפָר אַתָּה וְאֶל־עָפָר תָּשׁוּב

(3:19) ...until your return into the ground for from it, you were taken;
for dust you are and into dust, you shall return.

The "general" Adam, as explained in 3:19 was created from an element (dust עפר) from the ground (האדמה) mentioned in 2:7; but since he will eventually die and be buried (your return into the ground — האדמה) he will again become dust — the element from which he was created. A similar reference to matter (Clay) is found in the Mesopotamian "Enuma Elish" and in its Assyrian versions.[49]

Verse 2:15, thus, indicates that *a singular Adam* was taken from some locality; the transition from plural Adam of verse 7 to a particular one, therefore, has to occur in verse 8. A singular Adam had to be taken from among other already formed humans and put into the garden. These complicated verses, I suggest, should be read as follows:

(8b) And put [one of] the Adam which he formed.

(15) And Yhwh God took [that one of] the Adam;
And put him in the garden...

The validity of the above translation and interpretation rests on its logic but, as said all along, it also has to be supported by the text. It would have been simpler had the text presented in verses 2:8b and 15 the direct form מִן האדם — MIN Ha'ADAM instead of אֶת האדם — ET Ha'ADAM. This linguistic difficulty may be solved by adducing another case where ET serves as FROM: 4:1, "קָנִיתִי אִישׁ אֶת־יְהוָה I Have acquired a man FROM God", is a statement by Eve, where commentators regard ET as meaning 'from',[50] and the same interpretation and logic may be applied here. The above English rendering of verses 2:8b and 15, therefore, seems to provide an appropriate answer for the narrative's transition from the plural-Adam into the singular one.

Another alternative: a close affinity is suggested in *The Bible Dic* between 'to form — י.צ.ר.' and 'to gather — א.צ.ר.', which enables us to interchange them.[51] Thus, "ייצר" in verse 2:7 may be taken as 'to form', but in 8b and 19 it may be substituted by אצר. For 8b, this exchange implies that the creator took of the human stock he gathered (in previous creation), and for 19 — that he took from previously created animals. In both verbs, as discussed above, *it is not a new creation of new elements, but rather taking from existing stock.*[52]

> The literary use of "Adam" and "the Adam" regarding *the individual person* is interesting: although in 2:16 onwards "the Adam" refers to an individual, the article before the noun indicates that it is a mere noun, a synonym for 'the man'. In the summation of this individual's life (5:1) the author explains that "Adam" is the name of the species as well as that of the individual, yet all along the narrative he chose the reference "the Adam" — a nameless noun. This literary use is made clear if we notice that the first introduction of 'Adam' as a private name, without the article, occurs in 3:18, when God realizes that man's eyes "were opened" and thus he becomes more than a mere noun; the literary form for God's recognition is expressed when

God tells the future (לְאדם to Adam not לָאדם) and makes for them leather clothing (3:21 — לְאדם ולאשתו to Adam and to his wife, and not ...לָאדם).

It is only on this singular person, the individual in the secluded and secret garden — henceforth addressed as Adam — that an operation is to be carried out in order to form his partner, because, as will be discussed later, it serves the purpose of the secluded nature of the garden.

The above-suggested interpretation of "one of the Adam" corresponds logically also to Adam's isolation in God's private enclosure, an isolation which the author stresses twice — once after a single Adam is put in the garden (2:18), and again after the naming of the fauna (2:20b).

The creation of this Adam's female is a very picturesque one, and the phrasing of the actual process (21b, 22a) is similar:

(2:21a) And Yhwh God cast a dormancy on Adam, and he slept;

(21b) and took, one of his sides, and closed flesh, instead.*

* All translations of 2:21a use 'sleep' as verb and noun; the Hebrew uses two different words and the translation follows the Hebrew pattern by suggesting 'dormancy' as a noun ("sleep", n. New Collins Thesaurus; "dormancy", O.E.D.), and 'sleep' as the verb.

'צלע' is literally 'rib', but also 'side' (Rashi). 'Rib' is the common translation and the favorite one, probably because it is more picturesque and gives the reader a clear perception of the event. H. Goedicke (in "Adam's Rib", 75) suggests that the confusion about 'rib' as a member may derive from its writing in Egyptian: 'imw — rib' is a homophone with 'imw — clay' (Ibid., note 6) and says that "Adam's clay could in Egyptian be confused with Adam's rib". If the Egyptian story indeed nourished the Biblical one, the event should have been understood as one in which the woman is formed from the same clay element as Adam. The chosen translation of the elusive 'side' may come closer to the notion of 'Adam's clay' because it does not go into physical particularities.

(22a) And Yhwh God built the side that he took from the Adam, into a woman;

(22b) and brought her, to the Adam.

We have a sound ground to conclude, that in the second account, which is not that of the species but rather an occurrence in God's private enclosure, one individual was brought in, and another one formed — not originated.

In our conclusion of the first stage, viewed as part of the creation of the world, the transmission of authority was emphasized: God clearly devolves his responsibility on to the humans whom He has purposely created in His image. But when one of those humans is taken to the garden, the autonomy, which would logically be expected to devolve on him, is somewhat narrowed; it has limits. God develops a very peculiar relationship with the chosen human of which, at this stage, we mentioned only the unusual spouse. The relationship between the creator and this created one is expressed through the development of the personality of the human within the set limits, as will be discussed below.

3. The Created — Entity's Development

a) Introduction (2:15-17)

The individual in question was taken to a distinctive area which had no rains (2:5b) and was watered by subterranean waters, which practically points to natural irrigation, as we are told in verse 6.[53] He was put into a tree garden situated to the East of *a place* called Eden (8a).[54] The garden is suggested as "The House of God" and this is a deduction from parallel Mesopotamian compositions describing divine dwellings.[55] But such a perception is not conveyed by the text. God plants a garden, but it is his as is the whole of creation; the whole world is God's abode and "His house", in Biblical tradition, is the *man-made* sanctuary/temple. This particular garden is watered by a river that springs from

Eden (9a)[56] and it has all kinds of fruit trees, including two which are identified as “tree of life” and “tree of knowing good and bad” (9). There are several interpretations for what these symbolic titles indicate, and the subject will be discussed later on; for the moment it suffices to comment on the translation chosen above:

— “tree of *knowing*” instead of “knowledge” used by all translations. ‘Knowledge’ conveys a sense of a static philosophical wholeness whereas ‘knowing’ is an active continuous state which, I suggest, better corresponds to the infinitive of the Hebrew הַדַּעַת* and, as will be seen, suits the context;

— the term ‘bad’ was chosen instead of the commonly accepted ‘evil’, which implies intentional malice, whereas ‘bad’ is the opposite of ‘good’.

Adam is put there in order to till and guard the garden (15). For this he is entitled to eat from all the fruits but one, and a new verb (to command) is introduced regarding the instruction:**

* The verb 'י.ד.ע.' has various meanings determined by the context, and for here, “to analyze and distinguish by applying mental faculties” (The Bible Dic., 303, 5) is the proper interpretation.

The form הַדַּעַת is regarded by G. Bergsträsser (*Hebräische Grammatik*, 397) as “Verbalnominale Doppelnatur” of the infinitive (in Hebrew: "צורת היסוד השמנית־פעלית" of the verb), thus implying that it has two facets: noun and verb. His classification of Biblical occurrences of the infinitive is, ultimately, determined by his interpretation of the text. Thus, he regards הַדַּעַת as a noun (Ibid., 400), which fits the function it serves in the later books of the Bible (see Concordancia, 463). The literary rendering of עץ הדעת טוב ורע into modern Hebrew, according to the double nature of the infinitive, can be done by either an obvious static nominal mode עץ הַיֶּדַע של הטוב והרע (knowledge) or a verbal, more active one עץ יְדִיעַת... (knowing). As stated in the discussion, the second alternative was chosen for the English rendering of the phrase.

** 'צ.ו.ה.' is strictly an order; 'א.מ.ר.' is a general verb which denotes passing of information (ד.ב.ר. is the physical act of speech). M. Freilich

(2:16) And Yhwh God commanded the Adam, saying;
of all garden trees, *you may eat*.

(2:17) And from the tree, of knowing good and bad do not eat, of it;
For, when eating of it, *you may die*.*

The nature of Adam's task of "guarding" this particular garden can be explained by the presence of these trees. From their position in verse 2:9 as "inside the garden בְּתוֹךְ הַגָּן", it can be argued that the other trees might have been planted there as a sort of camouflage:

(2:9a) And Yhwh God caused to grow from the soil every tree desirable to sight, and edible

(2:9b) And עץ of life in the garden and עץ [of] knowing, good and bad.

(2:9b) וְעֵץ הַחַיִּים בְּתוֹךְ הַגָּן וְעֵץ הַדַּעַת טוֹב וָרָע׃

The use of the word "עץ — ETZ" in this verse is ambiguous: it is clear that it means plurality of trees [compare verse 1:29 "כל

---

suggests that צ.ו.ה. involves a conflict because it is followed by a sanction ("Myth, Method and Madness", 210), but sanctions are added also to א.מ.ר. (Genesis, 3:2), and צ.ו.ה. appears without them (Deut., 32:23). The issue seems to be not so much the sanctions but the implied quality of tone: צ.ו.ה. is a harsher expression where obedience is expected.

* "אָכֹל תֹּאכֵל" is translated as "thou *mayest* freely eat" [L], or "you are *free* to eat" [Speiser]. The two successive forms of the verb are difficult to render in English, and the 'free' in both cited translations is an interpretational deduction to which I agree. "מוֹת תָּמוּת", on the other hand, is translated as "you shall surely die" [L], or "you shall be doomed to death" [Speiser]. Neither of them retain the same rhythm of their previous suggested rendering of the first similar compound.

For the purpose of linguistic rendering, however, *the doubling of the verb into one compound should always retain the same form*, and this was achieved by the suggested translation of this paper for 16b and 17b, which omits the verbal 'free' and leaves it implied by the verb 'may', thus stressing the freedom of choice.

עץ — every tree"; literally all the trees] yet, further on, the text allows us to deduce that only one tree has been violated when the "tree of knowing good and bad" is mentioned. The conventional interpretation regards both special kinds of trees as single ones, and the question asked is — why the "tree of life" takes no part in the events of the garden, viz: why Adam and wife disregarded it and thus missed the chance of gaining immortality. The answers to this question vary,[57] but all are speculative, deriving from comparisons with similar motifs in other mythologies (the tree in the saga of Gilgamesh) and concluding that the author of Genesis was indeed referring to one fruit tree which makes it possible to attain immortality. The answer, I suggest, lies in the possibility of interpreting ETZ either as singular or as plural and, in this case, the text may give clues as to which is which, by means of the pauses and prepositions used:

a) The "tree of knowing..." has a pause after the word 'tree' (9b, quoted above), and thus the text accentuates and separates the noun:

> This tree is mentioned twice: in the first instance the author describes it to the reader (2:9), in the second, after it is known, in God's warning to Adam (2:17).
>
> There is a different punctuation in each verse — different kinds of pauses. When the tree is already known to the reader (2:17), the comma is but a grammatical means to clarify the subject and its predicative: "מעץ הדעת טוב ורע from the tree, of knowing good and bad" indicates that 'good and bad' are the adjectives of 'knowing' and not of 'tree'. But when the tree is not yet known (2:9), the author stresses its qualities twice:
>
> and a tree [of] knowing, good and bad". ועֵ֗ץ הדעת טוב ורע
>
> The first pause points to a peculiar nature of 'tree' and, as I suggest, may indicate a distinction between the two kinds of trees described in this verse; the comma in the second part, serves the same function as in 2:17.

On the other hand, the "tree of life" is stated without a pause and thus no element within its title is accentuated.

b) Only the "tree of knowing..." has an attributed preposition "from it" (2:17) and not "from them"; the "tree of life", on the other hand, has no preposition: "...and take also of the tree of life, and eat, and live forever", not "eat from it" (3:22).

From the different pattern of pauses explained in (a), one may deduce that the text distinguishes between the two kinds; and if the prepositions (b) explicitly suggest the "tree of knowing" as a singular, we may assume that the other kind, "the tree of life", is plural. The verse may be rendered thus:

(2:9b) And trees of life in the garden   and a tree   of knowing, good and bad.

(2:9b) וְעֵץ הַחַיִּים בְּתוֹךְ הַגָּן   וְעֵץ   הַדַּעַת טוֹב וָרָע׃

As Adam is permitted to eat from all trees of the garden (2:16) but one, the 'trees of life' is either a general title to all the garden trees or a separate category known as such *to the omniscient author* (2:9b), but not to his protagonist (2:17). This interpretation may imply that fruit trees of this garden, or perhaps all the fruits, granted immortal life; the garden's nature, apparently, was such that *eating from its trees constantly* ensured immortality.[58] That, perhaps, is why humans had to be expelled instead of supposedly one tree having to be removed. The individual Adam is merely the guardian,[60] and being the only human there he is the only one to know the one crucial tree's location and name (2:17).

This is the background against which Adam begins a phase in his life: he is a subject confined to the place and fulfils his task as a worker and guardian. The nature of his work, besides the physical element which 'to work' involves, is a matter of speculation;[57] the text, however, indicates by this verb that idleness is not part of life.

The development of Adam's personality from this stage of subjection to the realization of independence is set forth in three stages: the period of being alone, his relationship with his partner and, as a result of these — the concurrent relationship between him and the creator.

b) Adam alone (2:18-20)

Only one event is described regarding the period when Adam was alone: the naming of the animals (19, 20a):

(2:19) וַיִּצֶר יהוה אֱלֹהִים מִן־הָאֲדָמָה כָּל־חַיַּת הַשָּׂדֶה וְאֵת כָּל־עוֹף הַשָּׁמַיִם
וַיָּבֵא אֶל־הָאָדָם לִרְאוֹת מַה־יִּקְרָא־לוֹ
וְכֹל אֲשֶׁר יִקְרָא־לוֹ הָאָדָם נֶפֶשׁ חַיָּה הוּא שְׁמוֹ
(2:20a) וַיִּקְרָא הָאָדָם שֵׁמוֹת לְכָל־הַבְּהֵמָה וּלְעוֹף הַשָּׁמַיִם וּלְכֹל חַיַּת הַשָּׂדֶה

(19a) And Yhwh God had gathered out of the land,* all animals of the field and all birds of the sky and brought to the Adam to see, what he will call each one;

(19b) And whatever the Adam would call a living being, that was to be its name.

(20a) And Adam called names, to all domestic animals and birds of the sky and to all, animals of the field;

The placing of this paragraph between two phrases which point to Adam's social state (18, 20b; cited later) is usually interpreted as a way of emphasizing it: God did not find among the animals a suitable companion for Adam. It seems plausible because the two issues of the naming and Adam's aloneness are both mentioned in one verse (20). Colourful as this interpretation is, it has to be rejected on the grounds that the author thus puts God and Adam in an inferior state of awareness compared to the animals: every cat knows that among dogs or sheep it has no suitable partner.[61] The answer to this juxtaposition, I suggest, lies elsewhere:

When verse 20 is divided into its two different components (as is commonly accepted regarding the two issues in 2:4, see p. 68), one realizes that the first part (20a), as seen from the

* "gathered" and "land" for YiITZER and ADAMA respectively, is discussed on pp. 85-86.

verses quoted above, belongs to the previous issue while its last unquoted part (20b) "And to Adam [God] did not find a helping counterpart" echoes a different issue stated beforehand in (18b): "I will make him a helping counterpart". Both sentences have a common issue expressed by the same idiom "EZER Ke'NEGDO-עֵזֶר כְּנֶגְדּוֹ."

> The compound EZER Ke'NEGDO is problematic because 'help' is combined with 'against him' into a single expression. "A help *suitable for* him" [L]; "a help *fit for* him" [Speiser, R.V.]; "a *helpe meete* for him" [K.J.]; "companion *corresponding* to him" [P. Trible, God and the Rhetoric of Sexuality, 88]. All these translations do not project the element of encounter implied by Ke'NEGDO, and base themselves on what is supposed to be the traditional role of the female.
>
> The suggested, unidiomatic, "helping counterpart" was preferred because it retains both Hebrew notions of 'help' and 'counter'. However, Ke'NEGDO as 'counter' should not be understood simply as 'against' or 'contradicting' but rather as an equal power.[62]

Verses 19-20a cited above, on the other hand, form *a separate unit which stresses its issue by the triple use of the verb 'to call'*. Whenever the text intends to emphasize a point, one of the literary techniques employed is the use of the same expression three successive times [it appeared in the use of the verb 'to create' regarding the creation of humankind (1:27) and with the expression "the seventh day" regarding the Sabbath (2:2-3)]. The verb 'to call' in this unit, therefore, has to be the unit's focal interest and the text, thus, expresses the first intellectual activity performed by Adam.

The interpretation of the unit and its juxtaposition has to take this focal interest in account, because "before the intellectual work of conceiving and understanding of phenomena can set in, the work of *Naming*, must have... reached a certain point of elaboration. For it is this process which transforms the world of sense impression, which animals also possess, into a mental world, a world of ideas and meanings".[63] The unit, therefore, should be understood as *stressing Adam's intellectual capacity* rather than as presenting his social state of affairs compared to that of the animals. Its peculiar position between two statements denoting aloneness may be the author's indication, presented as God's point of view, that the quality required of the suitable companion for Adam is intellectual.

c) Adam and Eve

1) Introduction

Togetherness applies when at least two individuals relate to each other. The main protagonists of this state of togetherness are Adam and Eve, and for the purpose of this issue God and the serpent are secondary, regardless of the role they perform in the narrative. The text is neutral in its presentation, i.e., it stresses the point of view of each protagonist according to the action that takes place in the narrative, and thereby conveys a particular point of view at a given moment. The point of view of other participants is left to deduction or speculation.

As this book's point of view will be given in the chapter discussing the meanings of the story, the presentation at this stage will follow that of the text. The state of togetherness for humans starts with Adam's point of view and, in all, it is marked by four stages: acknowledging the phenomenon of togetherness, togetherness in tranquillity, in excitement and in the aftermath.

2) Acknowledgement of Togetherness (2:23)

(2:23) וַיֹּאמֶר הָאָדָם

זֹאת הַפַּעַם עֶצֶם מֵעֲצָמַי וּבָשָׂר מִבְּשָׂרִי

לְזֹאת יִקָּרֵא אִשָּׁה כִּי מֵאִישׁ לֻקֳחָה־זֹּאת׃

(2:23) And the Adam said:

This one this time, is a bone of my bones and flesh, of my flesh;

This one is to be called woman because out of man, this one was taken.*

Adam's first words when seeing the woman convey the idea of: "this one this time — is part of me". Remembering that Adam is one of the human beings and, like any other living creature, he knows how people are conceived (to deny him this intuitive knowledge would place him on a level below that of the animals), his reaction is understandable: this time, contrary to the natural process of procreation, זאת(ZOT; this one) is the one who was taken *out of him*. The triple use of the expression "this one" in the verses is noted; this very woman who was created in this particular way (not just 'a woman') is the focal point of the verse.** She is also the helping-counterpart that God provided for him, and Adam repeats this fact after eating of the tree: "The woman you gave me..." (3:12), and for the same reason — to stress that it was not just a woman, the snake or any other creature, but the particular one that God gave him.

The explicit and implicit meanings of the process of the woman's creation will be discussed further on, in the appropriate place. In the course of the narrative, and for this stage of our presentation, this process corresponds to similar mythological motifs of a female created out of male and, as she was not

* The suggested translation follows that of [L], only his suggestion for זאת הפעם-ZOT HAPAM as 'this time' seems to me incorrect because a subject is missing in the 23b sentence; in the rendering suggested in this paper, ZOT is the subject.

** P. Trible (God and the Rhetoric of Sexuality, 97-8) notes the triple stress on ZOT; however, because she regards the story as being that of the first humans, she shifts her attention to the sexual differentiation, and for her — ZOT "unmistakably emphasizes the woman whose creation has made the earth creature different, identifying himself as male".

brought into the garden from the outside world, it adds to the element of secrecy and seclusion of the garden.

3) Togetherness in Tranquillity (2:24-3:7)

'Tranquillity', for the purpose of this discussion, denotes times when Adam and Eve did not have to change the course of their life, regardless of what occurs in it. I am aware that this definition does not have the conventional meaning of "freedom from disturbances or agitation; serenity, etc." (O.E.D.). My approach is that the conversation with the serpent and the eating of the fruit are not disturbances; the word 'tranquillity', therefore, may be used in the suggested connotation but with the added subtlety: it is tranquillity because no change has occurred yet in their way of life. The tranquil times are narrated mainly in 3:1-7; verse 8 marks a change and thus belongs to another stage.

Togetherness in tranquillity is presented through two issues characterized by a social/philosophical connotation and through an incident involving another element of the garden. The two issues and incident will be discussed in the order presented in the narrative which shifts the spotlight from one protagonist to the next — the man, the couple, the woman, respectively.

a) For the man, the meaning of togetherness is suggested in verse 24:

עַל־כֵּן יַעֲזָב־אִישׁ אֶת־אָבִיו וְאֶת־אִמּוֹ
וְדָבַק בְּאִשְׁתּוֹ וְהָיוּ לְבָשָׂר אֶחָד

Therefore a man leaves his father, and mother;
And cleaves unto his wife and they became, one flesh.

This verse introduces a new vocabulary: man, mother and father, wife (literally — his woman). In the context of this story, the only אִישׁ—man under discussion is Adam, as he himself previously stated (23b: because out of man this one was taken); his woman (אִשְׁתּוֹ), therefore, is Adam's wife [and this very word is picked up, by the voice of the author, in the following verse which deals with a different subject — shame (25): "...Adam and his wife האדם ואשתו"]. Verses 23 and 24, therefore, have to be read as *a unit spoken by Adam* and not, as commonly regarded, as a general statement referring to a desired state of human behaviour.[64] These family relations with this particular woman are self-imposed by Adam, and our suggested interpretation of the verse makes sense in a situation where the union between Adam and wife is not a match arranged by the usual social involvement of the parents. Only in such a peculiar case, where *this woman* is taken out of *this man*, it does make sense to declare that he leaves his parents and cleaves unto his wife, contrary to the social custom, then and now in the Middle East, that a woman joins her husband's family. The obvious contradiction between the statement and customs cannot be excused as "a description of divine intention..." excused as poetic licence or as pointing to "the power of Love" (an expression not engaged in this text), [65] but rather to the peculiar circumstances that accentuate, by their very contrast, those customs. Adam's mention of parents is further evidence, supporting our interpretation of his being picked out from other humans (p. 90).

The implied togetherness that Adam expresses, however, is for becoming "one flesh" with the spouse, and it conveys a very specific social and philosophical perception of togetherness. It does not say that a couple becomes "one soul" but stresses "one flesh"; there is no elimination of the self in order to create a spiritual unity, but rather a union of two in order to procreate a physical one, of the flesh.[66] God's point of view, as discussed (p. 100), was to create an intellectual companion for Adam. The author's philosophical perception of a family unit, thus, can be deduced from that which he attributes to God's intentions and the reaction of his protagonists: a proper couple is one in which the helping-counterpart is intelligent, and both partners create a wholeness by a physical union.

b) The couple's joint perception of life in the state of togetherness is conveyed by the author's remark on their physical state of existence:

וַיִּהְיוּ שְׁנֵיהֶם עֲרוּמִּים הָאָדָם וְאִשְׁתּוֹ
וְלֹא יִתְבֹּשָׁשׁוּ

(25) And they were both naked the Adam, and his wife;
And not ashamed.

From a literary point of view, the intrusion into the text of such a verse presenting a certain state of affairs not seemingly relevant for the particular moment, is a stylistic device to prepare the reader for a further development, similar to the mentioning of Adam (2:8, 14) before the narrative actually dealt with him. The remark on the couple being naked and not "ashamed"[67] has physical and intellectual aspects:

— Being naked simply implies a physical fact. At this stage of their life Adam and Eve were walking around like animals — naked. Whether this necessarily implies a state of harmony with nature, is arguable.[68] Nakedness, however, does not necessarily imply defencelessness or helplessness for Man, more than it does for the naked animals.[69]

— Shame is something felt when one's actions, behaviour or state of affairs are considered as inappropriate. It presupposes a code of etiquette, and etiquette can be implied only in society — man alone manages without it. This verse, therefore, is but the author's way of expressing the absence of a particular social convention — shame; it does not convey any kind of positive feeling (e.g. harmony) that Adam and wife may had.

c) The conversation with the serpent is reported as being held only with the woman (3:1b, 2a, 4a), but the serpent addresses her in the second person plural — always as "you" (1b, 4b, 5), and the same applies to the woman's reply (2b, 3). Furthermore, her considerations about the fruit, eating and giving it to her husband, are all conveyed in the same verse (6) in a way that excludes a time span between her and his eating of the fruit. Moreover, the "opening their eyes" is a single occurrence, referring to both of them at the same time (7). It may be suggested, therefore, that the man was a silent bystander throughout the conversation with the serpent.[70]

The talking serpent is a strange phenomenon. As Skinner presents it: "It is the incomplete elimination of the mythological elements, under the monotheistic and ethical religion, which makes the function of the serpent in Genesis 3 so difficult to understand".[71] Some questions, however, become irrelevant when we deal with a Biblical text. To ask: "Does a serpent speak?" is as relevant as "does God speak", namely — one inexplicable phenomenon puts in question the other; and if one agrees that as far as for the personae in Genesis God talks, then the serpent can also talk.

Another question is "why a serpent?" The author states that it is the most cunning animal, but the fox is better known as a symbol of cunning and in ancient Egypt the ape was the attribute of God-Thut — the God of Wisdom. Serpents in Near Eastern cultures were metaphors for other things.[72] Let us discuss this issue of the serpent:

> An examination of the Hebrew noun נ.ח.ש. which alludes to the name of the species (נָחָשׁ) reveals its onomatopoeic affinities: whispering = לַחַשׁ, quiet sounds = רַחַשׁ and its basic meaning — a kind of whistle. All those verbs convey the sounds (sh, sh) made by serpents. *The active form of the verb נ.ח.ש. is Pi'el, and it means 'to divine'.* The Egyptian magicians used snakes as means for divining the truth, and whenever this verb appears in the early books of the Bible, (Genesis 44:5, 2 Kings, 17:17) it is always with the connotation of magic. These findings are echoed in the Genesis text: the author chose the serpent for its *practical usage* and not for assumed metaphorical meanings. His role in this narrative is clear: *to reveal the truth* as an oracle.[73]

The fact that he was punished for what he did, namely, being an accessory to a transgression, does not diminish the fact that his words, his 'guessing — נַחַשׁ' were the truth.

The snake stands as a metaphor for various things, (see note 72) but nothing is essentially 'evil'. True enough, the snake bites, but so do other creatures. The Biblical remedy for its bite was its own icon (Numbers, 21:8-9) which, in this case, renders the snake as a symbol of salvation, and that is why it took place in Israelite rituals until the middle of the eighth century B.C. (2 Kings, 18:4). M. Nadel agrees that in Israel there was no evil connotation to the serpent, and his conclusion, thereby, is that the story casting unfavourable light on the serpent is a much later literary product.[74] What is a later product, I suggest, is the story's unfavourable interpretation rather than its time of composition. The connotation of 'evil' must have been introduced as a result of the 'Fall' notion attached to the Eden story, probably as late as the first century B.C.[75]

Another facet of the author's choice of the serpent is a technical one: the conversation with the woman was held in a very low voice, assuming that the woman was answering in the same hissing tone. To derive from it that this was an inner voice[76] may raise the irrelevant equation, suggested above, that God's words as well are an inner voice.

Through this conversation the text exposes several points regarding the couple's level of understanding in the garden: although Adam was warned against eating the fruits of the specific tree 'of knowing good and bad', he is as ignorant about its nature and about the extent of the death-warning as is his wife, who even does not know the tree's name and identifies it by its location (3:3). Moreover, her statement that God "said" (אָמַר, not צִוָּה) to them not to "touch" the tree because they might die, points to the possibility that *she regarded God's words as a warning* rather than a prohibition.[77] Her words, thus, may indicate a lack of rapport between spouses, unless that is how Adam himself interpreted God's command. The tree, as long as they are sure that it brings death, holds no temptation for them; death is not tempting.[78] The tree becomes tempting only when the snake tells them what are its true effects:

(3:5) For God does know that, when you eat from it your eyes will be opened;
and you will be as God knowing, good and bad. [L]

The truth is told to them both, but it is the woman who is the first to seize the opportunity to acquire a certain kind of knowledge which will enable her to expand their likeness to God beyond that of form (3:6):

(6a) וַתֵּרֶא הָאִשָּׁה כִּי טוֹב הָעֵץ לְמַאֲכָל וְכִי תַאֲוָה־הוּא לָעֵינַיִם וְנֶחְמָד הָעֵץ לְהַשְׂכִּיל וַתִּקַּח מִפִּרְיוֹ וַתֹּאכַל
(6b) וַתִּתֵּן גַּם־לְאִישָׁהּ עִמָּהּ וַיֹּאכַל׃

(6a) And the woman saw that the tree is edible and lustful to the eye, and desirable for knowledge is the tree* and she took of its fruit, and ate;
(6b) And gave also to her spouse [who was] with her, and he ate.

The literary style here is revealing: eating is mentioned three times and therefore is the focal point of the verse; in 6a and 6b it appears as the last word of the sentence, thus underlining the important issue. But the sentence of verse 6a has two parts (divided above by the first comma) and the act of eating is reduced in it to an adjective (edible) in the middle of the first part. The stress, thus, moves away from "edible" to the part separated by the comma — "tempting for knowledge is the tree", making it a focal

* 'נֶחְמָד' as "delight to the eye" [Speiser], or "pleasant to the sight" [L] do not convey the essence of the verb ח.מ.ד.: *a wish to acquire*; this is rendered in the suggested translation as "desirable".

point and thereby connecting the act of eating to the practical *desire for knowledge*, rather than to a sensuous appetite for food. The verse is cleverly constructed so as to lead up to the act of eating — placed at the end of both parts of the verse, where the 'eating' is a result of the practical intention:

6a)	part 1 —	the woman's considerations are sensuous,	and practical
	part 2 —		her eating;
6b)		the woman's act,	his eating.

The man follows her, and the text does not indicate any contradiction or confrontation between them on this issue. Higgins suggests that "there is something comical in the image of the man standing there, never entering into the conversation, never interfering to stop the temptation... and only at the end reaching out his hand to accept and eat what his wife put in his hand".[79] It is comical only if an interpreter ignores the possibility that the man did not regard the event as "temptation" and therefore did not interfere. Adam's silence is comical only inasmuch as one expects the male part of the species to talk, think and decide, but not to accept and agree with the same actions taken by his spouse. Perhaps the author of Genesis had a clearer psychological, almost a modern, perception of the female drive, and hence the sincerity of the narration of this episode.

What started as an act of an individual, ended as a common step taken by the couple.

4) Togetherness in Excitement (3:7-19)

A. First stage: gaining of consciousness (3:7)

Togetherness is still in effect with the outcome of eating the forbidden fruit, when the couple goes through the first stage of excitement — a spiritual transformation overcomes both of them at the same time and changes the course of their life:

(3:7) וַתִּפָּקַחְנָה עֵינֵי שְׁנֵיהֶם וַיֵּדְעוּ כִּי עֵירֻמִּם הֵם
וַיִּתְפְּרוּ עֲלֵה תְאֵנָה וַיַּעֲשׂוּ לָהֶם חֲגֹרֹת

(3:7) And the eyes of them both were opened and they knew
that naked, they are
And they sewed fig leaves and made themselves, belts.

This verse, as the traditional pauses indicate, has five distinctive parts,[80] where each points to a different level of lucidity, each of which will be discussed:

a) opening of eyes, that is — the realization of an existing state of affairs;

b) knowing is separated from the rest of the sentence by a syntactical pause, and therefore I regard it as an autonomous issue. Although the text at this point does not specify what is known, nevertheless the context argues for "knowing good and bad";

c) comprehension of the nature of their nakedness, after which they perform:

d) their first act of creativity, which results in:

e) a product which did not exist before.

a) "Opening the eyes" is a general statement which conveys awareness, grasping the meaning of reality as it is; not seeing new things previously unseen, but rather acquiring a new perception of them.[81]

In the context of the story this means also that what was told by the serpent has been proven to be true: the creator withheld from them some essential and elementary faculty. The convention that God is righteous and means well[82] is an a priori assumption of interpreters. The author does not judge or argue for the creator, but conveys the information that Adam and Wife were not permitted to attain certain faculties and that the creator, using particular idiom, purposely misled them about a deadly result of eating from the forbidden tree: "You may die", as discussed (p. 95) does not indicate an immediate death, and might imply a possibility, a warning. God, thus, is a protagonist who leans on human fear of death in order to deceive.

b) "They knew". The nature of this knowledge has been widely discussed,[83] but the mountain of interpretations as to what kind of knowledge had been attained may be channelled into six main categories: carnal knowledge, knowledge of life and death, moral knowledge of good and evil, knowledge of the useful and harmful, knowledge of 'everything' and a moral autonomy.[84]

Carnal knowledge[85] seems to be the most popular interpretation because in the text the "knowing" precedes the consciousness of nakedness, and the immediate response to this is the covering — all mentioned in one sentence of continuous prose. 'Carnal knowledge' thus, seems to correspond contextually to the "knowing of good and bad". However, as the first mention of nakedness toward which the protagonists were indifferent (2:25) should not be taken out of context to allude to harmony with nature, so their awareness of it should not be taken to be more than what it is — awareness. Carnal knowledge [one wonders what can be "bad" in carnal knowledge or, for that matter, in any kind of pure knowledge] is something which the smallest being in nature knows instinctively; and there is no room to suggest that it was not known to human beings in a text which clearly states that they were created male and female and commanded to multiply (1:28). Such interpretations, in what easily can be labelled as "much ado about procreation", characterize both medieval Jewish and Christian attitudes toward the subject,[86] but they hardly fit into patterns of knowledge and thought in ancient times, where carnal knowledge or nakedness, despite complex taboos and rituals, was taken for granted and without inhibitions — as it is in so-called "primitive cultures". The problem in the text seems to be the question of *nakedness*, mentioned several times explicitly by way of emphasis (7, 10, 11), rather than that of an implicit possibility of procreation. Nakedness was not seen as negative in Middle

Eastern cultures: it can be seen in Egyptian wall paintings as well as in Canaanite statuettes which present people with exposed parts of their bodies (nakedness of the kind expressed in Greek art, though, is rare). The exception is the Hebraic one, whose negative attitude to it appears already in the historical sagas of Genesis: Canaan was cursed because of Noah's nakedness (9:22-23). Nakedness in the Bible is regarded not necessarily as immoral but rather as demeaning to those exposed, as in the case of Noah, as well as disrespectful to those who are present, be it only symbolically: the priest is prohibited from going up the steps on to God's altar, lest his nakedness be exposed there (Exodus, 20:26), and disrespect himself and God. In the East, clothing points to a social status: the poorer the person, the fewer are his clothes.[87] The same attitude, of *etiquette* and self-respect — not of morality, seems to be at work in the Eden story: Adam and wife are hiding because the belts that they sewed from leaves did not cover them in a decent way to appear before God:

וַיֹּאמֶר אֶת־קֹלְךָ שָׁמַעְתִּי בַּגָּן
וָאִירָא כִּי־עֵירֹם אָנֹכִי וָאֵחָבֵא׃

(3:10) And he said your voice I have heard, in the garden;
And I was affected with dismay because I am naked and I hid myself.*

The verb 'י.ר.א.' used here in connection with being naked, does not imply 'fear' in the usual sense of the word.** It would

* The first part of 10b is complicated: the common rendering in all translations of "I was afraid" is suggested here as "I was affected with *dismay* [dismay: "reduced to temporary despair or irresolution", (O.E.D.)]". The whole speech is said *as a continuous sentence* (unlike [L] who puts a comma in it) which conveys the idea of 'I felt uncomfortable because of my nakedness'. The word 'fear' is avoided for reasons explained in the next note.

** The verb "י.ר.א." has several meanings and comparative philology suggests for it both 'revere' and 'be frightened' (I.M. Gruber, "Fear have had this meaning, had the text said "I feared because I have sinned". The subtlety of the verb, however, implies here *a 'reverence' because of the nakedness*, and indeed later on God's reaction is to dress them properly with leather clothes (3:21).

Nakedness and procreation in this part of the text are are not correlated (the second element is introduced to Adam and Eve further on), and therefore carnal knowledge as the interpretation for "knowing good and bad" is inadequate.

"Knowledge of life and death", namely — consciousness of the potential of procreation, creation of life and realization of future death, is an interpretation which attempts to expand the scope of carnal knowledge by equating good = life, bad = death.[88] This equation, however, is rooted in the assumption that Adam and Eve, contrary to natural instincts, were ignorant of their procreative potential and their eventual death. We have already rejected this assumption about procreation, but equally unacceptable is also the claim regarding death. Every living creature is aware of death and instinctively acts to avoid it; even Adam and Eve were aware of it by not "touching" the tree.[89] This interpretation of "life and death" also fails to relate to nakedness which, as pointed out above, is a contextual imperative: the author puts it together with

---

anxiety and Reverence in Akkadian, Biblical Hebrew and Other North-West Semitic Languages", 412). In Biblical Hebrew and regarding God, however, it basically means respect and not fear or terror of him (*The Bible Dic.*, 340/2). Westermann quotes "who are no longer with God, are now possessed with "the fear of God" (Westermann, 254); but this does not correspond to the Hebrew notion; on the contrary, only pious people are "God-fearing" whereas sinners disregard him.

Westermann separates the verse into two statements (Westermann, 254): "I heard you coming, then I became afraid; I was ashamed, because I was naked. This is a prime example of how a division of the sentence determines its interpretation and stresses 'fear' as the main factor, against the function it holds in the continuous Hebrew verse.

"they knew" in the same sentence, and any adequate interpretation must take it into account.

Nakedness in this context, therefore, is regarded as a physical state of existence which, following "they knew" in verse 7, they realized and decided that it is a manifestation of disrespect to God.

Moral knowledge of good and evil[90] is an interpretation that assumes the existence of a certain moral code [set or invented by God?]. This knowledge is of a kind that one would expect God to give to humans; but the text relates that God conceals morality from man while, at the same time, tempts him to an act of disobedience that, according to that morality, is sinful. Another discrepancy is regarding humans' original state of nakedness which is considered as undesired; and the question arises, then, as to why God leaves humans to live in a state which is classified as "bad", a priori under this very morality. The contradictions between the moral assumptions and the facts in the text do not permit a response other than moralistic arguments of a theological nature, and these are outside the scope of this book. For the purpose of our discussion, therefore, the suggested interpretation of an existing moral code corresponding to "good and bad" is not valid. Similarly, the interpretation of "knowledge of the useful and harmful"[91] is invalid, as it implies that nakedness is harmful — again, an a priori argument of moralistic assumptions.

Knowledge of "everything"[92] or omniscience may be a human aspiration and is definitely a quality attributed to God; hence "you shall be like God" gives grounds for interpreting "knowing good and bad" as omniscience. 'Knowledge' as a quality which, to a certain extent, man shares with the gods and which distinguishes him from the animals, is a common feature of Near Eastern literature.[93] However, as omniscience is unattainable and, as a matter of fact, even after eating of the fruit humans did not achieve it, one must trust the author not to confuse wishful thinking with a fact of life when the reader knows the truth. Moreover, the context of the immediate stand against nakedness that humans take, implies that nakedness, as part of this 'everything', is classified a priori as "bad"; again, this is a subjective social attitude not necessarily congruent with pure knowledge. A careful reading of the text enables us to understand the serpent's words as referring not to knowledge in general [had the author meant it, the word "knowledge" without the adjectives would have sufficed], but of *a specific* kind of knowledge which automatically excludes any possibility of omniscience. The adjectives "good and bad" direct us towards an interpretation which involves a special kind of knowledge of classification or discrimination.

"Moral autonomy"[94] seems to be the correct answer to the faculty which belongs only to God and humans — the divine prerogative of determining *what* is "good" or "bad". In other words, man is now capable of setting for himself his own system of classification, *his own code of ethics*. The first to point to the direction suggested here was Spinoza, in his Ethics (IV. def 1-2). In the introduction to the chapter, he is aware that, as figures of speech, the expressions are subjective and *relative* (emphasis, added). The question why ethics are what distinguishes humans from other living beings, or why the author regarded them as a divine faculty essential to humans, will be addressed when we come to discuss the meanings of the story. At this stage, it suffices that this interpretation corresponds to the demand for a system of classification because it does not state that a priori there is one, but that the code is to be created by humans. It also corresponds to what is written in the text: after their eyes opened, they knew that they acquired a new faculty and they immediately implemented it *in accordance with, and relevant to, the setting in which they were living* — they decided that being naked is undesirable, so they sewed themselves belts; they set the first stage of etiquette by determining that appearing improperly dressed before God is a manifestation of disrespect.

c) "Comprehension of their nakedness" follows the act of "knowing" and not that of "opening their eyes" (3:7a). This is an important observation because it separates the awareness from the nakedness, thus expanding the scope of awareness which is usually narrowly interpreted only to embrace their nakedness. By juxtaposing the awareness of their nakedness after the acquisition of ethics and before the sewing of belts, the text conveys its perception of how to distinguish humans: as nakedness is an obvious common denominator of animals and humans, any kind of dress indicates the difference.

d) "The act of creativity" performed by the couple differs from the general course of work demanded in the garden (tilling and guarding) and thus it is an unnatural kind of work: it was not pursued by God or nature, but required an inventive and unnatural action. The fact that this inventive act follows the attainment of ethics and etiquette, in my opinion, indicates a philosophical attitude to ethics — they are regarded as a catalyzing force toward the fulfilment of practical purposes, because if one regards something as good, one strives and invents something to realize that good.

e) "Inventing a product that did not exist before" is the mark of creativity, or originating something new from existing elements; it equals God in his acts of creation, although on a smaller scale.[95] It is the last stage resulting from eating the fruit, last but not least — quite often the important part of a Biblical issue is presented at the end of a paragraph. In this case, the text emphasizes the product as the physical manifestation of human's spiritual similarity to God.

The text, as deduced from verse 3:7 on which we have elaborated for so long, presents the results of the eating not in the order of their importance but of their logical development, where each one adds another fragment to the formation of a conscious creative human. The results, therefore, have to be taken as one whole, where the "knowing" is as important as the final product — they all are but links in one chain.

The five results of eating the fruit discussed above were the first phase of togetherness in times of excitement and, as shown, the couple's actions and response were correlated and identical; including the hearing of God's presence in the garden: (3:8a) "And they heard Yhwh God's voice...". The act of hiding, however, is marked by a linguistic separation between man and wife — the text does not continue "and they hid" but rather states in a manner that leaves room to understand that, this time, the man was first:

וַיִּתְחַבֵּא הָאָדָם וְאִשְׁתּוֹ מִפְּנֵי יהוָה אֱלֹהִים...

(8b) and Adam hid and his wife, from Yhwh God...

This separation is continued in the confrontation with God which is held with each of them separately.

B. The second stage: the confrontation with God (9-19)

The exchange of words between God, Adam and Eve, has been the subject of several interpretations which, in most cases, have a recurring line of thought: humans in the state of innocence lived in harmony with nature — the 'paradise' notion; humans committed an act of disobedience — the notion of 'original sin'; humans realized it and were afraid; humans were punished.[96] This line casts an awesome spell over the conversation and the implied relationships and, therefore, requires counter-arguments:

— ***'Paradise'*** is a late concept for which the justification in the Genesis text is the name Eden. But the garden, as discussed (p. 93), was planted in *a place called Eden* (8a), and it is later named after this place (23a) and not vice versa. The narrative does not convey anything explicitly about life there besides the tasks of guarding and working, and epithets like "harmonious", "innocence", "paradise" or "peace and rest" added to it (see discussion p. 97) are not supported by the text.

— ***'Sin' implies*** an act contradicting a moral code, which at this stage of the narrative could not be committed because there was no moral code; therefore the notion of "original sin" cannot be applied.[97] The text employs expressions that point to disobedience; it may be considered as "bad" only if it is regarded as such by a moral code which, due to their lack of it at that stage, or the misunderstanding of the nature of God's warning (p. 106), was outside the scope of those particular humans' comprehension. Moreover, God's words on this issue are phrased in an indirect way.

(11b) is it from the tree, of which I have commanded you not to eat, you have eaten?

The syntax of the question is such that the part between the commas is an adjectival clause which relegates the 'disobedience' and emphasizes the act of eating juxtaposed at the end of the sentence. The straightforward way to ask whilst stressing the act of disobedience would be to isolate the offence by juxtaposing it at the end: have you eaten from the tree which I have commanded you not to eat from?* But the phrasing of the text, as discussed, relegates the accusation to a subordinate clause, and by this kind of question Adam is not yet fully aware of the importance of the clause, in spite of God's reference to the prohibition. A comparison with the verse where God explains the reason for the consequences of the eating (17a), shows a recurring pattern of the phrasing, but this time the offence is placed at the end of the

* Stressing the important issue in a sentence by its juxtaposition is possible in Hebrew's flexible syntax. Such is not the case in English, in which "I eat an apple" is an appropriate prosaic answer whereas "an apple I eat" is less, or almost never, used.

sentence. The syntax, therefore, clearly indicates that *this time* Adam understands that he has displeased God:

(17a) ...and you ate from the tree, of which I have commanded you saying you shall not eat, from it;

The assumption that they hid from fear when, as commonly claimed, they realized that they had committed a sin, is based on a misreading of verse 10. The worry, as discussed previously (p. 111), is that their nakedness might imply disrespect for God.

The questions asked by God in this narrative may indicate that we are not dealing with an omniscient God. Had he been such, he would have known the answer and the questions, thus, would have been redundant. Any reading, other than a literal one, projects a priori assumptions about God (which this book avoids) and thereby attributes to Him a sense of irony or regards the questions as a literary device, probably aimed at creating suspense.[98] The resonance of the conversation between God and each of the couple is a matter for the interpreter's discretion and suppositions; the text does not say that God was angry or whether he shouted, neither is it stated whether humans trembled, stuttered or cried. However, if read literally, and unprejudiced by one's notion of whether what happened is good or bad, the text conveys no anger and no emotions — God asks straightforward questions and the couple answers the truth as it is known to them and as it happened:

וַיֹּאמֶר מִי הִגִּיד לְךָ כִּי עֵירֹם אָתָּה
הֲמִן־הָעֵץ אֲשֶׁר צִוִּיתִיךָ לְבִלְתִּי אֲכָל־מִמֶּנּוּ אָכָלְתָּ׃
וַיֹּאמֶר הָאָדָם
הָאִשָּׁה אֲשֶׁר נָתַתָּה עִמָּדִי הִוא נָתְנָה־לִּי מִן־הָעֵץ וָאֹכֵל׃
וַיֹּאמֶר יהוה אֱלֹהִים לָאִשָּׁה מַה־זֹּאת עָשִׂית
וַתֹּאמֶר הָאִשָּׁה הַנָּחָשׁ הִשִּׁיאַנִי וָאֹכֵל׃

(3:11a) And he said who told you that you are naked;

(11b) is it of the tree, of which I have commanded you not to eat, you have eaten?

(12a) And Adam said;

(12b) the woman whom you gave me she gave me of the tree, and I ate.

(13a) And Yahweh God said to the woman, what is this that you have done;

(13b) and the Woman said the serpent HISHIANI, and I ate.

This conversation is almost unanimously interpreted as implying the disintegration of the unity between the couple, where each of them throws the blame for the sin on someone else.[99] But, as discussed before, in the couple's perception no sin has been committed. The conversation, therefore, yields another kind of interpretation, based on the context and the use of words in the above cited verses:

The inner divisions of the sentences point to a stable pattern of questions and answers. God asks Adam a two-part question — "who told you" and "did you eat" and one (underlined) adjectival clause; Adam answers in the same manner: "the woman" and "I ate" and an (underlined) clause. Only God's clause refers to the prohibition on the tree whereas Adam's refers to the woman who offered from the tree. The two clauses have the tree in common but they point to the alternatives Adam had between *God's explicit prohibition and the woman's suggestion.* Therefore God's next question addressed to her is about the essence and nature of her very act: "מה זאת עשית"-what is this that you have done (not "מה עשית-what you have done", which would have meant an interrogation about the deed, already known to God). This interpretation of the question is justified by the woman's answer: she does not explain *what* she has done, but *why*: "הנחש הִשִּׁיאַנִי-the serpent HISHIANI". The K.J. translation is "beguiled"; Speiser's is "tricked" and Westermann's "induced", all connoting, directly, something negative. But the verb נ.ש.א. in the Hiph'il form, in all Biblical references, is more subtle than the direct negative mentioned above, that could have been rendered by רִמַּנִי, הטעני, פתני respectively. לְהַשִּׁיא — Le'HASHI and its inflexions refer to those who believe that something good is awaiting them at the end of the road.* The serpent influenced her to act, because his words offered her a possibility of 'elevating herself' to God's state. As the serpent was proven to be truthful (they did not die immediately, and their eyes opened to realize that God had concealed from them an important faculty), her answer relates indirectly to her desire to acquire knowledge (ונחמד העץ להשכיל 6:3)** and indirectly to the motivation to reach a top (שִׂיא). The mere use of the word HISHIANI, however, does not necessarily mean that she regarded her ambition as negative!

A close textual reading justifies our suggested interpretation, because no hesitation is indicated in the couple's behaviour prior to the eating, no sense of guilt is heard in their response and — an important lacuna in the theory of them being aware of "sin" — *no words of regret are expressed.*

— ***'Punishment'*** is the notion that follows the supposition of a committed sin, but this too is not explicitly stated in the text. The persona God *explains* what will be the future life of the couple (in accordance with the author's intelligent observation of life). Had they acquired knowledge of 'everything', this whole paragraph would have been redundant; the necessity to explain natural life to the couple supports our interpretation of an artificial enclosure where God purposely kept its inhabitants in a state of ignorance (or innocence, if one prefers the glass half-full to half-empty)

* The Hif'il of נשא implies that someone aspires to raise himself up to a higher status or achievement: 2 Kings, 19:10, 18:29; Isaiah, 37:10; Jeremiah, 37:9; Obadiah, 1:3-4. Whether such aspirations are fulfilled or lead to a downfall is less relevant; in either case, it is summit 'שִׂיא' which is desired.

** The expression נֶחְמָד and its translation as "desirable" has been used also in regard to the presentation of both the trees (p. 95) and in the discussion of this very phrase (p. 107).

to the outside world. The necessity to explain everyday life to Adam who, as we claim, was taken out from an existing stock of humans, may point to his relatively young age; clarifications about life in this context, therefore, are not superfluous.

Two literary facts have to be noted: this future is explained to them *prior* to the expulsion from the garden, and to Adam it is phrased in the pattern of "because you have done so and so, then..." (3:17-19). The placing of God's clarifications as to the future, before the text tells about his consideration of expulsion and then its execution, justifies the interpretation of the above pattern as *clarification* — cause and effect — and not necessarily punishment, as it is usually interpreted. The more so, when the phrasing does not suggest a straightforward condemnation of Adam, as opposed to the serpent (3:14).[100] The text is so constructed that the last words of what is said to one, have the same subject-matter as the first words to the next, and the pattern is as follows:

serpent —	(3:14)	condemning him personally;
	(15)	relations between his offspring and the woman's. (
woman —	(16a)	her offspring's birth;
	(16b)	(her relationship with her husband.
man —	(17a)	his relationship with the woman;
	(17b-19)	his future on the earth.

Thus, in the first couplet the enmity between offspring is as negative a state of affairs as are the birth pangs of those offspring. The affinity between the second couplet is complicated and requires elaboration:

(16b) וְאֶל־אִישֵׁךְ תְּשׁוּקָתֵךְ וְהוּא יִמְשָׁל־בָּךְ׃

16b ...and for thy husband [is]your desise and he YiMSHOL-BACH

(17a) וּלְאָדָם אָמַר כִּי שָׁמַעְתָּ לְקוֹל אִשְׁתֶּךָ

17a ...and unto Adam He said, Because you has hearkened unto thy wife...

[L]

The crucial word of the relationship is YiMSHOL-BACH in 16b, translated as "he *shall rule* over you"* or "*he will rule* over you".** The difference is obvious — in the first case man is commanded to rule over his wife, whereas in the second it is presented as a future natural state of affairs. In both cases it does not complement the following verse which states that the man listened to his wife, and thus 17a changes the subject matter. The continuity of subject matter is reestablished if we translate the crucial word as *may rule*. This suggested translation is supported when this verse is compared to another, identical, verse in the Cain affair:

(4:7b) וְאֵלֶיךָ תְּשׁוּקָתוֹ   וְאַתָּה תִּמְשָׁל־בּוֹ

(4:7b) To you is his desire and you may rule over it.***

The essence of this translation appears in Speiser's Genesis, but worded: "yet *you can be* his master", and already in Rashi's interpretation: "ואת תמשל בו. אם תרצה תתגבר עליו". Whatever the expression used by the interpreter, it determines both for him and for the reader a philosophical perception of the relations existing between 'sin', as a powerful factor, and man: he is commanded to rule it, he will rule it, or as suggested here — if he wishes, he is able to rule it, thus given the freedom of choice. Rashi and Speiser suggest the last alternative, probably because 'sin' is an abstract entity which one does not literally 'rule over', indicated by the verb .מ.ש.ל. A textual reference: 4:7a suggests the alternative of: "*if* you doest well...".

The act performed, therefore, has to be an intransitive one,

* [Speiser], [L], [R.V.], [K.J.]. In 4:4, the R.V. employs "you *must* master it".

** P. Tribel, God and the Rhetoric of Sexuality, 127.

*** The translation follows M. Rosenbaum & Dr. A.N. Silberman Pentateuch (with Rashi's Commentary) 18. Leeser and Speiser use the verb 'can' which points at a *faculty* or ability, whereas 'may' points to a freedom of choice: one may or may not — it all depends on one's will.

directed at the person himself and not at an outside factor. A man, as the text is thus interpreted, has to rule over his own weaknesses regarding temptations and feelings in order to stand up to sin; the choice is his. By declaring that Man is able to overcome sin, the text does not diminish the powers of sin; it simply states that it can be combatted.

The same interpretation should have been applied to the verse stating the relations between Adam and his wife because the sentences are equally phrased:

(3:16b) וְאֶל־אִישֵׁךְ תְּשׁוּקָתֵךְ וְהוּא יִמְשָׁל־בָּךְ׃

(3:16b) ...and for thy husband [is] your desire and he, YiMSHOL-BACH

(4:7b) וְאֵלֶיךָ תְּשׁוּקָתוֹ וְאַתָּה תִּמְשָׁל־בּוֹ

(4:7b) ...To you is his desire and you TiMSHOL-BO

As this is another crucial philosophical issue, I would like to present several opinions:

> Westermann regards the pattern as a "mechanical citation which gives the words a quite different meaning in the new context".[102] The different approach suggested in this paper, i.e., that no citations are "mechanical" but intentional, implies a similar meaning to a new context. Unfortunately, Rashi makes no comment on this issue.
>
> Tur-Sinai (Turtchiner) is aware of the similar syntax of the verses and, like the approach presented here, he gives them a similar meaning.[103] But he bases his comparison on the grounds of 'need' or 'dependence': thus, because the woman desires the man, she needs him and thereby he rules her. His application of 'need' into the Cain story, however, involves the reading of חֵטא — sin as חִט — cereals, and an agricultural explanation is given as to why Abel needs Cain who, ultimately, will rule over him.[104] Although Tur-Sinai found a way out of the dilemma of how to explain the same pattern in different contexts, his system of changing the written text, in this case, is disturbing, because it is not a

minor change of a letter but rather a radical elimination of 'sin' in favour of an agricultural assumption of the shepherd's dependence on the farmer for cereals. But this is as valid an augument as is the farmer's dependence on the shepherd for wool, milk, and meat. A simple commercial exchange does not seem to be an issue of 'need' around which to build a crucial paragraph (for the same reason I reject the exchange made by Deurlo[104] who, as "dependency", extends it also to spouses, probably because he assumes them to be the only human family).

A better understanding of agricultural issues *per se* where 'sin' can be implemented in the Eden story, is suggested by W. Todd, (New Light on Genesis, 47); but his interpretation is relevant only for the Cain affair and, therefore, does not help to solve the problem of the similar linguistic pattern.

Although the woman is not an abstract entity, yet the same syntax-pattern used in both places in the text indicates that the same intentions are intended, namely — *to stress the factor of will.* Adam has to rule himself to resist the powers of the woman (which spring from her desire for him, thus projecting temptation[105]). The verse does not diminish her powers of persuasion by YiMSHOL-BACH, but simply states that man is able to resist her. This suggested interpretation of 16b corresponds to a logical contextual continuation, in which the following verse directed at Adam *picks up this very point*: (3:17) "because you have *listened to your wife*". Adam is told, also through God's words to woman, that he is able to rule himself against her persuasive power.*

* A similar opinion on women's power is expressed by Y. Zakowitz: "The subversion of the woman is the outcome of social organization; but Literature is capable of projecting the power within this subversion — a power which seemingly stands against conventional norms" ("The Woman in Biblical Literature", 22).

Togetherness in times of excitement, as we have seen, has two phases — the realization of a human being as an aware, conscious and creative creature, and the confrontation with God. The first phase formulates the personality of the couple and sets the ground for facing God — unashamed of deeds, respectful, offering explanations but not apologetic and, above all (as they have no sense of guilt), unrepentant.

5) Togetherness in the Aftermath (3:20-4:3)

The immediate state of affairs after the confrontation with God supports the suggested interpretation for the behaviour of the couple as being self-confident and guiltless: Adam, whom one would expect to be cross with his wife, if indeed there were truth in the allegedly 'lost paradise', acknowledges her importance — אם כל חי-mother of HAY and calls her חוה-HAVA (20). Adam's love and appreciation of Eve is not stated as a starting point, but as a stage reached, epitomized in the act of naming. The life episode in the garden, thus, requires the epithet "Love and Respect Gained" rather than "A Love Story Gone Awry".[106] Adam, equipped with ethics and all that they imply, is sent to till the land from which he was taken (3:23), and there he knows his wife and procreates his first son (4:1).* Although the chapter of the aftermath continues

* The syntax of this phrase "והאדם ידע — And Adam knew", viz: Waw attached to a noun, followed by a verb in the past tense, is systematically regarded by Rashi as past perfect, and hence his interpretation that Eve's pregnancy occurred before the expulsion. A past perfect event disturbing the narrative's logical continuity is not unusual, as we have seen before (2:7, 5:1b) but in this case it is unnecessary from the standpoint of the context; it raises unnecessary but unavoidable questions: did Eve conceive before eating the fruit? If so — all the assumptions of humans lacking carnal knowledge are invalid. If after it — there must have been a substantial amount of time between the eating and the expulsion, and this contradicts the spirit of the story where God is afraid to let the couple have access to the trees of life. [cont.→]

till Adam's death (5:3-5), the birth of Cain suffices for the purpose of the present discussion which is concerned with the personality development of the created ones and relationship established with the creator. Important in this context is the reason that Eve gives for the name of her first-born: (4:1b) "קניתי איש את יהוה" can be translated as: I *acquired* a man *with the help of* God[107] or, I have *created* a man *from* God.[108] The first one suits the concept of the humble Eve who acknowledges her debt to God; the second one follows the interpretation of "ET — from" (see p. 91), and corresponds better to our concept of the independent Eve who is proud that, like God, she is capable of creating life (in either case, the expression does not suggest that Eve was the wife of Yhwh and not of Adam[109]). This second interpretation can be regarded as sealing her confrontation with God, but also as acknowledging his superiority.

4. Conclusion: Creator-Created Relationship

The creator in the Eden episode appears to be a misleading persona.* The need to mislead in order to protect one's interests is an ironic situation for one who is regarded as almighty; the creator, thus, is reduced to the 'alazon' of Greek comedy, and I would like to address her, Good's explanation:[110]

> The 'alazon' is the pretender who affects to be more than he actually is. Humans, in this kind of Greek setting, are

---

An argument against a systematic application of the past perfect was presented (note II/46) and the same reasons are valid here: the narrative gives a logical order of occurrences and my interpretation, therefore, avoids unnecessary complications and takes the Hebrew particle "ו" as a regular conjunction 'and', describing the following event.

* The same motif, of a misleading clue in regard to profitable eating, is found in the Sumerian story of God Ea and Adapa; only in it the benefit derived from eating concerns immortality and not wisdom ("Adapa", ANET, 102).

the 'eiron', the sly, shrewd dissimulators who pose as less than they are. The conflict between the two is the basis of comedy.

Unlike the Greek comedy where the alazon puts on a false display, in the Biblical narrative God does not pose to be more than he is; the apparent pretence is the result of conventional interpretations which assumed for him the pose. Hence our claim that in the first chapters in Genesis he was reduced in stature. The sense of the narrative, I suggest, is ironic rather than comic. Moreover, God is presented as being threatened by humans; they have already acquired the divine faculty of determining their own code of ethics and they are capable of reaching his supreme prerogative of immortality (3:22). It is this threat which causes the expulsion from the garden (3:23),* and immortality is presented as an essential factor distinguishing God from humans.

The distinctive movement noted in the first account of the creation of the world, where God's authority over living beings is passed on to humanity, continues with humans acquiring the divine prerogative of determining their own ethics. If, in the first stage, the similarity between creator and created was that of form only, in the second stage it moves to the spiritual sphere which cuts humans off from animals and places them closer to God. The creator, whom one would expect to be angry and

* The reason given in the text contradicts Westermann who says: "The reason for the expulsion from the garden is... their disobedience" (Westermann, 271). He is not blind to the reason stated clearly in the text about the tree of life but, in light of his view of the story as one of 'crime and punishment', he dismisses it as an element of another composition, and claims that "The unity and directness of the narrative is destroyed *inasmuch as another reason is given in v. 22.*" (Ibid.; emphasis added).

The unity, I suggest, has to be sought for by including the reason given in v. 22 and not by ignoring it.

later on indifferent, cares about them, accepts the results of their transgression — the etiquette that they have decided upon, according to which nakedness befits animals — and makes them leather clothing (3:21).

The expulsion and the permanent inability of humans to acquire immortality determine the boundaries between creator and created: although one is destined to become the dust of which he has been made (3:19b), both have the same kind of spiritual autonomy. The creator, thus, remains superior to his created ones only where physical phenomena are concerned.

E. The Meanings of the Stories

1. Introduction

The lengthy discussion of the previous pages enables us to meet the aims presented in the introduction to this research: to determine *what* is written in the text, and thereby to look for the meanings.

The clarifications of words, phrases and issues presented many points differing from the conventional view of the text, to the extent that a new presentation of the narrative is imperative. In order to sum up the subject of the creation of humans, therefore, it will be necessary to go through all stages of a literary discussion, starting, in subtitles in this introduction, with a basic presentation of the narrative as it emerges from our examination, its literary analysis and its theme. The meanings of the text will conclude the discussion of the creation of humans.

a. The narrative

The fact of the creation of humans is mentioned twice in the text. The first instance (1:26-7), which does not mention elements, is a part of a chain of creation where their physical similarity to God is stated, in connection with His authority entrusted to them over other beings. The second instance is within the context of a particular area (2:4-6). Elaboration on the elements and the process of their creation are introduced (as I suggested) in order to clarify in due course the differences regarding mortality between the creator and the created. The second instance has been regarded as a literary flashback — not following logically after the first, but rather interposed as a clarification of a subject already mentioned.

The creation of humankind was intended to form a Godlike creature who will receive authority over the whole earth (1:28). The manifestation of authority or vocation to conquer the earth is determined by human needs, especially nutrition, which imply corresponding work: agriculture, livestock breeding and hunting. Later on, one of the species is taken from its land and put in a virgin area, in a place called Eden (2:5-6) where God plants a tree orchard of various kinds, among them two kinds which bear symbolic names: a group of trees which are "the tree of life" and a special one — "the tree of knowing good and bad" (8-9). The locality of that garden is given in geographical terms (10-15), and the man is taken to this garden to till and *guard it.* The latter task indicates the nature of the garden and the reason why only one man is there to till it — the garden is an enclosure created by God in order to hide the trees bearing the symbolic names, and the man is required to guard it from intruders. He is entitled to eat from all the trees, which implies also from the trees of life [later, to be understood as granting immortal life (2:17)], excluding only the "tree of knowing good and bad"; and he is warned that if he eats from it he might die. Not eating from it but from all other fruits, as can be deduced, would have left Adam (as suggested in the discussion about the trees) an immortal worker of the enclosure.

The narrative mentions animals in that garden, but the only relationship between them and the man specified in this part of the text is man's act of naming (2:19-20a). However, as this paragraph has to be taken as a part of the whole text, this act does not stand by itself but is connected with what was said beforehand about the animals: man who has already been given dominion over the fauna (1:26, 28), i.e., may use them for his needs, expresses this dominion, in addition, by giving each kind its name.

The state of solitude in which the keeper of the garden exists, without a companion, (regardless of the animals around him), is recognized by the creator as wrong (2:18, 20b). But being cautious about the secrets of the garden enclosure, God does not bring into it another of the species but rather forms from man's side a new creature (2:21-22). The man recognizes that the woman brought to him is an unusual phenomenon, and he expresses his astonishment and pride by naming her (Isha) after himself (Ish) because "this one" is part of his flesh (2:23).

The state of togetherness for the man starts with his self-imposed family ties: he has to disconnect himself from his parents and to cleave unto his wife in order to form a new family unit (2:24). Their physical existence in the garden is marked by similarity to the animals — both are naked and have no sense of shame about it (2:25). As the indifferent-toward-nakedness-Adam was taken from existing human stock, there is room to assume that either he was taken at an early age where 'shame' has yet played no role in life or, if taken as a mature person, that nakedness might have been common to other humans amongst whom he had lived.

The climax of the couple's life in the tranquillity of the garden is their encounter with the serpent (3:1-3) who cunningly introduces to them the possibility of eating from the forbidden tree, and thus acquiring God's faculty of "knowing good and bad", concealed from them by God's misleading warning of a possible death (3:4-5). Although during the encounter both Adam and wife are present, the conversation is held only with the woman, and it is her considerations and decision that lead them to eat (3:6).

The equation between "knowing good and bad" and 'moral autonomy' and its full meaning are expressed and explained as the result of the act of eating which changes their concept of life (3:7): a new grasp of reality leads to the formation of their ethics, according to which they reject the state of nakedness, and out of natural elements they create an unnatural product to cover themselves. When they hear God's voice, they hide in order not to show disrepect to him by their nakedness (8-10). The encounter with God takes the form of questions and answers (3:11-13) after which God, who is not pleased by their deed, as can be rightly assumed by the vocabulary used, punishes only the serpent for its catalysing role in enlightening the couple to the truth (14a). As a contradiction to existing human-serpent relationships, and perhaps in order to avoide more cooperation between them, enmity is created between the metamorphosed serpent and offspring and the woman and offspring (3:15). As for the couple, God accepts their ethics and etiquette and makes them proper clothing (3:21). As God's treasured faculty of moral autonomy is already common knowledge, he sees fit to tell them the full scope of life hitherto avoided: the woman, who is not a natural result of procreation and probably unaware of the facts of life, is told that she is destined to have abundance of pregnancies and birth pangs; her lust and desire for her husband give her powers of temptation but he will be able to "rule" himself to resist her (3:16). The man, accustomed to provide his food from the wildlife and fruits of the garden, is to change his way of life and depend on the hardships of agricultural work (3:17b-19).

It is precisely this change in lifestyle, as indicated by the position of this sentence, that causes man to call his woman חַוָּה-HAVA, because she was the mother of כָּל־חַי-KOL-HAY (3:20, discussed below). The change is needed because God worries that by staying on in the garden humans may also acquire immortality (3:22), and therefore he sends them away. Precautions are taken in order to obstruct the access to the trees of life (3:24).* They are

* The motif of 'Food of Life' is found in the Sumerian stories of "Enki

sent to the land from which Adam has been taken (3:23), and in the new/old land the woman conceives her firstborn whose birth she considers to equal God's creativity (4:1). The change in life pattern in comparison with the life in the garden is demonstrated by the occupations of their offspring: Cain tills the land and Abel is a shepherd (4:2); both living, as foretold by God, off the land, and in neither case does the text say that they are the first to do so (when the author wants to indicate a 'first', he does it with the expression "father of..."; e.g. — 4:20, 22). Adam and family, therefore, join others who live on the land, and amongst whom, later, Cain takes a wife (4:17).

b. Literary analysis

The analysis of the text as a whole has to start with the question "what is it all about?" and, as we have seen, the narrative described above conveys the author's interpretation for two phenomena: a) Man is the only living creature with the faculty of volition commonly attributed to God; b) unlike God, and like every other living creature, he is mortal. The first one is a quandary to which only a speculative answer may be given; the second is a fact of life which, however unpleasant, one has to accept.

The narrative suggests an enclosure in which the two are answered. The first one occupies the main part whereas the second is "solved" once the enclosure fades away. The explicit theme, therefore, does not seem to correspond to traditional titles of "paradise lost because of original sin", "crime and punishment", or a recent view suggesting "man's coming to an awareness of his utter dependence on the earth",[111] but rather conveys the development of personality of a chosen human being from

---

and Ninhursag" (ANET, 37) and "Adapa" (Ibid., 101-103), where eating fruits plays an important role; but the essential differences between them and the Eden story override the similarity.

dependence and unawareness to independence and consciousness. *Gaining of consciousness* is the narrative's highlight and subject matter; everything narrated leads to, and develops from it. This perception is evident also in the structure of the narrative, if the boundaries of the issue are determined at the point between Adam's coming into and leaving the garden:[112]

intr.

1. Adam brought to the garden (2:8-15)
2. God's warning — in the garden (16-17)
3. Naming of the animals (18-20a)

main body

4. Creation and appreciation of the woman (20b-24)
5. (narrative sentences) (2:25, 3:1a)
6. Conversation with the serpent (3:1b-5)
7. **Gaining of Consciousness** (3:6-7)
5'. (narrative sentence) (8)
6'. Conversation with God (9-19)
4'. Appreciation and naming of the woman (20)

conc.

3'. Distinction from animals — dressing (21)
2'. God's fears — in the garden (22)
1'. Adam expelled from the garden (23-24)

Parts 1-2 and 1'-2' have in common the same personae and place, but contradicting actions; 3 and 3' are units which do not strictly correspond [18 and 20b probably forming a different unit]; they might be connected as suggested above through interpretation. The proper division would be to relate to units 1-3 and 1'-3' as opening and closing paragraphs of the event (thus justifying the contradicting actions); the main even is emphasized between 4 and 4'. The correlation created in the central unit between 5 and 6 is a chiastic one, and the above scheme appears to present a coherent structure of the occurrences in the narrative.

The poetic style of the text cannot be defined in terms of any metric system[113] yet, its elements enable us to define it as poetic prose. The question, however, is — what is the literary purpose of this poetic prose? Once stripped of most of the supernatural connotations which go with "legend", the text is but *a record*, an historical account of events which the author saw as important and as fit to report.[114] That, perhaps, may be the reason why the author did not write in a distinctive poetic style such as ceremonial incantation of praise to the creator[115] but rather in prose, although poetic, as befits a record. The poetic patterns introduced, I suggest, are but a sylistic device to imprint the accounts more firmly on the memory, because in this way it could have been passed down orally through generations of illiterate people. Just for the record: the first mention of writing in the Bible is in Moses' time (Exodus, 17:14). Abraham's contacts with his family, via his slave Eliezer, were by word of mouth and not by tablets or papyri, even when it concerned the important and crucial subject of Isaac's wife.

A comparison of structure between the narratives, that of creation of the world and that of occurrences in the particular area, shows a similar pattern of "before, after and conclusion": the narratives state an existing situation before the main subject is discussed (1:1-2, 2:4b-7),[116] and then follow occurrences which start with an action (1:3, 2:8). Both parts are concluded by a similar sentence stating that "these are the generations of..." (2:4a, 5:1). The similar structure, I suggest, is another argument which justifies our claim on the unity of the text.

c. Theme

Gaining of consciousness — the philosophical issue of "Knowing good and bad", the faculty which, prior to the act of eating, distinguished God from humans — was found to be the structural highlight of the Eden story; it has been interepreted as 'moral autonomy' — Man's autonomy to shape his own ethics, i.e., to form his own code of values. Philosophers of all ages have discussed ethics, values and morals, and one of the central lines of thought was and is: "what is the 'good' to which we should aspire, and what is the 'bad' we should avoid?"[117] Usually, discussions on these issues concentrated on, or sought to improve, relations between man and society; they have almost never pointed out or emphasized that *ethics are essential to man's mere existence.*[118] We shall endeavour to explain it, and moreover — to point out that within this perception lies the explicit meaning of the Eden story:

> Man, as known to the observant author, has no automatic code of survival; his consciousness has to discover what goals to pursue, what course of action to take and what means will achieve them; and for this he needs to determine a code of 'good' and 'bad'. Because where no alternative exists, no goals and no concept of values are possible. The right goals for man to pursue and the values his survival requires are the questions answered by ethics, and this is why man needs a code of ethics.[119]

The author, as may be deduced from the discussion on the five stages of Adam's gaining of consciousness, saw the knowledge of 'good and bad' as an essential factor for Adam's development and he points to an external factor which causes the changes in human existence.[120] By presenting at first 'a natural Adam' in the garden, the story expresses the idea that living in God's enclosure without consciousness is possible only when man's state is similar to that of animals: they have an instinctive perception of safety and reflex course of action. In Adam's case, the similarity is manifested by nakedness as well as by the automatic cyclic actions of tilling and guarding, but without personal goals except mere existence guided by instinctive knowledge. By acquiring a moral autonomy, a code of ethics, Adam gains conceptual knowledge of the alternatives 'good and bad' and distinguishes himself from other living creatures who act on their instinctive knowledge. Although the act of eating fruit is a rational act, the connection between a physical act and its spiritual outcome in this story is less self-evident and requires elaboration:

> The motif of acquiring a spiritual faculty through food is quite common in primitive as well as in sophisticated legends and quite frequent in the Mesopotamian ones (cited from ANET): Enki eats the trees and is cursed by Ninhursag that she "shall not look upon him with the 'eye of life' ("Enki and Ninhursag", 40); Enki, the God of wisdom, "knows the food of life" ("Inanna's Descent to the Nether World", 54); Gilgamesh and the the tree of life ("The Epic of Gilgamesh", 96); Adapa is offered the bread and water of life ("Adapa", 101-2). This motif was probably used by the author in order to convey a transformation in the human phase for which he did not have (as neither do we) a proper explanation. The Biblical stories, however, are reflections of cultivated and sophisticated urban societies which have very little in common with everyday life of primitive tribal totemistic cultures. Therefore, comparisons between Biblical stories and totemistic notions may be rejected on the grounds that the civilization gap is big enough to enable primitive concepts to have sunk deep into the oblivion of the unconscious. The Biblical stories, on the other hand, reflect a clear and calculated consciousness.
>
> This, however, does not mean to ignore the fact that primordial concepts still retain a hold in the consciousness

of much later eras, and the so-called silly element in this story, as it is in myths of civilized people, "as a rule, is either a survival from the period of savagery, or has been borrowed from savage neighbours by a cultivated people, or is an imitation by later poets of old savage data".[121] The notion of 'eating a quality' is amongst them: eating a member (either of animal, of another human being, or even a plant which corresponds to human form) has the notion of acquisition of its attributed qualities — brain, heart, penis, etc. Thus, when T. Reick suggests that eating the fruit in the garden is a similar act to the primordial eating from Father's body,[122] it makes sense *only* inasmuch as eating from "the sacred tree [which] is the totemistic god" reflects the notion of acquisition by eating of the Father's attributed *faculty*. The Biblical author's use of the motif of eating from God's tree, thus, seems to be a literary use in order to explain a phenomenon, the attainment of a quality explicitly stated as the special kind of wisdom; not, as Reick suggests, immortality.

The literary connection made by the Genesis author between the physical act of eating and its spiritual outcome is thus understandable.

The fact that ethics, "knowing good and bad", are considered as God's prerogative, brings the discussion back to the starting point of God's creativity: God is presented as an entity with goals to achieve and, like the self-enlightened man, He chooses the right actions and means to achieve them. Without an ultimate goal or end, there can be no lesser goals or means; it is only an ultimate goal, an end in itself that makes the existence of values possible. Metaphysically, 'Life' is the only phenomenon that is an end in itself — a value gained and kept by a constant process of action. When the text expresses, through Adam, that Eve is the mother of “כל חַי-KOL HAY” it does not necessarily mean “the mother of all living beings” which, as a matter of fact, is untrue. This verse (3:20) about Eve’s name and function comes *before* the text states that she had conceived and, furthermore, where the role of women in the process of procreation is an instinctive knowledge for Adam and deserves no special praise. But by the title “mother of KOL HAY” the text, through Adam, conveys the idea that this particular woman is the mother of what can be determined as Life — HAY; she is responsible for the acquisition of ethics which determine the values according to which the pursuit of life and its goals is achieved.

Gaining of Consciousness, therefore, is not only the structural highlight of the Eden story (p. 133), but also its theme and message: the narrative illustrates how consciousness was gained by eating or, in other words, *how and WHY a special kind of authority had been acquired.*

2. The Explicit Meanings

Let us now, sum up our records:

The account of the ‘Creation of Humans’ was presented in its two stages, each having its own characteristics. The first stage was a brief presentation, due to the text’s clear and coherent perception. The second stage was elaborated at length, due to the complexity of vocabulary and subject-matter. The account has logical items which correspond to our understanding of natural phenomena, and as such they present no difficulties and require little elaboration; others are tinted by legend and, although intriguing, they seem to be out of place in the overall logical narrative. It is these peculiar parts that draw the reader’s attention, and interpretation of some [the trees of life, the talking serpent, the cherubim] lead to a clarification of their apparent legendary quality.[123]

The common denominator of the two stages of the creation of humans and the explicit meanings of the narrative have two aspects, physical and philosophical, both unnatural or logically questionable. They are presented in the following scheme which, when read horizontally, conveys the opinions already discussed:

Stage	Physical aspect	Philosophical aspect
I	God gives humans His shape and form.	God passes on to them His authority over the earth and everything on it.
II	A female is produced out of the male.	Man gets himself another kind of divine authority.

For the conclusion, a vertical reading is required:

The physical aspect relates to creation: in the first stage a human author bestows divine form upon humanity; in the second — he produces a female of the species out of, or by, a male. Both manifestations are universal motifs which preceded the Biblical account (e.g., the male Egyptian god Ptah-Nun, the father who beget Atum; ANET,5) and continued up to the familiar classical mythologies where they appear in several variants: gods assuming human form, Athena born out of Zeus and Galathea formed by Pygmalion are well-known examples. The literary reason for these motifs in this text, as argued before, may answer to the narrative's logical necessity, in the first stage, of forming man as the bearer of authority, in the form of the creator who gives him His authority; in the second stage, of creating a special female in order to conceal the secret of the garden. But the question "why the author chose irrational literary motifs, borrowed from an existing body of legends, as a solution for a rational situation"[124] lies in the implicit meaning of these motifs, and will be discussed with other mythic motifs of the text in the final chapter.

The philosophical aspect relates to authority: in the first stage of the creation of humans, it is given by God; in the second stage it is taken by man from a reluctant God. ***Shift of authority,*** therefore, is the main characteristic of the creator-created relationships narrated by the author.

3. The Implicit Meaning — The Mythic Motif

The implicit meanings derive from the explicit ones, as emerges from the two aspects of the scheme discussed above:

The physical aspect conveys the aspiration of humans which goes beyond mere 'authority' to the spheres of adopting divine form and the divine ability of creation. The assumption that humans are reflections of divine forms, in the first stage of their creation, is a universal motif and a purely philosophical speculation which, needless to say, cannot be proved. Its importance lies in the facet of the human psyche that it projects: the universal need to familiarize the divine which thus a) becomes an object to identify oneself with and b) a model of imitation:

> a) In psychology, this is considered as a process of idealization, i.e., "mental process by means of which the object's qualities and value are elevated to the point of perfection. Identification with the idealized object contributes to the formation and elaboration of the individual subject's ego-ideal.[125]
>
> b) The ego-ideal is a term coined by Freud for an agency of the personality which constitutes a model to which the subject attempts to conform.[126] In psychoanalytical practice, this agency is considered as resulting from the coming together of narcissism (idealization of the ego) and identification with the parents. For the purposes of literary search of the mythic motif, God (as will be pointed out — p. 234) is exchangeable with the Father.

Concluding this issue, we may state that familiarizing the divine makes it more accessible and better comprehended.[127] The mythic motif of this physical aspect, thus, may be titled as ***the aspiration to the divine***.

The mythological nature of the creation of the woman, or the universal mythic motif of a female created out of male and thus inverting the natural process, in the second stage of creation of humans, is regarded in psychology as ***the male's "womb envy"***.[128] In Genesis it is associated with Eve's claim that procreation equals God's acts of creation (4:1), and this appears to be the general common perception. But by denying the female her prerogative, be it only for one instance as it is the case in Genesis, the male authors of mythologies usurp this prerogative for their sex, and thereby achieve their unconscious unfulfilled desire to 'create':

> K. Abraham examines the Prometheus saga (the acquisition of the divine fire), and his conclusions suit other sagas with the same motif of acquiring a divine faculty. What he says in his research is valid also for the story of Eden: "I have not yet referred to a very remarkable characteristic of the Prometheus saga: that it is a pure masculine saga. The procreating man appears in it as well in the form of a person... [this type of saga] had the tendency to proclaim the masculine power of procreation as a principle of all life" and he adds: "That is the sexual delusion of grandeur of all mankind even to the present day".[129]

The philosophical aspect, in both stages, presents 'authority' as the author's distinct theme. Whether given (first stage) or taken (second stage), the implicit mythic motif it represents is a desire for it; ***the desire for authority*** (discussed on p. 60) is its mythic motif. In the second stage, because of the clash of interests between creator and created over a certain kind of authority, this mythic motif assumes the notion of "Father-Son Conflict".[130] Unlike interpretations of this concept as connected with sexual aspects (the well known Oedipus complex), the Biblical story does not hint at sexuality, as we have seen in the interpretation of 'knowing good and bad', but rather at authority — as the Oedipus saga probably does too.[131] The Genesis text expresses the Son's attempt to acquire the powers of the father by a protagonist who gains consciousness and a Godlike moral autonomy via transgression, and thereby gains control over Life.

The conflict of interests between humans and God resulted in the establishment of a new kind of creator-created relationship: not that of master and his obedient servant, typical to other mythologies, but rather that of a master who has to take the will and wishes of his created one into account. This unique relationship is fully manifested in the account of the creation of a nation which will be discussed in the next chapter.

Chapter IV
CREATION of a NATION

A. Introduction

'Nation' is understood in the O.E.D. as "people distinguished by community of descent, language, history, as to form a distinctive race or people, usually organized as a separate political state and occupying a definite territory". In early examples, states the dictionary, the racial idea is usually stronger than the political, whereas in recent use — the notion of political unity and independence is more prominent. The O.E.D. perception of 'nation' is related to the concept of 'a people' viz., a body of persons comprising a community, tribe, race or nation. Both concepts do not comfortably fit the Jews: are they a nation? a religion? a people? The disputes on the issue seem to be everlasting, and they continue also into the entity of the modern Israeli state.[1] The lack of clarity emanates from the fact that for most of their history, Jews lacked the above mentioned elements of political institutions, a common *spoken* language or a territory.

On the other hand, Jews had and still have *a cultural common denominator* ('culture' being an attitude of mind which determines values — p. 25) which resulted in a unique sense of purpose to their existence as a distinctive group, and this has been the case since the dawn of the Israelite entity. The common ancestral origin, no doubt, is a strong common denominator of the cultural sense. However, I suggest that it is not mere blood ties with the ancestors but rather a common cultural backbone which gives the ties its unique significance, mainly — the pact with God.[2]

But abstract cultural notions are not part of the above mentioned commonly accepted definitions, and as this paper has no intention of solving a millenium-old quandary about how to define the Jews, a self-imposed attitude is required for the following discussion. Leaving aside the disputes of sociologists, and for the reasons given above, it is now agreed (and we shall elaborate upon it further on) that Jews are a nation as well as a people or, in Biblical terms — GOY and AM.[3] The relevant questions arising from this statement are: who creates the nation, how many people are needed in order to constitute such a body, and how or when is it actually realized. The answers to these questions have to be looked for in Genesis; our aim is to find what are *the author's answers* and how they are expressed.

Nations in Genesis are mentioned as a matter of fact (chapter 10), where the name of the nation's founder becomes the name of the nation, and it is not characterized further. Among the nations which are naturally formed by accumulation of social and historical factors (not elaborated in the Genesis text), only the one nation under discussion is described as a preconceived one, the artificial result of a private pact between God and one person.

Thus, the text answers clearly the first question of "who" — God proclaims its intended creation, and its realization in Genesis is conditioned by the will of a chain of three generations of one family to hold on to this pact, and to perform certain acts in order to retain it. The answers to the question of who actually were the forefathers of the nation have two principal trends: demythologized Gods or indeed human beings. For anthropology, and also in the case of Mesopotamian God-Marduch who was the forefather of Erech, the first trend prevails; for Biblical research, the second.[4] For the purpose of this literary research they are protagonists considered by the text to be humans.

But one person in each successive generation does not constitute a nation; the text clearly states that only in Egypt nationhood will be self-evident (45:3) as well as its commonly acknowledged national name 'Israel' (Exodus, 1:7). For our research, however, the creation of the nation is not the stage where its existence is taken for granted but rather *the formation's process*; 'Creation', where the nation is concerned and as it has been in the previously discussed creations, embraces the span between the declaration of intention to a degree of realization, where more than individuals are involved and where the group receives its name. Jacob and his direct family who number seventy (46:27b, not including the uncounted household members), form such a group which corresponds to our requirement.

> The text never relates to household servants as part of the family, although it tells that Abraham (who had enough of them to form a small army (14:14), circumcised them, thus indirectly made them members of the pact. It can be assumed that by the time Jacob went to Egypt, i.e., within the span of time embraced by Genesis, they were quite numerous.

For the purpose of this research, therefore, Jacob and his household represent the turning point from individuals to a nation, and they justify the restriction of the research on the subject to the book of Genesis. The fact that the cultural common denominator, the sense of purpose, continues developing beyond the Genesis narrative, is beside the point; no living social group retains, forever unchanged, the same cultural platform.

Answering the question of HOW the nation is realized, therefore, is the aim of the following discussion, relating to Genesis only. From chapter 12 onwards, Genesis and most of the other books in the Bible deal, between the lines of the history of a particular nation, also with its relationship with its God. But unlike previously discussed creations, there is no one verse, chapter or continuous narrative, which can be singled out as indisputably indicating 'lo, a new nation is created here'. Mainly, because the abstract factor of cultural entity, that is — the sense of common purpose of a group which singles out the Jews as a nation, develops gradually and is not 'made' or 'created' in one act.* It is the outcome of the evolution of the pact between God and Abraham via his heirs, culminating in (Exodus: (6:7a):

וְלָקַחְתִּי אֶתְכֶם לִי לְעָם   וְהָיִיתִי לָכֶם לֵאלֹהִים

"And I will take you to me as my people   and I will be to you for a God".

[L]

This evolution is expressed in Genesis through encounters in which messages and promises are communicated to the patriarchs. The questions whether the promises are an integral part of the text or later additions and what is the amount of historical truth in the stories,[5] are irrelevant to the *literary truth* discussed here about the relationship with God. On the other hand, the question raised by Z. Weisman: "Did the national religious consciousness embodied in the promises originate the narratives or did it establish itself upon existing narratives?" is not a simple riddle of what preceded what, and it also evokes previously discussed questions of authorship. In his conclusion that the stories about Jacob contain earlier promises regarding the national consciousness as well as earlier religious strata than the stories about Abraham and Isaac, Z. Weisman points to the first alternative, that is — an achieved, existing phase of the national consciousness which originated the narratives; he justifies it by relying on the Documentary Hypothesis.[7]

The approach of this book, based on a rejection of 'documents', tends to support the second alternative, i.e., that the national consciousness established itself upon existing narratives. In other words, the narrated *historical events* provided the theoretical-

* I find a support for this argument in Z. Weisman's statement that the stories are "not dealing with *a single national historical conception* regarding the origins of Israel" and that in the patriarchal promises "it represents the collective consciousness of settler tribes rather than that of a nation or of a kingdom", while pointing to an early phase of the *development* of the national consciousness.[6]

theological grounds for the national consciousness. This approach is explicitly expressed in Exodus: Moses employs the national memory on the patriarchs in order to evoke the national consciousness (Exodus, 6) and the detailed narratives may have followed. These narratives[8] which express the evolution of the relationship between God and his created nation are presented by encounters, spread throughout Genesis. The final stage is reached when, according to the self-imposed attitude discussed earlier, the group acquires its national name (35:9-10). Therefore, there is a need to accumulate a reference text [henceforth to be called 'the narrative-body'] consisting of isolated verses where communication between both parties occurs, and the exchanges concern the characteristics of a nation (population, territory, and name/identity). The encounters which constitute the narrative-body will be presented in their chronological order and identified henceforth by their number.

B. The Narrative-Body

Eight encounters between Abraham and God are mentioned [the names Abraham and Abram will be used in accordance with the text in question (see encounter 6 below)]; two other encounters are marked A, B, and the intended discussion will justify their exclusion from the general list. The following presentation of encounters includes direct communications — when God speaks, and indirect ones — when his angel speaks or when the protagonist is not aware of the deity. Each presentation points to characteristics of subject matter, and in small print in parentheses — to the protagonist's age and location.

1. The Call: God speaks to Abram, promising him a status of nationhood if he leaves his country and goes to a new place chosen by God (12:1-3);

[communicated in Haran — Abram is 75 years old].

2. Arrival to Canaan: God reveals himself to Abram, and promises him the very land into which he came — Canaan (12:7); [communicated in Elon-Moreh near Shechem].

3. In Canaan: God presents the whole promised land to Abram, who is told to walk through it; many descendants are predicted for him (13:14-17); [communicated between Beit-El and Ha'ai].

4. The first covenant: between God and Abram (15) involving God's passing between the pieces and promises of descendants and territory;

[in Elonei-Mamre, near Hebron; Abram is about 85 years old].

5. Hagar and YHWH's angel: An indirect communication (between God's messenger and Hagar) where the name Ishmael is suggested (16:7-13);

[communicated in the southern road of Shur; Abram is 86 years old].

6. The second covenant: God reveals himself to Abram — the second covenant involving Abraham's circumcision and new name (17:1-22);

[in Elonei-Mamre near Hebron, Abraham is 99 years old].

A. Abraham and three messengers: they travel to Sodom (18:1-22); one of them promises a son within a year.

[Time and place as in No. 6].[9]

B. Abraham and one messenger: An indirect communication with God (18:23-33) who proclaims the destruction of Sodom. [the above time and place].

7. The expulsion of Ishmael: God suggests that Abraham accept Sarah's decision to expel Ishmael (21:12-13);

[in Gerar, Philistine land; Abraham is 101-2 years old*].

* Ishmael was expelled after Isaac's weaning period ended, 1-2 years

8. The binding of Isaac: Direct and indirect communication with God — sacrificing Isaac (22);

[Isaac — unknown age*, with his mother in Hebron (23:2); Abraham in Bèer-Sheba (22:19)].

Abraham was 75 years old when he first heard the call to go (No. 1); the last direct encounter with God was when he expelled Ishmael (No. 7), and he was then 101-2. As he died at 175, his six direct communications with God (1-4, 6, 7) took place in a span of 25 years in mid-life.**

After Abraham's death, God continues the intimate relationship with his son Isaac, and the text records only three encounters:

1. God speaks to Rebekah, predicting two nations from her (25:23); [in Be'er Lachai-Roi, Isaac is 60 years old].

---

after birth; Abraham was 100 when Isaac was born; hence Abraham's estimated age of 101-2 when Ishmael was expelled.

* The text does not specify either when in Abraham's life the event occurred or Isaac's age, Isaac's title 'נַעַר' — NA'AR (a boy) does not clarify the issue because it indicates an emotional connection between the protagonists rather than an age [this will be explained in the due discussion of the issue, p. 198]. As for Isaac's age, the issue remains unsolved. *Bereshit Rabah,* 58:5 deduces, from the juxtaposition of Sarah's death immediately after the event, that her death occurred by a stroke after she heard of Isaac's tribulations. This is an implausible suggestion, as Sarah died at the age of 127 (23:1) and she gave birth at the age of 90; Isaac was 37 when she died and, thus — according to *Bereshit Rabah,* the same age at the Binding. It is hard to accept that a 37 year old man, silently and without comment, would let himself be tied to an altar by an elderly father, 137 years old.

** Abraham lived 175 years (25:7); at the time of his first Call he was 75 (12:4), and the last direct comunication was in encounter No. 7, when he was 101-2. Therefore, no direct communication with God is reported in the first and the last 75 years of his life.

2. God reveals himself to Isaac, asking him not to go to Egypt, (26:2-5); [settling in Gerar; see Abraham's No. 7].

3. God reveals himself to Isaac, promising him many descendants (26:24); [in Be'er Sheba].

The route that Abraham took in one direction has been trodden by Jacob twice, and in both directions he has been guided by encounters with God:

1. Jacob's dream: God speaks to him, promising him peoplehood and the land (28:12-15); Jacob's response (28:20-22); [in Luz, Beit-El].

2. Leaving Haran: God tells Jacob to go back to his homeland (30:3, 11-13); [in Haran].
   A. Jacob meets with God's angels (32:2-3). [in the land of Gilead].
   B. The encounter at the Yabbok (32:25-31); the first mention of the name of the nation, Israel, repeated later on in 35:9-10. [in Gilead].

3. God summons Jacob to Beit-El: thanksgiving (35:1, 6-7) and God's promises to him — descendants and his father's land (35:11-15); [in Beit-El].

4. God encourages Jacob to go to Egypt: the promise about nationhood and the return from the exile given to Abraham is repeated (46:1-4); [near Hebron].*

* Genesis 37:1 states that Jacob lived in his father's area, which in 23:2 and 26:23 is Hebron. Later on, Jacob sends Joseph from Hebron to visit his brothers in Shechem (37:14).

These are the encounters to which the forthcoming discussion is to relate. One feature that stands out is the different marking (letters) given to Abraham and Jacob's encounters with beings called angels; the difference of these encounters from others will be clarified in the discussion on word analysis.

C. Word Analysis

1. Introduction

The above presentation of isolated sentences which do not form one continuous narrative, requires general agreement regarding linguistic expressions and synonyms. Our discussion will analyse the vocabulary used in regard to the following concept — deity, nation and land — and will attempt to find what it expresses at each particular point in the text. Since, in this paper, we have not accepted the 'documentary' approach, our analysis will attempt to find a coherent unifying meaning for each expression in regard to the whole. The relevant terms for the above mentioned concepts are: Elohim/Yhwh/angel/El; nation/people; and the extent of the promised land. The terms will be discussed in this order, examining the vocabulary used for each concept throughout the encounters presented above.

2. Elohim / Yhwh / Angel / El — אלהים, יהוה, מלאך, אל

a) Introduction

The expressions אֱלֹהִים and יְהוָה [hereafter — Elohim, Yhwh], why and when they occur, indicate for the European School of interpretation different authors/sources of a text; and in light of the difficulties facing a reader who is looking for a coherent *literary* answer to each expression, the Documentary-Hypothesis poses an irresistible temptation to help manoeuvre oneself out of the literary dilemma. But this hypothesis results in dividing a logically continuous narrative such as that of chapter 35 into a patchwork of verses [1-8, E; 9-13,/P/; 14,E; 15,/P/; 16-20,E; 21-22a,J; 22b-29,/P/] (Speiser) which cannot constitute any literary work.

Regardless of 'documents', 'Elohim' is usually comprehended as a generic form of the noun, whereas 'Yhwh' is either a synonym for the noun, or a specific/private name[10] acting as the private or the national god of the protagonists concerned. If we return to the texts which we discussed earlier, we shall see that this basic distinction is justified: 'Elohim' in the chapter of the creation of a world, can indeed be regarded as the generic entity, whereas 'Yhwh-Elohim' as a name of the account of locality, for the protagonists involved, is a more private entity. An interesting suggestion, for the *meaning* of this compound is made by Ellen Van Wolde: as YHWH he is the one who exists in continuity and represents eternal life; as ELOHIM, he is the one who creates, discriminates and differentiates.[11] As a private *name* the linguistic use of 'Yhwh' in the subsequent chapters, seems to point to the personal God of Adam's descendants after Enosh (4:26b). But in the story of Noah both expressions are used, and the reasoning behind both synonyms requires interpretational speculation as to how to justify the use of each.[12] On one occasion, however, the distinctions suggested above seem to be explicitly supported by the Noah narrative — in the poetical phrase of Noah himself:

(8:26a) בָּרוּךְ יהוה אֱלֹהֵי שֵׁם

(8:26a) ...blessed be Yhwh, the God of Shem;...

whereas for Yapeth the author uses the general name:

(27a) Elohim will enlarge Yapheth... (27a) יַפְתְּ אֱלֹהִים לְיֶפֶת

'Yhwh', in this context, is a word used by Noah to describe the deity of one of his sons, and the syntax of the cited verse may imply that it is a private name, long before the Hebrews related it as a personal name for their national God. But how is this verse to be interpreted — as the voice of an omniscient author from a later period who is aware that Yhwh is a private name, or perhaps as *a literary* vacillation of a synonymous noun in order to avoid repetition and achieve a poetic effect? A possible explanation in the literary direction may be the linguistic premises: whereas 'Yhwh' always stands as it is — uninflected, 'Elohim' lends itself to inflexion ...אלֹהֵי...אלֹהיך... etc., and thus the use of expressions may be determined by literary necessity.

The issue is even more complicated in the narratives of the patriarchs, in which only the encounters with the Almighty concern us. Since He is their private God, the use of 'Yhwh' should have been prominent if not absolute, both by the author who no doubt regarded Yhwh as his personal God, and also by the protagonists who consciously perceived him as such. This, however, is not the case, and here we shall adduce one of Abraham's encounters to illustrate the complexity of the issue:

Encounter No. 6 is linguistically important because three synonyms are used: 'Yhwh' opens the encounter conveying the voice of the author (17:1); then *the deity introduces himself* for the first time in the text of Genesis by a version of the local name 'El' thus indicating for the reader that this is how Abram relates to him: "I am El-Shadai" (17:1b); the following designation is 'Elohim' — the generic name for the deity which, again, presents the author's voice (3b onwards).

'El-Shadai', the name by which God presents himself to Abraham and later on to Jacob (35:11), is formed upon the Canaanite designation for the deity of locality 'EL';[13] the others mentioned in Genesis are "El-Elion" (14:18) and "El-Roi" (16:13); apparently, in all cases the compound points to a quality.[14] This name, as later on told to Moses, is the only facet of God presented to the forefathers (Exodus 6:3):

וָאֵרָא אֶל־אַבְרָהָם אֶל־יִצְחָק וְאֶל־יַעֲקֹב בְּאֵל שַׁדָּי
וּשְׁמִי יהוה לֹא נוֹדַעְתִּי לָהֶם׃

And I appeared, to Abraham to Isaac and to Jacob, as El-Shadai;

and my name Yhwh   I did not make it comprehensible to them.*

If the integrity of the text is agreed upon and the use of 'Yhwh' in the Exodus verse cited above accepted, then throughout Genesis 'Yhwh' should be regarded only as a noun, a synonym for 'God', even when the context enables us to interpret it as a private name. The use of designations or their vacillation, therefore, may be regarded as merely literary devices which has no bearing on their meaning.[15] Apart from this alternative of a literary nature, no other suggestion, unfortunately, is plausible enough to explain all the occurrences of God's designations in the text.[16]

The following discussion aims to find the *nature of the deity as it is exposed in the text* by whatever synonyms used to represent Him, rather than to argue the unsolved quandary — their literary use in Genesis as a whole.

Much has been written on the consonants YHWH (see note 6) and the issue is still undecided. Linguistic issues as such are outside the scope of this paper, but I allow myself a brief comment:

* Leeser renders: "And I appeared... by the name of God, the Almighty, but by my name The Eternal was I not made known to them"; Motyer (The Revelation of the Divine Name, 12): "...and I showed myself to Abraham... in the character of El-Shadai, but in the character exposed by my name Yahweh, I did not make myself known to them." Leeser adds 'name' to the first part and Motyer 'character' to the second; in both cases they are not part of the text.

The suggested translation of "בְּ — as" in 2a conveys the essence of *quality* for which Motyer adds a new word; that sense is retained in 2b by the Hebrew "נודעתי": the basic verb implies comprehension and knowledge, and the exposure is not of the mere name but also of the implied quality ("ידע", The Bible Dic., 304/2); hence the choice "I did not make it comprehensible to them". The name, as such, was known, but not its full exposition (Motyer, Ibid., 30; W.R. Garr, "The Grammar & Interpretation of Exodus 6:3", 385-408).

With great respect for the work of the voweller Ben-Asher, I take the present form יְהוָֹה — YeHOVA to be the correct one, and the question should be: how and why we have the recent form.

God says his name 'אֶהְיֶה — EHYE' (Exodus, 3:14). It is first person, and God calls himself as such. But one should use for Him the polite third pronoun; אֶהְיֶה-EHYE thus becomes יִהְיֶה- YiHYE. The tetragrammaton 'יְהוָֹה — YeHOVA' may have resulted as an *intentional exchange* of "י" with close consonant "ו" of the group אהוי", probably *in order to distinguish the name from the future tense conjugation* [a linguistic tendency in spoken Hebrew, which is not taken in account by a recent study which stops at אֶהְיֶה (C.R. Gianotti, "The Meaning of the Divine Name YHWH", 38-51)]. An explanation for Ben-Asher's YeHOVA may be that although it avoids the form of strict grammatical conjugation, it embraces the three tenses of the verb 'to-be', thus indicating the eternal existence of the deity — הָיָה, הֹוֶה, יִהְיֶה = יְהוָֹה HAYA, HOVE, YHYE = YEHOVA.

E. Cassirer says about this tetragrammaton, that "here all separate and individual divine names have been resolved into one name of Being... From here it is but a single step to the fundamental idea of monotheism" (Language and Myth, 76).

The relevant issue, while examining the use of vocabulary regarding the deity, is to find *how He is viewed by the protagonists* and what the reader understands from the encounters. These aims require to limit the discussion on creator-created relationships to the practical/material manifestations of the intercourse between God and the three patriachs (questions about religion are outside the scope of this paper). Not that the deity evolves, i.e., changes his very nature in the course of events; but the text is structured in such a way as to expose, gradually, the facets of the deity and his nature. This, however, is stated regarding Genesis only. As for the

Bible as a whole — it is unreasonable to assume that the concept of 'God' did not undergo a process of change, due to cultural and social changes during a period of millenia.[17]

b) Abraham

1. The Call (12:1): Yhwh *says* to Abram.

The text, at this point, does not tell us how God reveals himself or how Abram refers to Him. The nature of communication follows the hitherto described relationship between God and individuals: God *speaks*, and we have to take this statement as a narrative fact because the text states it (a similar issue has been discussed in the previous chapter regarding the serpent; p. 105). For theological interpretations, this is a priori an unasked question; for a literary approach, however, every question has to be asked of a text. *Speaking*, thus, is a method by which, as the text tells us, God usually approaches protagonists in Genesis: Adam and Eve, Noah.

Encounters 3, 6, 7 which mention only speech but do not contribute to further our understanding of the nature of God will not be discussed.

2. Arrival to Canaan (12:7-9): Yhwh *is seen* וַיֵּרָא by Abram.

An exposure of the deity is mentioned for the first time in the narrative of Genesis, but the reader is still in the dark as to what Abram saw. Also, for the first time, the author adds that Abram built an altar and "calls in Yhwh's name וַיִּקְרָא בְּשֵׁם יְהוָה" (8). The altar is the conventional appendage of worship, probably involving sacrifices, and has been mentioned before (8:20). The notion of 'calling in Yhwh's name' also appeared before, and is usually interpreted as a use of the word 'Yhwh' made by the people in Enosh's days (4:26). The text in both instances, however, reads as *a report by the author using the expression* and not necessarily as what was expressed by the protagonists.

A comparison with another instance in Genesis may be helpful: Hagar names "the Yhwh who speaks to her, You are El-Roi... וַתִּקְרָא שֵׁם־יהוה הַדֹּבֵר אֵלֶיהָ   אַתָּה אֵל רֳאִי" (16:13), and the phrasing as well as the Massoretic punctuation clearly indicate that 'Yhwh' is the author's word for God and not Hagar's. The same, I suggest, should be applied in the case of Enosh and Abram — 'Yhwh' is used by the author who thereby conveys the generic name, a synonym for God. In both cases, contemporaries of Enosh and Abraham, invoked the deity, i.e.,acknowledged their affinity and used the word, but not in reference to the particular Hebraic entity.*

4. The first covenant (15:1):

Yhwh speaks to Abram *in a vision* — בַּמַּחֲזֶה.

Vision[18] involves seeing (in a dream), and the author's elaboration of the communication's method at this point in the text is necessary in order for God to execute the physical act of moving between the pieces. This method of 'vision' seems to be a reasonable alternative for an author who keeps the events of his narrative within the confines of the logical and the natural, while, at the same time, retains the unworldly or incorporeal nature of the deity; God appears and acts in a vision/dream. Support for this argument can be found in God's communication with the king of Gerar and with Jacob's father-in-law Laban: the text explicitly states that God revealed himself in a night dream (20:3) and talked to them in a dream (20:6, 31:24, respectively). A further step is

* In light of what was said before it makes no difference: the name may have been used as a noun, but not with the meaning which later periods attached to it. Regarding Abraham as "the founder of the worship of Yahweh" (Skinner, 126) is therefore inadequate, as Skinner himself cannot conjecture what historic reminiscence, if any, lies behind verse 8 which he regards as "this remarkable statement" (Ibid.).

made by the author, in this encounter, in exposing a form by which God appears when he performs a physical act: as smoke and fire (15:18) and the same physical manisfestations of smoke and fire are evident throughout the wanderings in the desert (Exodus, 3:2, 14:19,24, 19:18).

The chapter presents two occurrences separated from each other by the span of daylight (15:5 — night; 15:12 — next evening); this does not necessarily imply two different stories, but rather *two stages of the same event.** They are required because the sceptical Abraham is not satisfied with God's words of the first stage (15:8) and preparations for the second stage are needed (15:9-10) so that God will perform a physical act (15:17).

In their conversation, Abram addresses the deity as "Mylords Yhwh" (15:2, 8) which can be regarded as a synonym for "mylords God" — because Abraham never addressed the deity impolitely by the use of the singular form. An allusion may be made, at this point, on the use of 'us' in the creation story: whatever the designation of God, the plural form is but a coinage of polite manners (as it is in contemporary spoken languages). The same attitude is at work with Moses: although God presents himself as Yhwh (Exodus, 3:15), it is used in the narrative by the author and the deity only; Moses addresses Him in the plural "mylords" (4:10).

* The conclusion that the event described is conjecture of *two separate stories* (e.g., M. Anbar, "Abrahamic covenant — Genesis 15", 35; note 3 cites other commentators of the same opinion) is a logical one if wording and subject matter are taken at face value. But the *whole event* is entitled by the author "בַּמַּחֲזֶה", a title which actually suits only the second stage; had they been two occurrences, a mere 'Speech' would have sufficed for the first one. The author's placing "בַּמַּחֲזֶה" before the first event occurs, requires us to approach the whole as *one literary unit*, and analyse it as such; it will be done in the main body of the discussion.

5. Hagar and YHWH's angel (16:7-13): Yhwh's *angel* speaks. The context of these verses concern Sarai's maid Hagar and not Abram. But in the action required to help her (not in a dream but in her actual distress), the author exposes a different facet of God: Yhwh's angel. An angel, strictly speaking, is a messenger,[19] and God's angel is therefore his messenger. Quite often he is regarded by people who see him as God himself,[20] as can be understood from the text: although the author stresses three times (16:7, 9, 11) that it is God's angel who speaks to her, he adds her reaction to the apparition she saw by using a designation of the deity himself:

(16:13) And she called the name of Yhwh who spoke to her You are EL-Roi;
because she said, it is also here that I have seen, after Ro'i.*

Although Hagar recognizes the outstanding nature of the being she saw — Yhwh serves the author as a noun — she calls it by her version of the local name El. But the narrative gives no indication as to what it was she actually saw.

A. Abraham and Three Messengers (18):
God is seen as a member of a company of three men:

(18:1a) And Yhwh appeared to him in Eloney Mamré;
and he was sitting in the tent entrance, in the heat of the day.
(:2a) And he lifted his eyes and saw lo three people standing by him;

The verses are the author's comments, telling us what Abraham saw. Although in verse 3 Abraham talks to "Mylords", he apparently addresses one of them in the main, as indicated by the following forms of speech in the second person singular (18:3): תַעֲבֹר...בְּעֵינֶיךָ, and the plural "mylords" has already been

* The translation of 13b is complicated because the Hebrew syntax is not clear; rendering, therefore, is interpreting. The given phrase follows the Hebrew pattern where "Ro'i" is kept due to unclarity (see: Skinner, 288; Westermann, 247-8).

mentioned as a polite form when addressing a single person. In the following verses of the conversation (4-6), however, Abraham uses verbs conjugated in the plural, and there he is obviously addressing the whole group. The conversation between Abraham and Sarah and the three people is marked by the constant change of plural-singular speaker: "they said" (9) is immediately followed by "he said" (10), thus impressing the reader that at first two of the group ask "where is your wife" (9) and afterwards one of them prophesizes "*I will* come back at the proper time when Sarai your wife has a son" (10). The singular speaker is identified in the text as Yhwh (18:13), forming an interesting linguistic pattern — he, Yhwh, he: verses 10 and 15 do not mention him, just the pronoun — "and he said", whereas in verse 13 *the author states* that it is Yhwh who speaks. At most, one may assume that the author who relates the event is interpreting it as a 'theophany'; but the text indicates that Abraham is not aware of it, by rendering the person's speech as if Yhwh is not present — relating to Him in the third person instead of the first: (14a) "is something beyond Yhwh's capacity" and not "my capacity". The speaker goes on repeating his prophecy without identifying himself as God:

(14b) in the due time I will come back to you and Sarai will have a son.

When the guests depart, the text repeats the expression "people — ANASHIM":

(18:16) And the people got up from there and looked over Sodom
and Abraham goes with them to see them off.

In this encounter, the author leaves no doubt as to his perception of how God reveals himself, when it is not as smoke and fire — it is a human form and human nature: the messengers eat, drink and rest.* The text's treatment of God's messengers, thus, corresponds

* Rodin-Oberski (*The Patriarchs in Hebron and Sodom*, 35) regards them as ahuman figures, in spite of the fact that they eat and drink; consuming food, she suggests, does not comply with later apparitions

to the initial philosophy laid down in the chapters of creation: humans were made in God's form and image. Therefore, it is reasonable that *the apparition seen by people is that of humans*; as the text indicates, Abraham sees humans whom, all along, he regards as travellers and guests who intend to reach Sodom (as indicated in 18:16, cited above).

B. Abraham and One Messenger (18:22, 23a, 33):
God figures as a person talking to Abraham.

The vocabulary asserts the already stressed human nature of the deity: Abraham stands in front of him (22) approaches him and talks to him (23), and when they finish their conversation, *the author* states that Yhwh "goes" and Abraham returns to his place — they depart (33). During the conversation Abraham addresses *the person* he talks to by the polite plural form "Mylords -אֲדוֹנָי" as he did at their meeting (18:3). The interpretation of the group as a central figure and two messengers makes sense in view of the vocabulary used by Abraham. *But the identification of the central figure as Yhwh is made by the author* — nothing in the text indicates that this is how Abraham regards it! While they converse, the two other people reach Sodom; and while the author in his narrative calls them "angels" (19:1, 15), he uses the expression "people - אֲנָשִׁים" when Lot is involved with them (19:10a, 12a, 16) — because Lot, like Abraham, sees people.

Both encounters A and B, as far as Abraham is concerned, are with people.[22] Their designation by letters rather than numerals within the general list of numeral encounters, in our opinion, is justified because although illuminating our understanding of the

---

of angels (Judges, 6:2, 13:16, Tuvia, 12:19). But whether an angel in a narrative eats or does not eat, does not necessarily imply ahuman nature. The act of eating, of not eating, or of burning the food, seems to me to be a literary device which serves the nature of the narrative in which it occurs.

concept of angels, they make no contribution to our main issue — the nature of the *direct* relationship between God and Abraham — because of Abraham's ignorance of His identity.

8. The binding of Isaac (22:1):

The God הָאֱלֹהִים[23] speaks with Abraham.

This chapter, regarded by traditional interpretation as the peak of Genesis, the epitome of obedience and blind devotion of man to God,[24] is linguistically devoid of any personal touch of the author toward the deity mentioned, because throughout the whole personal affair only the generic 'Elohim' is used. The intervention of the angel brings back for the reader the missing sense of intimacy: the author uses "Yhwh's angel מלאך־יהוה"[25] who speaks from the sky to save Isaac, as against "God's angel" who saves Ishmael (21:17). In both cases the intervention came "from the sky", and the interpretation of this form of communication can only be speculative. On the one hand, until now the text has left no room to suspect that angels were anything other than messengers who had gradually exposed their human form and nature. On the other hand, neither Abraham nor Hagar have seen these angels but only *heard* them. A mystical interpretation might regard it as a kind of revelation; a logical one, which this research supports — and which later on will be discussed in greater detail — regards it as an inner voice of the unconscious surfacing and gaining control over a stressful situation, as today we psychologically observe and explain:

> "Auditory Hallucinations — ...the individual may hear voices telling him what to do...may result from a variety of biological and psychological conditions. Among these are...exaggeration of the ego-defence mechanism."[26]

c) Isaac

Isaac's encounters with God follow two of the patterns prevailing in the narratives about Abraham: God speaks to Rebekah (25:23) and presents himself — וַיֵּרָא to Isaac (26:2, 24). No indication is given in the text as to how and in what form it has happened but, alluding to Abraham's encounters, we may assume that it was in a "vision". As no further development in the nature of God comes to light, the encounters will not be discussed.

d) Jacob

In Jacob's encounters the author employs a complicated vocabulary regarding the deity, its nature and names:

1. Jacob's dream.

Verse 28:12 does not only stress the dream as a means of communication but also implies a vision without literally saying so. Both elements, a dream and a vision, were expressed in Abraham's encounters with God; the pattern, therefore, has already been used in the text. The differences lie in the particularities: whereas in Abraham's vision God takes the form of smoke and fire, in Jacob's dream Yhwh "stands" there and "speaks" to him (13a). The verbs which anthropomorphize the deity are not employed merely to allude to a human figure but, as discussed in Abraham's encounters No. A, B, they actually imply a real one. The phrasing of the sentence, thus, gives ground to suggest that in his dream Jacob saw a human figure whom he interpreted as God.

The God of the fathers is presented as "Yhwh", but the reason for the word in this very place might be due to syntactic convenience: the deity states his *nature* by saying "I am Yhwh"; had the author written "I am ELOHIM, אֱלֹהִים" this would be tautologous when he continues with inflection ...and ELOHEY. As the word Yhwh cannot be inflected, the use of Yhwh in cases like 13b seems to be a linguistic variety which sounds better. 'Yhwh' therefore, is a more limited word when it comes to describe qualities or attributes.* Verse 28:13, thus, is constructed in a way that avoids immediate repetition of expressions; "I am Yhwh" means that He is the noun Yhwh, who is the forefathers' God.

Jacob's verbal response is presented in three stages and with a different vocabulary at each:

a) he declares that "there is *a Yhwh* in this place" (28:16);

אכן יש יהוה במקום הזה

b) he suspects that the place is the "house of God — בית אלהים" (17b) and calls the place by the local name of the deity El — "בית־אל — BEIT-EL" (19);

c) he vows that if Elohim (20b) will help him, then "Yhwh will be my God: והיה יהוה לי לאלהים" (21b).

As all these statements are made by the same person, it might have been predicted that after the protagonist's comment on "a Yhwh", the text would continue with the same designation "Yhwh's house" and call the place "Beit Yhwh". But the text presents in (a) two synonyms for the deity — El and Elohim, and in Jacob's vow that follows (c) a mixture of "Yhwh" and "God". From a literary point of view, regarding 'form', the vacillation between the designations may suggest a deliberate avoidance of consistency in favour of presenting the synonyms in chiastic and parallel word-play. The surfacing pattern is thus:

(12, 13a)	the dream:	God's angels,	**Yhwh** —
(13b)	God's words:	**Yhwh**,	God
(16, 17)	the response:	**Yhwh**,	God's house.
(19)	naming of place:	Beit-El	
(20, 21b)	the vow:	God,	**Yhwh** my God
(22)	dedication of place:	God's house.	

* A random example: (Deut., 6:15a) "כִּי אֵל קַנָּא יְהוָה אֱלֹהֶיךָ"; 'El-Kano' is the quality which describes Yhwh, the private God/Elohim.

The literary use regarding content, however, may suggest an unconventional use of the deity's designations — as a coinage for 'awe'. The leading clue is found in 31:36-42, in Jacob's words to his father-in-law:

> The whole paragraph is constructed poetically by parallel synonyms, thereby doubling each issue:
>
> (31:36) What is my trespass what is my sin מַה־פִּשְׁעִי מַה חַטָּאתִי

Verse 42 is constructed the same:

The <u>God</u> of my father, the <u>God</u> of Abraham, and the **Pahad** of ISAAC...

לוּלֵי אֱלֹהֵי אָבִי אֱלֹהֵי אַבְרָהָם וּפַחַד יִצְחָק...

and God of Abraham, thus parallels PAHAD Isaac; PAHAD, said by Jacob, stands for God. This coinage seems to be at work by the voice of the author also in 31:53.

Coining a popular use from God's designations could have been an awkward suggestion, had it not been previously seen functioning also as an adjective.* Jacob's words in 28:16, 17b, thereby, acquire a different meaning (respectively):

a') he declares that "there is an awe, in this place";

b') he suspects that the place is a fearful one, 'house of awe' which to him is the gate to the sky — the way to the netherworld; the narrating voice of the author precedes Jacob's statements of awe by a comment on Jacob's fear (28:17a). The whole unit (28:116-17) focuses on fear, where 'Yhwh' and 'God' are its synonyms.

<u>2. Leaving Haran</u>.

God's call to return is conveyed in two phases: at first *the text states* that "Yhwh said to Jacob" with no further elaboration as to how (31:3); afterwards, when Jacob tells his wives about it, he is more explicit:

(31:11) וַיֹּאמֶר אֵלַי מַלְאַךְ הָאֱלֹהִים בַּחֲלוֹם, יַעֲקֹב...

(13a) אָנֹכִי הָאֵל בֵּית־אֵל אֲשֶׁר מָשַׁחְתָּ שָּׁם מַצֵּבָה אֲשֶׁר נָדַרְתָּ לִּי שָׁם נֶדֶר.

* As in "awesome wind" (1:2); see translation on p. 56.

(31:11) And God's angel said to me in my dream, Jacob;...
(13a) I am the God of Beit-El where you have anointed there a stone
to whom you have vowed there, a vow;

The communication, as suggested all along, is in a dream; the name of the God mentioned is not Yhwh but the God of locality — El. The personal name Yhwh in 31:3, therefore, is the author's voice who thus states that the speaker is God himself; but when he narrates Jacob's transmission of God's message to his wives, he uses a vocabulary which implies that Jacob actually relates to His representative — 'God's angel' (31:11), who embodies the deity of locality — "I am the El Beit-El" (31:13a).* The same linguistic ignorance of 'Yhwh' as a private name is evident when the text gives the wives' response which uses 'Elohim' (31:16).

Later, when Jacob gets his new name and settles near Shechem, he builds an altar which he calls "El, the God of Israel אֵל אֱלֹהֵי יִשְׂרָאֵל" (33:20); hence, for Jacob "El" is the designation of the deity's name.

A. Jacob's meeting with "God's angels".

The affair (32:2-3) does not involve a long narrative, but the two verses point to something different from the verbal encounters dealt with until now: "וַיִּפְגְּעוּ־בוֹ VAYIFGEU-BO" points to a warlike encounter,[28] and although the text does not elaborate what kind of encounter occurred, it indicates that Jacob came out of it safe and mostly sound. Like Abraham's parallel A-encounter, it is relevant to our discussion because it helps to clarify the meaning of the

* It seems that *the place* is called "El-Beit-El" (35:7), but the phrase should be rendered as "El *of* Beit-El". The Hebrew verse lacks the particle 'of', but its synonym is found in the twice repeated "שָׁם" in the continuation of the verse; the place factor is the common denominator to the three-part verse and ties its poetic essence. This is important because commentators interpreted the verse lacking the particle as an idiom which stands for the name of the place.[27]

'angels' in Genesis. The problem, in this case as well as in others, is how to interpret 'God's-X', i.e., when the suffix God indicates a noun in the possessive-construct or, as discussed before, when it is an adjectival suffix for an exceptional phenomenon.

The verses tell of a camp, called by Jacob "God's camp מַחֲנֵה אֱלֹהִים" (3) which corresponds to its inhabitants who are called by the author "God's angels" (2); *immediately afterwards* the author juxtaposes "angels מַלְאָכִים" which are sent by Jacob to his brother (4), and in this case one is sure that the messengers involved are humans. Therefore, there is room to assume that all 'angels' are of the same nature. This issue of 'God's angels' may be better clarified in Jacob's next encounter which, as implied by the text, occurs immediately afterwards.

B. The encounter at the Yabbok.

The text clearly states, that it occurs between Jacob and *a man* (32:25) with whom he fights all night. As until now this is the only place in the text where *a physical struggle* is specifically narrated, there is no room to suggest, as opposed to the "man" explicitly mentioned in the text, that the fight was held against any kind of deity.* The physical wound that Jacob carries with him

* The man's request to be released when daylight breaks is generally interpreted as a sign of an unnatural phenomenon: Skinner regards this point as a survival of the widespread belief in the spirits of the night who cannot stand daylight (Skinner, 409), and Westermann is on the same path with "all suit the hostile demon, an evil spirit..." (Westermann, 516), both noting Frazer's Folklore in the Old Testament, (412-24) who suggests this subject to be a river spirit (for a parallel ancient story, see: M. Tzevat, "Two Old Testament Stories and Their Hitite Analogies", 321-323).

Westermann, however, is aware that any interpretation of an unnatural nature collides with fundamental beliefs ["religion", in his text] of either Israel or of the patriarchs (Westermann, 515); and in spite of the logical explanation which he provides: "just as the robber must take care not to be arrested, so must the attacker watch out for the break of the day...

indicates a physical factor that caused it,[29] and the interpretation of the event has to take this factor into consideration.[30] Likewise, there is no room for an interpretation of the event as describing a state of mind: had the author wanted to confront Jacob with a spiritual encounter, then, like the previous cases with Abraham and Jacob, he would have narrated a physical action taking place in a dream — 'בַּמַּחֲזֶה'. This physical struggle is one among several dangerous encounters which Jacob, according to the text and as stated by the man when Jacob demands his blessing, has faced (32:29):

(:29a) וַיֹּאמֶר לֹא יַעֲקֹב יֵאָמֵר עוֹד שִׁמְךָ כִּי אִם־יִשְׂרָאֵל

(:29b) כִּי־שָׂרִיתָ עִם־אֱלֹהִים וְעִם־אֲנָשִׁים וַתּוּכָל

(:29a) And he said, not Jacob shall any more be called you name but Israel;

(:29b) because you have striven with ELOHIM and people, and have prevailed.*

The danger to Jacob's life, as Jacob states in 32:31 (cited below), is because he "saw a God face to face", a danger from which he was saved — "וַתִּנָּצֵל נַפְשִׁי".** But as in the preceding

both must conceal their identity, their names" (Ibid., 516), he goes on regarding the event as 'animistic belief in spirits or demons" (Ibid., 515).

I choose to follow the logical part suggested by Westermann and the wording of the text which explicitly states that a man fought Jacob.

* The first part of the verse — [L]; the second follows the vocabulary but alters the syntax. "שרה", The Bible Dic., 812: to overcome with his power.

** The traditional explanation of this verse may be epitomized by Eichrodt's explanation (Theology of Old Testament, vol. I, 35): "It is true that *a concrete conception of Panim* is also found in the popular tales of ancient Israel. Thus Jacob was astounded that he should have escaped with his life in spite of having seen the divine being" (emphasis in original).

Since our approach is to relate to concrete concepts, the interpretation suggested in this discussion conforms with Eichrodt's notion of the concrete but rejects the 'divine being'.

verses the author tells us that he fought *a man face to face*, the two declarations, therefore, have to accommodate each other:

"אֱלֹהִים — ELOHIM" expressed by the man in this context (32:29), is merely a synonym for 'the awe, the dread' which endangered Jacob; it equals Jacob's expression in the same context, because Jacob does not say אֶת אֱלֹהִים ET-ELOHIM (32:31) but ELOHIM. We may deduce from the missing particle that Elohim/a God is not a designation or familiar object that he saw, but something unexpected, frightening (similarly to our discussion on ELOHIM in Jacob's dream, p. 167).

As for the nature of this awe and what it represents, it is worth noting the similarity of this verse to the vocabulary used when Jacob meets his brother. The two verses state:

(32:31b) כִּי־רָאִיתִי אֱלֹהִים פָּנִים אֶל־פָּנִים וַתִּנָּצֵל נַפְשִׁי

(33:10b) כִּי עַל־כֵּן רָאִיתִי פָנֶיךָ כִּרְאֹת פְּנֵי אֱלֹהִים וַתִּרְצֵנִי

(32:31b) because I have seen a Elohim face to face and I survived it.*

(33:10b) because I have seen your face, [and it was for me like] seeing ELOHIM's face, and you were pleased with me.**

The identical pattern in the first part of the verses is intentional,(*) and the author, as it emerges from the above discussion, builds this narrative gradually: Jacob encounters a

* The translation follows the vocabulary used in [K.J.].

** [K.J.], [R.V.] and [L] render "ותנצל נפשי", each in its version of life being *preserved*. The suggested "survive", on the other hand, conveys the sense of being *saved*, which better corresponds to the Hebrew meaning of the root .נ.צ.ל; unfortunately for our suggested translation, the Biblical passive form (Niph'al) had to go.

(*) Emanueli, 440, touches the delicate point of comparing God to Eusab, but claims that *the author was not aware* of the complexity of the comparison (Ibid., 441; emphasis added). The problem seems to be solved and the author's honour restored, once the synonyms 'dread' or 'fear' are accepted. There is nothing awkward in comparing Eusab to a dread; the literary work thus gains its unity, and the honour of the author lost in Emmanueli's interpretation, is restored.

group of messengers — מלאכים; later he has a duel with one of them — "וַיֵּאָבֵק אִישׁ עִמּוֹ..." and when he meets his brother amongst his men he identifies the *face* who threatened his life (32:31b, "I have seen ELOHIM face to face").[31] His statement to Esau: "and you were pleased with me" (which structurally parallels "and I survived" in 32:31b) may be not only flattery but rather a silent reminder that he, Jacob, won a struggle and was blessed by Esau (or his man) whom he fought. Because immediately afterwards comes a more explicit reminder, an allusion to those blessings, when he beseeches Esau to accept his presents which he calls "blessing" (33:11).

> Jacob's fears of a direct confrontation with his brother, epitomized by finding and bribing his way out of Esau's anger (32:21b) is usually misunderstood as a reflection of a physically and spiritually weak person.[32] As I do not go into details which do not correspond to the main track of our subject, two brief remarks on this issue of Jacob's nature will suffice:
>
> a) Jacob's physical strength is manifested by his single-handed removal of the well stone (29:10) as well as by his struggle at the Yabbok; the description of his character as "איש תם יושב אהלים — A plain man, dwelling in tents" [L] (25:27b) does not indicate less physical strength than Esau's assumed strength as a hunter, but rather points to vocational tendencies. On the other hand, the text gives no indication of Esau's physical strength — it mentions only his bad temper.
>
> b) Jacob's reluctance for physical confrontation seems to result from his awareness of his own strength and the possible consequences of committing fratricide; the text points to this possibility as the reason for Jacob's journey to Haran ordered by Rebekah (48:45b). Jacob's life story appears to be one of avoiding physical confrontations, a tendency which is quite often misinterpreted as cowardice.

The nature of angels and the use of vocabulary are thus made clear: the angels seen by Jacob (Encounter A) are intimidating humans, and the use of the suffix 'God' is but an adjectival suffix which aims to stress their awesome nature or an awesome occurrence.[33] This interpretation, if accepted, eliminates the enigmatic motifs traditionally applied to both encounters, and "angels", thus, are not relevant to our discussion on direct relationships with *God*.

This long discussion sums up our analysis of the various expressions relating to the creator in all their manifestations. In other encounters with God (3, 4), the use of vocabulary follows the preceding patterns — God "speaks" where no indication is given as to how (No. 3), and speaks in a night dream (No. 4).

Let us continue now into the expressions relating to the created ones - the nation.

3. Nation/People — גוי/עם

The historical-sociological division into different groups of humans occurs, according to Genesis, only after the affair of the tower of Babel, in days of Peleg, the son of Ever (10:25) — the fourth generation after The Flood. Beforehand, humankind was united by language and concepts:

(11:1) וַיְהִי כָל־הָאָרֶץ שָׂפָה אֶחָת
וּדְבָרִים אֲחָדִים:

(11:1) "And all the land had one language;
and the same concepts"*

* The translation of 1b seems to raise a problem of comprehension: [K.J.] — and of one speech; [R.V.] — and few words; [L] — and of one kind of words; [Speiser] — The same words.

The adjective אֲחָדִים is rightly translated by Speiser as 'the same' (Speiser, 74, note 1), but דְבָרִים has its subtleties ("דבר" *The Bible Dic.*, 161-2) and in picking up one of them, subjective logic takes over: if the author wants to convey the idea of a unified society, then 'language' and

The author calls that union, or rather, unity — one people:

(11:6) וַיֹּאמֶר יְהוָה הֵן עַם אֶחָד וְשָׂפָה אַחַת לְכֻלָּם

(11:6) "And Yhwh said, this is <u>one people</u> and one language to all..."

The first expression in the text indicating a subtle distinction of nationality occurs when it names Noah's descendants after the Flood (10:1). The three sons, Yapheth, Ham, Shem, are discussed in reverse order of their birth; 10:1 states the chronological order of their birth, whereas the report on nation starts with the last one (10:2a) and ends with the first one — Shem. As the narrative continues with Shem and his offspring, the reason for this literary inversion becomes clear: to reach the final point of the report with the one who is the main subject, regardless of chronological order.

After their descendants are named, a summarizing verse states in each case (10:5, 20, 31): "these are the sons of... to their countries — אַרְצֹתָם, to their language — לְשֹׁנֹתָם, to their families — מִשְׁפְּחֹתָם, to their nations — לְגוֹיֵהֶם. These four elements — family, language, country and nationhood/peoplehood — are repeated in almost the same order:

10:5	—	Yapheth:	<u>countries</u> ... language ... <u>families</u>... nations;
10:20	—	Ham:	families ... language ... countries ... nations;
10:31	—	Shem:	families ... language ... countries ... nations.*

The word 'family' has to be understood here as implying more than the extended family,** and the word גוי [hereafter: Goy] requires clarification:

'concepts' convey this message; 'words' and 'language' are but synonyms and convey only part of the message.

* The two underlined words in Yapheth's line create the discord; had they been exchanged, the pattern would have been the same in spite of linguistic alterations.

** E.A. Speiser ("'People' and 'Nation' of Israel", 165) suggests that the main difference between contemporary 'people' and 'AM' lies in

A new word, אֻמֹּת — UMOT, is introduced when the sons of Ishmael (who also is destined to become a Goy — 21:13, 18) are mentioned:

(25:16a) אֵלֶּה הֵם בְּנֵי יִשְׁמָעֵאל וְאֵלֶּה שְׁמֹתָם בְּחַצְרֵיהֶם וּבְטִירֹתָם
(:16b) ...שְׁנֵים־עָשָׂר נְשִׂיאִם לְאֻמֹּתָם׃

(25:16b) ...twelve chieftains to their UMOTAM.

And a similar word of the same origin, לְאֻמִּים LEUMIM, is used of Esau and Jacob at their birth:

(25:23a) ...שְׁנֵי גֹיִים בְּבִטְנֵךְ וּשְׁנֵי לְאֻמִּים מִמֵּעַיִךְ יִפָּרֵדוּ

(25:23a): ...Two GOYIM are in thy womb and two LEUMIM shall be separated from thy bowels [L]

The text of Genesis, therefore, suggests four expressions, גוי, עם, אֻמֹּת, לְאֻמִּים — GOY, AM, UMOT, LEUMIM. An attempt to analyse these latter terms on the grounds of what is written in Genesis only,* leads to the following observations:

About Ishmael, the text states (25:16b cited above) and:

(17:20b) ...twelve chieftains he shall beget** and I will make of him a great Goy.

(25:16b) ...twelve chieftains to their UMOTAM [Speiser]

---

the suggestion of blood ties and the emphasis on the individual — both features which are peculiar to the Hebrew term. But the expressions in Genesis, 10, reflect a period where the mass of humanity was smaller in numbers and the blood ties among them more obvious; it seems that מִשְׁפָּחוֹת — families corresponds better to Speiser's comprehension of Am.

* Speiser (Ibid.) ignores UMOT, and therefore the above discussed verses are not included in his discussion.

Basing his suggestions on the uses of AM in *the whole* Bible, on extrabiblical data and on Ancient Israel (in the light of the combined data), Speiser states that "the problem of Am and Goy... is yet far from settled" (Ibid., 161). The system employed in this paper refers only to Genesis, and the different approach results in different conclusions.

** The translation follows Speiser's vocabulary.

Hence, Ishmael, with all his many chieftains is many 'Umot' but one Goy.

'Umot' probably means 'tribal groups' [Speiser] but words like chieftains, courts, encampments (see 25:16 English rendering below), point to a social organisation rather than a mere group of people. Therefore, when the text uses a word of the same origin, LEUMIM לְאֻמִּים, as a parallel to 'Goy' (in 25:23, cited above), it is not a synonym but a different entity. The Hebrew verses cited above may be rendered thus:

(25:16) These are the sons of Ishmael and these are their names by their courts and encampments; twelve chieftains, to their tribal groups.

(25:23) ...two nations are in your womb and two tribal groups will depart from your bowels.*

The distinction between 'Goy' and 'Am' is a complicated one and Speiser's suggestion for 'Am' as something subjective and personal and 'Goy' — objective and impersonal,[34] is accepted here but with a slightly different emphasis: 'Am' is the mass of humanity, whereas 'Goy' is the entity or frame which they form. This definition of 'Goy' enables inclusion of several 'Umot' within it and thus, perhaps, the distinction between the expressions is clarified: the scale of these expressions is suggested here as — family, (several of which combine to form) a tribe, (several of which combine into a social organization called) Uma, several of which combine to form a Goy. All these entities in Genesis relate to blood connections and none is explicitly related to territory; this can be seen already in the first instance where these expressions are used (10), when the text mentions separately territory, language and other human factors.

The translation of 'Goy' into 'nation', therefore, does not have

* The translation follows Leeser's vocabulary; but as explained, for LeUMIM — 'tribal groups' is used, as in 25:16.

the same contemporary connotation suggested in the introduction to this chapter. The question of contemporary sociology, whether the Jews are a people or a nation, therefore, is irrelevant to the biblical text, because in Biblical terms Israel was both 'Goy' and 'Am' — as stated in the Bible:

(Deut., 4:6) "but a wise and understanding people is this great nation". [L]

רַק עַם־חָכָם וְנָבוֹן הַגּוֹי הַגָּדוֹל הַזֶּה

After clarifying expressions relating to the creator and the created, we conclude by investigating the meaning of the last component of a nation: its territory. The survey will follow the promises given to the patriarchs in the encounters.

4. The Promised Land

a) Abraham

1. The Call: The promise of the land is treated primarily as an outcome of, or a supplement to, being a nation. In their first encounter God's promise is that of a nationhood conditioned, as stated, on Abram's reaching an unidentified land (12:1). For childless Abram, the identity of the land or its borders is an academic question in comparison with the promised descendants and, apparently, that is why God does not elaborate on the subject beyond "the land that I will show you" (12:1). The direction of Abram's wanderings was laid down by his father Terach, who initiated the departure from Ur for Canaan; Terach's death in Haran dictated only a temporary pause in Abram's journey to Canaan (11:31-32).

2. Arrival to Canaan: Only after Abram executed God's will, by leaving his country, was the land in which he arrived promised as a territory for his descendants:

(12:7) And Yhwh appeared to Abram and said to your descendants
I will give, this land;*

3. In Canaan: After Abram's return from Egypt, God is more specific about the land (13:13b-14a). In this encounter the issue of land precedes that of descendants (15a), and concludes it (17); the land, despite the impression made by the numbers of descendants promised, is the focal point of this encounter, as can be seen by the structure of the promise, delivered in a poetic manner achieved through the repetition of the words Land and Seed:

Land	...	to thee will I give it	(15a)	לך אתננה	...	ארץ
	seed		(b)		זרע	
seed	Land		(16a)		ארץ	זרע
Land	seed		(b)		זרע	ארץ
Land	...		(17a)		...	ארץ
		to thee will I give it	(b)	לך אתננה		

The land, as seen above, receives the central attention, more so when its multitude is employed as a metaphor for the descendants (13:16).

4. The First Covenant: the promised land, which in the previous encounter was the land of Canaan Abraham could see around him (13:14-15) while standing near Beit-El (13:3-4), is not the same area in the first covenant (15:18):

(15:18a) On the same day, Yahweh made a covenant with Abraham saying;
(15:18b) to your descendants, I have given this land from the river of Egypt
unto the great river, the river Euphrates. [L]

The boundaries described above are not those of Canaan, which are (10:19): from Sidon [Lebanon] to Gerar [in the land of the

* The vocabulary follows [L], but the syntax tries to convey the traditional pauses and thus — the stressed words in the sentence.

Philistines, near Gaza], to Sodom and Gomorrah. This, practically, is the west bank of the River Jordan and, needless to say, cannot be seen from Beit-El. Among the nations enumerated afterwards (19:21), three are clearly eastern and not Canaanite.*

The area encompassed by this description of 15:18 is practically the whole southern part of the Fertile Crescent of which Canaan is only a part — a narrow strip along the banks of the River Jordan. This covenant preceded Ishmael's birth and therefore the promised area, minus Canaan which was later explicitly promised to Isaac, is due to Ishmael.[36] A comparison with the wording of what is said later about Ishmael's territory supports this interpretation, because the author uses regional synonyms for the rivers mentioned above in 15:18:

(25:18) And they dwelt from Havila unto Shur which borders with Egypt going unto Assyria;**
bordering all his brothers he resides.

* Genesis 10:15 names the eleven sons of Canaan. Also in 15:19 ten are named, among them only seven are known to be of the locality of Canaan; three — Kenites, Kenizites, Kadmonites [L] — are distinctively eastern nations.

M. Anbar explains the author's choice of three eastern nations as aiming to reach the number ten, and also because their archaic nature suits the ancient list.[35] This claim, I suggest, is arguable: if the author's intentions indeed were to employ archaism or a sacred number for the story, he could have found local archaic Canaanite names. The fact that he found *eastern* names may indicate that he wanted to point to areas and nations who lived east of the river.

** The Hebrew "בֹּאֲכָה אַשּׁוּרָה" is problematic:

[K.J.] and [L] — "as thou goest toward Assyria"; but the text does not say 'as'. Omitting the 'as' we are left with the fact that from the Egyptian border one is asked to go to Assyria in the north, thus encircling the area suggested in this discussion. Hence my suggested translation "unto Ashur".

6. The Second Covenant: The sixth encounter, the request for circumcision, precedes the birth of Isaac. Following the suggested approach of the previous encounter, it seems that a limited area within the larger one already promised is destined for descendants of Isaac's line (17:8a):

> And I shall give to you and your descendants after you the land of your dwelling, the whole land of Canaan an everlasting possession;

The suggested interpretation of the promised land makes sense inasmuch as borders are concerned. These are not different areas from different 'documents', but a logical development in accordance with reality: first, the whole is given to Abraham. When a second heir is due, a part of it is given to him, leaving the rest to the first born.

b) Isaac and Jacob

The 'promised land' for Isaac is defined in unclear language and repeated twice (26:3, 4) as "these countries". The text does not clarify, at this point, which countries unless the concept of Canaan and its peoples' territories which were promised to Abraham are implied automatically as being promises also to Isaac. Moreover, the expression "descendants" is not specified, as Isaac has two sons.

Although in his blessing to each of his sons Isaac does not mention the land, it is through Rebekah that the author clarifies what the second generation to the pact understood as the promised land: Rebekah sends Jacob away with Abraham's blessing about inheriting *the land of his dwelling* — "the land which God gave to Abraham" (27:4). Canaan alone, therefore, is Isaac's promised land, and it corresponds to the above suggested interpretation of the apparent discrepancy in the promises given in the two cases of the covenants.* Later the author repeats this notion when relating

* Speiser, among others, regards them as belonging to different authors: verse 15 as J/E?; 17 as P.

that Esau leaves Canaan to Jacob (36:6). The same concept is evident to Jacob, as stated in his encounters with God: "the land which you lie upon" (28:13) or "the land which I gave to Abraham and Isaac, to you I shall give it" (35:12).

The outcome of the above discussion on the land discloses the author's favourable attitude toward Ishmael who, in practice, gains the larger part of the whole area promised to Abraham's descendants, whereas the line of Jacob receives only Canaan. Other sons of Abraham (25:1-4) are settled east of Canaan (25:7) bordering on Ishmael's territory, as stated in 25:18: "עַל־פְּנֵי כָל־אֶחָיו נָפָל ...of all his brethren [L]"; brothers, i.e., more than one; and therefore they are Abraham's other sons. Esau is confined to the mountain of Seir (36:8).

D. Creator and Created

1. Introduction

We have now the linguistic clarifications for looking into creator-created relationships. The narrative-body of accumulated encounters, suggested as "The Narrative Body" describes several events, and there is no alternative but to regard each of them as a mini narrative. The following discussion, therefore, will elaborate on each one, focusing *only on the issues concerning the inner relationship revealed* between God and each of the forefathers, while excluding other aspects which do not illuminate this concern. Attention will be devoted to the literary methods in which each encounter is constructed.

Until now, the subject of religion (which has been defined as "a system of faith and worship", p. 23) could be ignored because the previous discussions on creation did not involve any of its manifestations: the text is mute on Adam and Eve's religious practices or beliefs. Some remarks on religion in relation to the forefathers, however, are needed because 'relationship with

God' is usually regarded, as "a concept or idea of God".[37] Still, one has to bear in mind that Hebrew does not have a word for 'religion' (discussion p. 22), and relating to "The Religion of the Patriarchs"[38] is questionable. I agree with Westermann that a comprehensive study of the religion of the patriarchs, taking account of all perspectives, remains to be done. However, scepticism regarding the findings is bound to prevail.

The approach of this book, on the other hand, is based on the assumption that the nature of the relationship with God does not necessarily imply a system of faith and worship because *all beliefs* include a relationship with a god, and religious appendages of altars and sacrifices are common to many. *The uniqueness of the forefathers' relationship with God* is neither in the existence of religious appurtenances nor in God's designations (of which 'El' was common to other cultures) or their manifestation of gratitude; it *is rather in their peculiar nature*. This is the issue which our discussion seeks to illuminate.

2. God and Abraham

a) The Encounters

1. The Call[11]

(12:1a) וַיֹּאמֶר יהוה אֶל־אַבְרָם   לֶךְ־לְךָ מֵאַרְצְךָ וּמִמּוֹלַדְתְּךָ וּמִבֵּית אָבִיךָ

(1b) אֶל־הָאָרֶץ אֲשֶׁר אַרְאֶךָּ

(2a) וְאֶעֶשְׂךָ לְגוֹי גָּדוֹל   וַאֲבָרֶכְךָ   וַאֲגַדְּלָה שְׁמֶךָ

(2b) וֶהְיֵה בְּרָכָה

(3a) וַאֲבָרְכָה מְבָרְכֶיךָ   וּמְקַלֶּלְךָ אָאֹר

(3b) וְנִבְרְכוּ בְךָ   כֹּל מִשְׁפְּחֹת הָאֲדָמָה

(4a) וַיֵּלֶךְ אַבְרָם כַּאֲשֶׁר דִּבֶּר אֵלָיו יהוה ...

(12:1a) And Yhwh said to Abram get yourself out of your country and birthplace, and out of your father's home;

(1b) to the land, that I will show you.

(2a) And I will make of you a great nation and bless you and raise, your name;

(2b) and you shall be a blessing.

(3a) And I will bless those who bless you and your curser, I will ban;

(3b) and in you shall be blessed all, the families of the earth.

(4a) And Abram departed, as Yhwh had told to him; ...*

The poetic quality of God's first call to Abraham is clear, and the literary structure of the straightforward and clear message[39] may be analysed in a number of ways.[40] Its opening and ending are correlated by subject matter:

ויאמר	יהוה אל	אברהם	לך לך...
יהוה אליו	כאשר דבר	אברהם	וילך
said	YHWH to	Abraham	Get thee Going...
to him YHWH	As said	Abraham	and he went

and the same correlation can be seen in the blessing, where there are blessings for Abram and Abram as a blessing:

(2a) ואעשך לגוי גדול

(2a) ואברכך

ואגדלה שמך

(2b) והיה ברכה

(3a) ואברכך מברכך

ומקללך אאור

(3b) ונברכו בך

כל משפחות האדמה.

* On the translation:

"לך לך" is in Speiser "Go forth"; [K.J.] & [L] — "get thee out". The suggested one follows the last sources.

"ואגדלה שמך": the common "and I will make your name great" lacks the nuance which 'raise' conveys, and which suits the Hebrew.

"מקללך אאר" uses two distinctive separate verbs: ק.ל.ל. is to curse, but א.ר.ר. is 'to ban' (see: *, p. 000). Surprisingly, Speiser renders אָאֹר as 'banned' in 2:14, and 'curse' in 12:3 *for the same root.*

In 3b, the vocabulary follows [L].

Blessing Abraham	Abraham as a blessing
(2a) And I will make of you a great nation	
(2a) and bless you and raise your name	
	(2b) and you shall be a blessing.
(3a) and I will bless those who bless you and your curser, I will ban	
	(3b) and in you shall be blessed all, the families of the earth

Verses 2a, 3a present the same subject matter of God's blessings, although with a different structure: 2a suggests three successive blessings, repeating the three-factors pattern noted also in 12:1a, whereas 3a is a chiastic structure of contradicting notions. 2b and 3b are blessings resulting from Abram: in 2a Abram will be or will project a blessing (for others, as is apparent but not stated, and in 3b it is repeated, explaining for whom — families of the earth, alluding to nations. This echoes the nation, Goy, of the first isolated part in the diagram and thus presents the same subject, nations, at the beginning and end of the utterance.

The relationship between God and Abram revealed here is a peculiar one. God is not presented as the Almighty who deserves automatic obedience, but rather as a side to a pact: *if* Abram will commit himself to some action, he will be rewarded. The nature of this reward is also peculiar and reveals what Abram's price is (assuming that at the end of the day everyone has his price): in legends and fairy tales the reward is material (wealth) or spiritual (fame); for Abram who, according to the text, was then childless, 75 years old, well established and prosperous, it is the promise of a kind of immortality — not just sons and heirs, but founding a great nation. When Abram accepts the Call of God, therefore, he is not an obedient servant of the deity; he is a partner in a contract.

The frequency of God and Abraham's three first encounters and the time span between them is unclear, and can be estimated by deduction. The first one discussed above had been when Abram was 75, when he left Haran (12:4); the second — when he arrived in Eilon-Moreh near Shechem. The first and the second might have a time span of approximately a year.* The third one is after he returned from Egypt and settled near Hebron and the time span would no doubt have been greater; it takes more than one year's drought to force migration, and the return journey would take place only after a year's rain. An estimation of three years, therefore, is reasonable. The following, yet undiscussed encounter (No. 4, the first covenant between God and Abram) is ten years after arriving in Canaan, after Hagar was given to him for the purpose of having a child (16:3). Abram was 86 when Ishmael was born (16:16) and this fourth encounter, in all probability, occurred before Ishmael was born; it seems to follow the explicit pattern of the narrative on Isaac's birth, i.e., a covenant entered a year before the event (encounter 6, 17:1). The juxtaposition of this covenant in the text just prior to Sarai's handing over of Hagar, seems to support this assumption. This is a reasonable deduction from the structure of Genesis, where similar events are indicated by almost identical vocabulary and structural pattern:

> The first covenant (chapt. 15) precedes Hagar's conception (chapt. 16). Thirteen years later, the second covenant takes place (chapt. 17) and the text tells that a year later Sarah has a son (chapt. 21). This juxtaposition is but one factor pointing

* The estimated time required for the journey with flocks and household by way of the fertile crescent would be, according to my discussion with S. Avitzur (Prof. of the material cultures of ancient Near East, Tel-Aviv University) about six months. In order to allow for breaks in the journey, I have doubled the estimated period to one year.

to a similar pattern between the stories of covenant-son; others will become evident in the discussion on issues.

The first covenant, thus, probably occurred when Abraham was 85.

From the above deduction one may conclude that only four encounters occurred in a time span of ten years, of which the first two were close in time, followed by a slightly greater interval before the third and an even greater interval till the fourth.

The promises to Abram, within that time span and the long intervals between them, exhibit an escalating order of temptation: in the first encounter, it is not merely descendants for a childless person aged seventy-five, but abundance in this respect — a nation (12:2) which will leave its mark on humanity (12:3). In the second encounter, after Abram leaves his homeland for a destination already planned by his father Terach (11:31), God promises the land in which he arrived (12:6-7) and which he can survey from the standpoint of Beth-El, in the midst of the mountains. After the forced exile in Egypt, God sees fit to repeat his promises on both subjects — the land (probably because this element seems to be a crucial one after the trip to Egypt), and the descendants (12:15-17). God's escalating rhetoric of promises and constant repetition of them, therefore, are logically compelling in a situation of uncertainty and of infrequent encounters which characterizes the Abram-God relationship, and are not a mere literary device.*

* Adherence to the Documentary Hypothesis, for this very issue, has two aspects: it regards these repetitions as resulting from different sources (e.g., Speiser: chapter 15 — J/E?; 16 — J/P; 17 — P; chapter 21; 1-2a — J, 2b-5 — P, 6-21 — E), and it asks if we can "recognize a specific type or genre of promise-narrative" (C. Westermann, The Promise to the Fathers, 27). This approach of regarding the promises as elements which do or do not conform with an assumed genre or fixed pattern of "promise-narratives" (Ibid., 28) or "family history" (Ibid., 34), seems

The author conveys through the escalating rhetoric of the first three encounters a sense of passing time, where fulfilment of promises is not evident in human terms, and where Abram needs reassurances of mounting force; the peak is reached in the fourth and most important encounter.

4. The First Covenant

The conversation in the fourth encounter, the covenant,[41] is revealing as far as reassurances are concerned. Abram does not accept blindly what God tells him, dares to doubt a ten-year-old unfulfilled promise and asks for reassurances for whatever is promised. Thus, when God promises that he will exceed his reward (15:1b), Abram is quite cynical about it and, politely, with the due respect of "Mylords Yhwh", says "What can you give me — מַה־תִּתֶּן לִי" (2). The "can" is omitted from the Hebrew answer (see quotation below), but is implicitly conveyed by the subsequent complaint about the unfulfilled promise and the unhappy state of affairs created by it: Abram is still childless and the heir-apparent is Eliezer of Damascus (15:2).[42] Apparently God does not respond straightaway, and the text indicates it by twice repeating the opening "and Abram said" and the complaint; the whole paragraph reads:

(15:2) וַיֹּאמֶר אַבְרָם אֲדֹנָי יְהוִה מַה־תִּתֶּן־לִי וְאָנֹכִי הוֹלֵךְ עֲרִירִי
וּבֶן־מֶשֶׁק בֵּיתִי הוּא דַּמֶּשֶׂק אֱלִיעֶזֶר׃
(3) וַיֹּאמֶר אַבְרָם הֵן לִי לֹא נָתַתָּה זָרַע
וְהִנֵּה בֶן־בֵּיתִי יוֹרֵשׁ אֹתִי׃

(15:2) And Abram said, Mylords Yhwh what will you give me and I, continue childless;
and my household-member is, Eliezer of Damascus.

---

to me to deny them a literary flexibility and development of their own, which has little in common with the Icelandic patterns of millenia later, cited by Westermann.

(3) And Abram said to me you have given no offspring;
and therefore my house-member, inherits me.*

The aspects of the poetic structure and vocabulary are overlooked: the Hebrew stresses the alliteration of the sound [ee] created by the endings of most parts of Abram's speech; thus, there is an element of incantation rather than merely being two separate sentences. The vocabulary reveals them to be more than simple repetition of the subject, because Abram's complaint presents a development: in the first part Eliezer is a household-member and in the second part, the general objective noun "household" becomes more intimate — בֶּן־בֵּיתִי "of my house".** The development of subject occurs because the one who is a member (2b) becomes, due to Abram's lack of children, a substitute for a son, an inheritor (3b).

* The suggested translation of this paragraph was influenced (in 2a) by the vocabulary in Speiser. The rest is a result of the literary analysis discussed below.

The suggested "household-member" is based on "מֶשֶׁק", The Bible Dic., 518, which regards the noun as a synonym for 'custom'; thus משק בית is 'household customs'. 'בֵּן' is a member; likewise — 'בני ישראל' the members of the nation of Israel.

Traditionally, Eliezer is regarded as the same person who was sent to Haran to fetch a bride for Isaac (Rashi, 4-5), because the confusion of "בן־משק בית — household-member" and "בן ביתי — house-member" of 15:2, 3 with "*the eldest of his house, who ruled over all he had*" (24:2, [L]). But of the latter, the text clearly states that he is *a slave*, and during the whole Haran-affair he is called "Abraham's slave"; he is no prospective inheritor, as there are two sons. Eliezer, on the other hand, is a member of the household and not a slave, and this distinction is what makes him a prospective inheritor.

** Speiser notes the alliteration of the title Ben Meshek and the town Damessek, but his translation for it is primarily based on the issue of inheritance and therefore he renders it as 'successor' (Speiser, 111). In his interpretation, the two sentences become parallel statements of the same subject; my rendering, as can be seen, suggests development.

Only after the complaint is thus repeated, and reaches the crucial issue of inheritance, does God answer. And again, the wording indicates a kind of a pause — not an immediate answer by the customary phrase "and God said", but:

וְהִנֵּה דְבַר־יהוה אֵלָיו לֵאמֹר (15:4)

(15:4) And behold Yhwh's discourse to him saying...

As the whole affair takes place in a vision, the suggested intervals may well be short within the overall framework. Another one seems to occur in verse 7, when the text separates the promises, of an heir and of the land, by presenting between them a God who introduces himself to Abraham. Such pauses or introductions, when not interpreted as resulting from sources[43] or different stories[44], require *a literary* explanation for their apparent unity, and this is attempted further on. Whether or not God's answer is belated, it does not satisfy the sceptical Abram and a more tangible offer is in order. God takes him to see the stars, and the same kind of comparison as previously suggested with the dust of the earth (13:16) is employed — Abram is asked to count the stars, and is told that his descendants will be equally innumerable (15:5). After this demonstration the text tells us something about Abram's belief in God (15:6):

And he believed, in God — וְהֶאֱמִן בַּיהוָה

and *he* regarded it, a TZEDAKA. — וַיַּחְשְׁבֶהָ לּוֹ צְדָקָה

Abram, the text tells, believed in God, and *he* regarded it, as TZEDAKA. This sentence has two ambiguities: who is "he" and what is Tzedaka. Rashi suggests "he" to be God, who regarded it as Abram's righteousness; Tzedaka, thereby, takes the meaning of "integrity and just in his ways of life".[45] Rambam (Nachmanides) regards "he" to be Abram, and this alternative allows us to offer a different interpretation of verse 6:

Tzedaka has also the meaning of an act of charity[46] and if "he" is Abram, then the sentence may be rendered as: "Abram believed in God, and thought of it (ויחשבנה) as a charitable act (צדקה)". Blasphemous as it may sound, the text gives it some grounds: by using the past participle when he talks of Abraham's belief — והאמין ביהוה (the proper conjugation should have been וַיַּאֲמֵן ביהוה — VAYA'AMEN in YHWH; but the author writes "וְהֶאֱמִין ביהוה — VeHE'EMIN in YHWH", which points to a distant past;[47] by a hint of scepticism in Abraham's response, by the context of unfulfilled promises and by the necessity for God to employ physical demonstrations and metaphors. All these factors point to the unconventional and unreligious attitude suggested here, rather than to the conventional interpretation of this verse as portraying various degrees of what amounts to blind faith.

Abram's faith, the text goes on telling us, is not blind, and it requires proof, something more tangible than mere words in order to believe in the promised land:

(15:8b) אֲדֹנָי יְהוִה בַּמָּה אֵדַע כִּי אִירָשֶׁנָּה

(15:8b) Mylord Yhwh whereby shall I know, that I shall inherit it. [L]

After which God, in a dream (15:12), passes between the animal pieces (15:17), which was the custom when entering into a commitment.

The text presents in this encounter a sceptical Abram whose faith has to be underpinned. There is nothing self-evident or certain about Abram's belief; it has to be acquired by a covenant between him and God, *where only God is committed*:[48] He is the one who passes between the pieces and commits himself, through this act, to give a huge area to Abraham's descendants, without naming any specific one amongst them. The juxtaposition of Ishmael's birth immediately afterwards indicates that Ishmael is high-ranked, and that the author is less nationalistically orientated than most of his interpreters. The first one is Moses' contemporary Joshua, who mentions the Euphrates among his intended borders (Joshua, 1:4); but the Euphrates is not mentioned when God shows the promised land to Moses (Deut., 34:1-4). Joshua's mention of places which Moses did not, may indicate that Genesis stories were well known to and understood by the author who wrote Deut., and less so to the one who wrote the book of Joshua and who gave to the first conqueror-general aruguments which are based on a wrong interpretation of Genesis stories. The general, thus, seems to have had grander territorial aspirations than the political leader who preceded him.

6. The Second Covenant

This encounter (ch. 17) is one in which God's words are delivered in the longest speech in Genesis, and in which he finalizes his intentions and obligations to Abraham. After the introductory phrases (17:1-2) which Abraham acknowledges by throwing himself on his face (3), God continues, and His long speech is divided by the phrase "And God said to Abram" into four parts (4-8, 9-14, 15-18, 19-21):

The introduction (17:1-2). This encounter takes place when Abram is 99 years old, thirteen years after the previous one; *a long period for any kind of relationship*. Perhaps that's why the author sees fit to use an introductory phrase which presents God to Abram as if he might not remember him: "I am El Shadai" (1b) says the deity, and it is the first time that the protagonist God introduces himself by any name. In the previous encounter long ago (15:8) he was "the Yhwh who took you out of Ur" and, as suggested, 'Yhwh' serves as a synonym for the noun 'God'; but now the deity, perhaps because of the gap in time, finds it necessary to be more personal, and he introduces himself not as a mere deity but by a name which indicates a quality.* He reminds

* The name has already been mentioned on p. 155. The three main explanations are: 'God of the mountain' which assumes the Canaanite Sadu = mountain; 'God of plentitude' derived from "שדי = mother's breast"; 'God almighty', based on Rashi's interpretation "אני הוא שיש

Abraham of the pact between them and thus evokes, without explicitly mentioning it in this stage, the nationhood and territory which are conditioned upon Abraham's adherence to God. The author constructs God's words cleverly, as he did in The Call — first comes the request and afterwards the reward:

(17:1b) ...I am El-Shadai follow my steps, and be immaculate (TAMIM).*

(:2a) And I will give my covenant, between me and you;

(:2b) and I will multiply you, exceedingly. [L]

The first part of God's speech (17:4-8). It states the promises of nationhood and territory already known to Abram, and it has two distinctive literary units of vocabulary and subject matter:

— the first unit is created by a repetitive use in each verse (4-6) of the expression 'GOYIM — nations' which Abraham is destined to become, and thus the subject matter of this part is conveyed: as Abram has already one heir who will become a nation, the promise of nationhood is now extended to other sons and, therefore, his name is changed accordingly — father of many nations, (5b): "כִּי אַב־הֲמוֹן גּוֹיִם נְתַתִּיךָ".

— the second unit, 7-8, is noted for the repetitive expressions: three times "you and your descendants", double mentioning of becoming a personal God, double mention of the promises as "everlasting".

"די במהותו לכל בריה". For summaries of the view regarding this divine name, see: note 49.

* 'תמים' (17:1b) is rendered by Speiser as 'blameless'; [K.J.] & [L] — plain. The same idiom referring to Jacob — איש תם was rendered by the last two sources as 'retiring man'. "Immaculate" was chosen here because it conveys *for both verses the same sense* of 'man of integrity, doing the just thing'.

The second part of the speech (9-14). It introduces an action demanded of Abraham — circumcision. In the first covenant before Ishmael's birth, it was God who had to perform an act to ratify the pact; before the birth of Isaac it is Abraham, and the reason is clarified here as "to be your God וְהָיִיתִי לָהֶם לֵאלֹהִים". This notion is emphasized twice more at the end of the encounter.

The author presents God's demand in this paragraph by repetitions of four subject matters: the covenant; the parties to it (God, Abraham and his descendants); the act requested (circumcision); and the foreign household members who should be included. These subjects are not arranged in the paragraph according to a fixed pattern, but their constant repetition lends it a poetic sense.

The third part of the speech (15-18). It consists of a conversation between God and Abraham, in which each says one sentence:

(15) God changes Sarai's name to Sarah because she will be mother of nations. Abraham's silent reaction has two facets: he falls on his face and laughs (16), and he says in his heart:

(17:) ...הַלְּבֶן מֵאָה־שָׁנָה יִוָּלֵד וְאִם־שָׂרָה הֲבַת־תִּשְׁעִים שָׁנָה תֵּלֵד

(:17) ...will a hundred years old procreate and Sarah will a ninety years old, create*

Abraham's silent scepticism is important because he considers his chances of becoming a father as reduced to nil — *it is not only Sarah's fault, but his too*; this point is stressed because this issue will recur later on.

* The Hebrew text uses twice the verb 'י.ל.ד.'; the English translation suggested here plays on Eve's verse 'קניתי איש' and its meaning 'I have created a man' referring to bearing a child (p. 126); thus the translation retains the same verb in both parts of the verse.

Abraham's spoken answer is sceptical as well, as can be deduced from the fact that he does not respond on the subject of Sarah's child but refers to the child he already has, asking that God may keep him alive:

(:18) "Let but Ishmael thrive if you so will it." [Speiser]

God's answer to Abraham's scepticism (19-21). It is constructed in three parts: it starts with a repetition of Sarah's forthcoming child who will be called Isaac, corresponding to the laughs of both Sarah and Abraham in 19a. (The issue of "laughing" related to two protagonists is regarded by commentators as a repetitive account[50]). God continues on to emphasize that the everlasting covenant is with Isaac and his descendants:

(:19b) and I shall establish my covenant with him into an everlasting covenant, for his descendants after him. [L]

and although Ishmael will be granted abundance of descendants (20), still — the pact will be carried on through Isaac whose birth is soon due (21).

God's final answer, thus, stresses twice the continuation of his pact with Abraham through Isaac and his descendants. This, I suggest, is the main difference and *the spiritual one* between the two covenants: when only God is performing an act (chapter 15), there are rewards for Abraham and all his descendants — nationhood and territory; when Abraham is required to perform an act (chapter 17), beside the practical rewards, it is the future descendants who will carry on with the special relationship between God and Abraham, as emphasized in verse 7: "I will be their God".

The very same idea will be expressed in the next encounter: God, who supports Sarah's demand to expel Ishmael, justifies it by saying (21:12) "כִּי בְיִצְחָק יִקָּרֵא לְךָ זָרַע — Isaac is the one *to carry on your name*", while at the same time repeating His intention to make Ishmael, as Abraham's son — כִּי זַרְעֲךָ הוּא, into a great nation (21:13).

7. The Expulsion of Ishmael

Verses 21:9-19 constitute a narrative with several distinctive features:

— for the first time in the encounters, as well as in Genesis as a whole, God intervenes in a family argument and takes sides, telling Abraham to listen to Sarah (12).

— Abraham's reaction to Sarah's words is stated explicitly (11), the only time where a protagonist's judgement is thus expressed.

— God is presented as a catalysing force at the beginning ("and God said...", 12) while actually withdrawing from the event itself; at the end, it is an angel's voice from heaven which brings salvation (17).

The feature of God as a family counsellor presents the deity in a close relationship with Abraham who obeys him. But the act of obedience, which contradicts Abraham's natural paternal instincts and is carried out with reluctance, takes place only after God promises a reward: the expulsion will not hurt Ishmael's prospect of becoming a nation (13), which implies that his life is not in danger. The principle guiding the relationship between Abraham and God in all previous encounters is still at work in this one — a deed or action performed in exchange for a reward.

Abraham's personal attitude is conveyed in the expression "וַיֵּרַע — VaYERA" and this word echoes the subject of 'good and bad' discussed earlier. It does not convey emotions as such,* but rather a judgment — *Abraham regards the demand,* according to his code of ethics, *as 'bad'*. That a priori this is not the case, can be

* [K.J.] & [L] render it "grievous"; [R.V.] "displeasing"; [Speiser] — "distressed"; all convey a certain kind of feeling which makes sense, and is accepted later on — but only *as a reasonable result of the case*, not as a translation of the text.

deduced from God's admitting to it and from the rationale behind it. For Abraham, however, the case was regarded as 'bad' and the verse, therefore, is rendered thus:

(21:11) וַיֵּרַע הַדָּבָר מְאֹד בְּעֵינֵי אַבְרָהָם עַל אוֹדֹת בְּנוֹ:

(21:11) "And Abraham regarded the case, concerning his son, as a very bad one"*

Abraham's reaction concerns only his son; the woman who bore him is irrelevant, as she was when Sarah ill-treated her.

This is evident from the verse which reports Abraham's attitude, as well as from the text's vocabulary concerning Hagar: in the whole of chapter 16, Hagar is "שִׁפְחָה" [hereafter — Shif'hah]. When Sarah complains of Hagar's impertinence, Abraham reaffirms her status as *Sarah's servant* — שִׁפְחָתֵךְ, neither his nor the household's, in spite of her being pregnant with his child. Only after Ishmael's birth her status seems to change, because the author omits all mention of it (16:15-16). But when Sarah demands Hagar's expulsion, she talks of her by a different status-word: as 'אמה' [hereafter — Amah]. Shif'hah, in general, is a regular, lower-status slave, practically the female form of 'slave'; Amah enjoys a higher status, a household person closer to her master.[51] To relate to Hagar as "the other woman in Abraham's life",[52] is to put into the text something which is not there; the contrary is manifested in Abraham's indifference to her status (16:6), or lack of concern (16:11).

God is not involved in the actual narrative of the expulsion: Hagar is lost (14b), in desperation she throws her boy under a bush

* This translation, due to difficulties in rendering the content, has to avoid our usual tendency of following the Hebrew pattern and its division into sentences; hence its presentation in one line which uses the vocabulary of both parts.

(15-16a), cries (16b) and is saved by the voice of God's angel. As the issue under examination is the role of God and his relationship with Abraham, Ishmael's expulsion seems to be relevant only inasmuch as it discloses new facets of this relationship: in the first encounter involving Hagar (No. 5) the text introduced the motif of the angel; in this encounter it introduces, for the first time, "an angel calling from heaven". In the chapter on Word-Analysis (p. 164), it has been suggested that the use made by the author of this concept might be logically interpreted as a literary device to present a state of mind rather than a state of affairs. This was suggested on the grounds that psychology has been always known to humankind even if it lacked our contemporary vocabulary: "Long before abnormal psychology became an area of scientific study, the masters of fiction and drama developed many brilliant and moving characterizations of abnormal behaviour. Such literary classics, in their description of human [behaviour] in all its infinite subtleties of degree and variety, often achieved a lifelike, vivid and an emotional force that science cannot achieve" suggests Coleman.[53] The author of Genesis, therefore, does not say that a protagonist has hallucinations; he narrates someone hearing voices from an unexpected place.[54]

Bearing this in mind, we may understand why the text of Ishmael's expulsion and God's place in it acquires a peculiar dimension:

a) God approaches Abraham (12) and asks him to act against his better judgment; an inevitable state of personal distress caused by inward feelings ensues, which the author conveys by the degree 'very bad' "וַיֵּרַע מְאֹד" with which Abraham perceives Sarah's demand.

b) Hagar is in a state of distress caused by the external factors of expulsion and thirst, and it is implied in her actions and her words: she leaves her son under a bush and, crying, sits far away in order not to see him dying (16). Her distress is such that she cannot see that the instrument of her salvation lies in front of her.

When she relaxes after hearing the angel's voice and comforting words (17-18), her eyes are opened (19) to what she was not aware of until then* — a well of water. God's participation is conveyed by the author's voice in the first and last statements: "and God heard the voice of the boy" (17a), "and God opened her eyes" (19a). Hagar, as the text tells, is not involved with an angel of the kind she earlier had seen in reality (17:7-13); she *hears a voice* which helps her out of her distress.[55]

c) The role of Ishmael in this narrative is reduced to nil. Not that he was not hurt by the expulsion; this is conveyed artistically by twice relating that God heard the boy's cry — once by a direct comment (17a) and once through the angel's voice (17b) — but the boy's cry is not part of the narrative which treats Ishmael as an object. Moreover, Ishmael's first epithet "child יֶלֶד" (14a, 15b, 16a) is as misleading as the second — "boy נַעַר" (17, 18a, 19b, 20a) — neither of them gives a proper indication of Ishmael's age or state in life because the epithets describing the Biblical protagonists seem to change in accordance with the subjective attitude of people around them, as in the case of 'boy-son'.[56] In the Abraham narrative, as well, they connote a subjective attitude toward the person involved. Thus, it is "the maid's *son*" by Sarah (21:11), whereas Abraham gives Hagar "the child" (21:14). Hagar, in her distress, throws "the child" under the bushes (21:16-17); but when salvation comes, she gives water to "the boy" (19). Only afterwards, when apparently they become close, does the author tell that "his mother" took him a wife. In a single narrative of one event, the author uses 'son, boy, child' (*respectively, in reduced order of intimacy*) where all the epithets refer to the same person: for Abraham's household he is reduced from 'son' to 'child', and in his relationship with Hagar he raises up from 'child'

* The same expression is used with regard to Adam and Eve (3:7, p. 109, and the same interpretation applies in both cases.

through 'boy', ending with 'son', when she actually becomes 'his mother'. Ishmael's relevant age and state of affairs, however, require further elaboration in regard to his silence:

> Ishmael was thirteen when circumcised (17:25), fourteen when Isaac was born a year later, and fifteen or sixteen when Isaac ended his weaning period.[57] In the everyday life of the period, Ishmael was probably a working member of the household.
>
> An analogy should be made with Jacob's sons who, in spite of their father's wealth, were working (37:12). In contemporary Israel, until the law obliged Beduin children to attend schools, a boy (or a girl) as young as eight years old could be seen shepherding a small herd of domestic animals.
>
> The event that triggered his expulsion is explicitly stated in the text (9): "And Sarah saw the son of Hagar the Egyptian whom she conceived by Abraham, METZAHEK." In other words: in the heat of the feast (probably involving drinking and gaiety and what we would call a certain amount of free behaviour), Sarah saw Ishmael indulging in sexual games — METZAHEK,[58] and for the first time she realized that *he was physically a mature youth.* The epithet "child", thus, has to be interpreted in the above suggested order of intimacy.

Therefore, the silence of Ishmael in the expulsion context, when he is almost sixteen years old and probably already experienced in desert conditions [as deduced from his age and from the text's twofold repetition of the nature of the place in which he will live from then on (21:20b, 21a)], makes sense only if there was no real threat to his life and the whole stressful situation occurred in Hagar's mind.

The outcome of the above points (a-c) results in two protagonists, Abraham and Hagar, in distress, and an affected youngster who witnesses them in silence. The state of distress is the main factor of this event, and justifies its interpretation as a state of mind. As such, this encounter belongs to the category of 'encounters with God' only inasmuch as all intercourse with God is considered a state of mind. But the author distinguishes this encounter from the previous ones, which projected positive states of mind, by stressing this time *a negative state of the mind* and by introducing the *voice of the angel coming from heaven.* This encounter, therefore, belongs to a different category from previous encounters, and it has a distinctive structure: God is understood as ordering Abraham to perform an action which contradicts Abraham's paternal instincts; the action is perfomed; a happy ending is brought about by the intervention of the voice of the angel.

8. The Binding of Isaac

The last encounter (22:1-13) follows the subject matter and the structural pattern of the previous one, only this time it involves Isaac. Both encounters display similar elements:

a) God asks Abraham to execute a painful act against his sons (21:12, 22:1-2 respectively);

b) Abraham accepts God's request (21:14, 22:3-10);

c) The intervention, the salvation of Ishmael and Isaac, comes through the angels who speak from heaven (21:17-19, 22:11-13).

The differences, however, are cardinal. As discussed earlier, there is a logical explanation for Ishmael's expulsion (21:9-10), and its painful impact is softened by Abraham's knowledge, explicitly expressed by God, that a happy ending is intended (21:13). The request to sacrifice Isaac, *as the author states*, comes to test Abraham (22:1a). The literary technique of describing an event as 'a test' and thereby notifying the reader of a happy conclusion, is suggested as a literary device to capture the reader's interest while freeing him from concern at the outcome of the plot and drawing his attention to the ideological message.[59] But for Abraham the request has no logical explanation — the same God that asks for Isaac's sacrifice jeopardizes his own promise that in Isaac Abraham will have an heir to the spiritual pact between them.

The similarities in subject-matter and structure of the last two encounters (a-c, mentioned above) compel a similar interpretation, despite the differences in detail. If the voice of God's angel coming from heaven is merely a state of mind for Hagar, it has to be so for Abraham. Both encounters thus form a separate unit within the larger body of encounters and deserve to be analysed as such — with greater attention to their similarity. This will be done below in three parts: the narrative, its analysis, and the emerging relationship with God.

b) The last unit

1) The narrative (21:8-22:19)

The unit has an introduction which tells of Isaac's birth (21:1-7), three parts which are relevant to our discussion and a geographical interlude [the incident with the Philistine king of Gerar about the wells (21:22-34)] which indicates that Abraham was then, and for many years (31-34) living in Beer-Sheba which was then a Philistine area. Each part is distinguished by the actions of the personalities involved — Sarah, Hagar, Isaac, in this order. All parts have two common denominators: the participation of Abraham, and what was previously defined as a 'state of mind' implied in the author's literary presentation and deducible from the narrative's details.

The first part starts with a happy ending: Sarah and Abraham miraculously have a son (21:7). The claim of a miracle is based on Abraham's own estimation, stressed beforehand, of himself and Sarah as future parents (17:17). Sarah's elder surrogate son is fourteen years old and the text does not indicate that his presence in the household is regarded as a disturbance. The peaceful state of affairs continues for a year or two until Isaac is weaned, and it explodes only after Abraham throws a party to celebrate it (8); only then does Sarah realize that Ishmael is a mature youngster (9). She demands his expulsion (10a) because she worries for her son's inheritance prospects (10b). Abraham resents this request (11) but God supports Sarah's demand and promises Abraham good fortune and future for Ishmael (12-13).

The second part is the story of Hagar: Abraham obeys the merciless demand, sends her and Ishmael away with provisions (14a). She undergoes her ordeal in the desert of Beer-Sheba (14b-16), from which she is extricated by the voice of God's angel (17-18); she acts accordingly and saves Ishmael (19). The happy end is conveyed by the author's voice who describes Ishmael's future (20-21).

The third part is the story of Isaac: Abraham obeys the merciless demand (22:1-2), takes Isaac and provisions (3) and both undergo an ordeal (9-10) from which Abraham is extricated by the voice of Yhwh's angel (11-12); he acts accordingly and saves Isaac (13-14). The happy end is conveyed by the angel's promise about Isaac's prospects for the future (15-19).

2) Literary Analysis

The similarities in the narrative structure and the subject-matter of the two last parts have already been discussed, where we interpreted the two affairs to be that of a state of mind (p. 201). The first part, in this respect, seems to be different, but a closer examination displays a great deal of structural and interpretational affinity:

(21:9)	וַתֵּרֶא שָׂרָה אֶת־בֶּן־הָגָר הַמִּצְרִית אֲשֶׁר־יָלְדָה לְאַבְרָהָם מְצַחֵק
(:10a)	וַתֹּאמֶר לְאַבְרָהָם גָּרֵשׁ הָאָמָה הַזֹּאת וְאֶת־בְּנָהּ
(:10b)	כִּי לֹא יִירַשׁ בֶּן־הָאָמָה הַזֹּאת עִם־בְּנִי עִם־יִצְחָק׃

(21:9) And Sarah saw the son of Hagar the Egyptian whom she had borne to Abraham, METZAHEK.

(:10a) And [she] said to Abraham expel this maid, and her son;

(:10b) because the son of this maid will not inherit with my son, with Isaac.

What seems to worry Sarah is not so much the inheritance as a material loss; nor that this is how the author regards it. This interpretation is supported by the following facts in the text to follow: Ishmael receives his share of land (p. 142, 144) and presents from his father (25:6a). Moreover — when Abraham dies, he is the only other son mentioned by name who comes to bury him (25:9). The issue that concerns Sarah, at this stage, is rather the fear that the baby Isaac has no chance to survive against the alternative heir, a mature son, whose name she does not utter. The text's avoidance of the name Ishmael conveys Sarah's inner state of mind: the long synonym (9, underlined) as well as those expressed by Sarah (10, a, b, underlined) indicate a break in the relationship that undoubtedly existed between Sarah and Ishmael; because in all aspects, apart from the actual pregnancy, Ishmael had been Sarah's son. She initiated his birth (17:2) not only so that Abraham would have a son but also in order to become a mother "אִבָּנֶה" "מִמֶּנָּה", Hagar being merely her maid (17:1b, 3, 5a, 6a). Moreover, the surrogate motherhood lasted for fourteen years — a substantial amount of time to enable a close mother-son relationship to develop. The text indicates this closeness by the juxtaposition of Ishmael's expulsion not immediately after Isaac's birth but almost two years later; had Ishmael been estranged to Sarah, she immediately would have predicted a possible enmity and conflict of interests between Isaac and Ishmael. The time gap between Isaac's birth and Ishmael's expulsion suggests a state of previous harmony which had to be broken — a process that took place in Sarah's mind only after she realized that he indeed is a grown-up person. This kind of realization characterizes a loving mother who retains the notion of 'my little boy' when everyone else is aware of the contrary; it takes an extraordinary occurrence to create such a realization, and for Sarah it was to see Ishmael METZAHEK. The break in her attitude is manifested by her avoidance of the name "Ishmael" and the almost frantic repetition of "this maid's *son*" in contrast to "my *son*" concluded by stating the alternative name "Isaac".

> The text depicts Hagar only as being Sarah's slave. From verse 21:9 *as it stands*, it can be deduced that Hagar had another son or sons whom she bore to someone else (increasing the numbers of a household is a common practice in slave societies). Such a reading of the text makes sense because Sarah was not looking to provide a concubine or "the other wife" for Abraham, but a surrogate womb for herself; the womb, therefore, had to be a sure bet where fertility is concerned. Verse 21:19 leaves room to deduce that Hagar had other children, because the author points to *the one conceived by Abraham*. To relate to her as a virgin, in the circumstances of Sarah's need, is somewhat out of place.[60]

Taking in account what was said regarding the epithets 'son' and 'child', we may notice that even in the crucial moment Sarah retains the notion of 'son' toward Ishmael, be it other woman's son.

In contrast to Sarah's sentiments to Ishmael the author conveys Hagar's attitude by using the general expression 'child — יֶלֶד'. The more intimate 'boy — נַעַר' is used by Hagar only after she gives him water (19b). The ties between the natural mother and her son apparently developed only after Ishmael leaves Sarah, and Hagar is explicitly regarded by the author, for the first time in the text, as "his mother — אִמּוֹ" (21b). Thus, by the subtle use of different expressions for one concept and their careful juxtaposition in the narrative, the author conveys the state of affairs in Abraham's household as well as the change in state of mind that Sarah undergoes in order to protect her baby.

Another possible implication of Abraham's personal life may be deduced from Sarah's frantic repetition of "this maid". Later the text tells of another woman and her children (25:1-2) who probably were around when the event of the expulsion of Ishmael occurred [Sarah died at the age of 127 (23:1) and Abraham was by then 137; if at 100 years it was considered a miracle for Abraham to have a baby (17:17), then at 138, after Sarah's death, to start a new family with six children is an extended miracle which the text does not indicate.[61]

The above analysis suggests the following structure of subject-matter which relates to Sarah in the first part of the unit's narrative:

a) a realistic state of affairs is observed;

b) a state of mind is implied by the wording of (c, below) —

c) a request/demand put to Abraham.

The next parts (expulsion and binding) which have the same subject matter present a mirror-pattern of structure:

c') a request/demand is stated to Abraham;

b') a state of mind is implied by the protagonist's actions

a') a realistic state of affairs is observed.

The first part conveys Sarah's stress within a logical situation; in the second part, the stressful situation temporarily takes a hold on Hagar's mind. Both parts are connected not only because the first one is the logical justification for the events in the second, but mainly because it puts Abraham into a continuous stressful situation which, in the first instance affects Hagar, and in the second its outcome affects Isaac. The first and second part, thus, involve the three protagonists in a circle of stress, and God, who talks to Abraham, is only a bystander.

In the third part God creates the stressful *circle* only for Abraham because feelings of guilt are the usual consequences of doing something that is felt to be wrong, and it may be particularly stressful if it seems that nothing can be done to rectify the error:

> "Thus, when an individual behaves in ways that *he views as immoral*, he experiences not only self-devaluation but apprehension as well... As a consequence of this orientation, he may... search back through his past life, locating and exaggerating misdeeds that have presumably led to his present difficulties. This process is especially obvious among severely depressed persons" (emphasis added, to remind the reader that knowing good and bad has been defined as moral autonomy; p. 114).[62]

We use the word "circle" instead of "situation" advisedly, because Abraham's sense of guilt pushes him to re-enact, to a heightened degree, past events, and it is suggested by several linguistic expressions which allude to it. E.g., by the incantation of the noun 'son', echoing Sarah's demand from the first part and, in a subtle way, putting the blame on Sarah whose care for her 'only son, whom [she] loves' triggered the chain of events:

(21:10b) בֶּן־הָאָמָה הַזֹּאת עִם־בְּנִי עִם־יִצְחָק

(22:2) אֶת־בִּנְךָ אֶת־יְחִידְךָ אֲשֶׁר־אָהַבְתָּ אֶת־יִצְחָק

(10b) the son of this maid <u>with my son</u> with Isaac

(22:2) your son <u>your only son whom you love</u> Isaac.

Or, the request to sacrifice Isaac which echoes the original Call by the use of the same verb 'to go', noun 'son' and the unknown destination:

(12:1a) ...לֶךְ־לְךָ מֵאַרְצְךָ וּמִמּוֹלַדְתְּךָ וּמִבֵּית אָבִיךָ

(:1b) אֶל־הָאָרֶץ אֲשֶׁר אַרְאֶךָּ

(12:1a) ...get going from your country and from your birthplace, and from your father's house;

(1b) to the land, which I will show you.

(22:2a) ...אֶת־בִּנְךָ אֶת־יְחִידְךָ אֲשֶׁר־אָהַבְתָּ אֶת־יִצְחָק וְלֶךְ־לְךָ...

(:2b) ...עַל אַחַד הֶהָרִים אֲשֶׁר אֹמַר אֵלֶיךָ

(22:2a) ...your son, your only son whom you love, Isaac and get going...

(2b) ...on one of the mountains which I will tell you.

The epithets of place have in 12:1a three synonyms and so do those for the son (22:2a); the same command "לֶךְ לְךָ" underlines the difference of goal: the first goal is meant for the descendants who will become a nation whereas the last one is intended for the sacrifice of the very descendant who was supposed to become that nation.

Other similarities, besides those already mentioned, are the early hour of the day in which each event starts, the act of walking and the taking of provisions (21:14a, 22:3a).

A crucial distinction between the second and third part is Isaac's participation (contrary to Ishmael's silence). The elaboration of the text on the conversation between Abraham and Isaac, besides the dramatic effect,[63] reveals two more spiritual elements:

— Abraham's love can be deduced from the use of "son" throughout the ordeal. When Abraham talks of Isaac to his servants, he says "the boy" (22:5) which is less intimate but not as indifferent as 'the child'. But when Abraham talks to Isaac, or when the text describes his actions, it is always as "son" (6-13).

— Abraham's belief is put on trial. The text states that God demands the sacrifice of Isaac in order to put Abraham to the test; it does not say how this communication has been transmitted, and the assumption that it was in a dream is supported by the conclusions reached in our discussion of this issue (p. 159). The demand, conveyed by a similar vocabulary and sentence-pattern as the Call, contradicts God's promise of a pact with Isaac's descendants to the extent that Abraham's faith challenges his logic. It seems that Abraham succumbs to his faith: he takes all the necessary steps to carry out the demand. However, in his conversation with Isaac he says:

(22:8) ...אֱלֹהִים יִרְאֶה־לּוֹ הַשֶּׂה לְעֹלָה בְּנִי...

(22:8) "...God will suit himself [with regard to] the lamb for an offering, my son..."*

* "יִרְאֶה לוֹ" is "provide" [L], and "see for himself" [Speiser] which, in

meaning: I am not the one who makes the decision as to what pleases God; He is the one who makes His choices. Abraham's answer can be interpreted as replying to Isaac's curiosity but, by stressing God's role of suiting himself, Abraham turns the tables on God's attempted trial — *Abraham is now putting God to test*:[64] will he choose himself a human sacrifice? Will he choose thereby to break his promise? What is now on trial is the extent of Abraham's belief and, in a way, the situation echoes Jacob's decision to put God on trial (28:20a) — *will God come up to expectations*? Whether the demand of sacrificing his son originated in Abraham's guilty conscience which re-enacts a morbid version of the expulsion of his first son, or whether he believed his dream to be God's wish, God ultimately is the one whom the text puts to the test.

The intervention of Yhwh's angel and not of the deity himself is a surprising element; one would have expected that the voice which gave the order would be the voice bringing salvation. But the voice coming 'from the sky' hints that the narrative, in spite of the discrepancy and perhaps accentuating it, deals with a state of mind out of which the protagonist wakes up to reality. An animal for sacrifice is suggested as a substitute. In Abraham's case, God came up to expectations.

Abraham sums up the event by a peculiar naming of the place:

(22:14) And Abraham called the name of that place, YHWH Will See (YIR'EH);
as it is said to this day on the mount of YHWH, it will be seen (YERA'EH).*

"God will see" is an explicit allusion to Abraham's expectations

---

my opinion, are not satisfactory. The notion of pleasing oneself is better rendered by the suggested translation.

* The translation follows [L] but the last parts of the lines were arranged symmetrically.

as expressed to Isaac (22:8);[65] but the phrasing of the sentence and the use of the verb 'to see — .ר.א.ה', echoes Hagar's use of the verb in her first encounter with God's angel:

(16:13) And she called the name of the Yhwh who spoke to her You *are* El-Ro'i

because she said, also here I have seen after Ro'i

(14a) Therefore <u>he</u> called the well Lachai-Ro'i well...

This "He", in all probability, is Abraham,* and the wording, as well as the use of the verb .ר.א.ה is his naming (in Isaac's affair) indicate that Abraham knew of his first son's tribulations.[66] The correlation between the two incidents is not mere linguistic play of the verb .ר.א.ה by the author but indicates that both he and his protagonist Abraham made a clear connection between the two events. This correlation, therefore, supports the assumption that Abraham's actions and reactions are a literary narration of a state of mind: in regard to Ishmael it corresponds to a painful reality, whereas The Binding is its heightened nightmare.

c) Relationship with God

The overall picture of Abraham's relationship with God, in spite of the constancy of the pact between them, undergoes a change: it evolves from a pure belief (encounters 1-5) to something which can hardly be regarded as "YIR'AT YHWH, 'יראת־יהוה'", in spite of what is said to Abraham by voice of the angel (in 22:12b);[67] because what emerges from the discussion is scepticism

* This suggestion stands in contrast to all renderings who regard the Hebrew על־כן קרא לבאר in the general sense ([K.J.] & [L] — ...the well was called; [Speiser] — ...the well is called). My reasons for relating it to Abraham are twofold: the conjugation used is in the third person active past קָרָא, not the passive form 'יִקָּרֵא', and the following verse which seems to pick up this very notion of 'Abraham ...... calling/naming' when referring to the name Ishamel (15b).

(encounter 6) and a protagonist who puts God to test (encounter 8). This relationship which started in good faith by a trusting partner to a pact, ends up with that pact being continued by a confused believer.

3. God and Isaac

The similarity of life patterns between Abraham and Isaac is extended also to their relationship with God, inasmuch as the conventional means of communication are expressed: God speaks to him and "is seen — יראה " which, as has been suggested, takes place in a dream. Isaac, as said before, carries on the pact with God and passes it on to his son Jacob.

In the two direct encounters that Isaac had with God (No. 2, 3), the shadow cast by Abraham's pact is evident: God repeats his promises about descendants and the land, and in both encounters stresses it as a commitment to Abraham. But as the fulfilment of God's promises is conditioned on Isaac's accepting God's words, i.e., carrying on with the pact (26:5), Isaac's place in the chain of creation of a nation is crucial. His life story in this respect does not exhibit any characteristics which differ from the patterns of his father's life, but on the other hand he is the only one of the forefathers who was born in the promised land and never left it.

4. God and Jacob

The first link between God and Jacob is established by his father Isaac who sends him to find himself a wife, saying to him:

(28:3a) And El-Shadai will bless you make you fruitful, and multiply you;
(3b) and you shall become, a multitude of people.
(4a) And he shall give you Abraham's blessing to you, and your descendants with you
(4b) to inherit your dwelling land which God gave, to Abraham.

The underlined repetition of "Abraham" and "Blessing" in the above verses (forming a pattern of a, ba, b), the triple repetition "you" in one sentence (4a), the alliteration of the sound ךָ ×ֵ throughout the blessing, and in 3a the three successive blessings bestowed upon Jacob, are the devices that give the whole unit a sense of poetry.

But this is more than a blessing emanating from a father's heart, as might be interpreted from the preceding verse 1a: "and Isaac called Jacob and blessed him", because afterwards there is a change in subject matter and Isaac orders him (וַיְצַוֵּהוּ), giving him instructions regarding his marriage (1b-2). This juxtaposition of subject matter suggests a separate, unspecified, fatherly blessing beforehand (in 1a), and after giving Jacob his instructions (2), Isaac *transmits the spiritual inheritance* which distinguishes the chain of Abraham (3-4, cited above). Isaac, thus, is but its transmitter, because if there is a gap between the declaration of blessings and the actual elaboration which specify them as Abraham's, then one may assume that the title 'blessings' concerns emotional personal matters and are followed by the equally personal issue of marriage.

There is not much novelty in its content, as it repeats what was previously said to Abraham. But it is worth noting that Isaac transmits to Jacob the name of the God who gave those promises to Abraham as "El-Shadai" — the name by which God presented himself to Abraham (17:1). Jacob's departure from his parents marks the beginning of his relationship with the family God, as presented in the following encounters:

1. Jacob's Dream

Jacob's first direct encounter with God happens immediately after Isaac's blessing (28:12-15) and the importance of this encounter is not so much in God's familiar promises as in the nature of Jacob's response: the pattern established by Abraham of "give and take" is here reinforced. But while this kind of relationship has been offered to Abraham and Isaac by God [*if* you'll leave your country, *then* I'll reward you; *if* you'll follow Abraham's footsteps *then* I'll keep my promises, respectively], the order of things with Jacob is different: first, God introduces himself (13a), then he promises the country (13b) and descendants (14) and at last he promises to help him in his intended journey until his return home (15); no implicit "ifs" are mentioned by God. It is Jacob who conditions his relationship with God and puts it to test:

If God will be with me...	(28: 20a)	אִם־יִהְיֶה אֱלֹהִים עִמָּדִי...
Yhwh shall be my God. [L]	(28: 21b)	וְהָיָה יהוה לִי לֵאלֹהִים

This statement is a reverse pattern of what is said by God (Exodus, 6:7), which in itself is the marriage contract formula in ancient Near East.[68] The God-nation relationship, therefore, is alluded into wife-husband relationship, a notion which will be elaborated upon by the much later prophets: "I remember unto thee, the kindness of thy youth, the love of thy espousals..." (Jeremiah, 2:2, or 31:3). In Jacob's case — he takes the role of the husband.

2. Leaving Haran

God, as portrayed in the text, shows signs of a controlled sense of humour toward Jacob's practical attitude, because in the second encounter He does not reproach him for setting the terms in what might be considered as unprecedented impertinence [in Abraham's case it is the well-mannered ironical scepticism of "מַה תִּתֶּן לִי - what will you give me" (15:2)]. When the time is ripe, that is, when God has come up to expectations, He reminds Jacob (31:13) of the commitment expressed in Jacob's vow; and although there are no direct references to the deal set by Jacob, God ironically points to it by engaging the same vocabulary referred to Jacob (pillar, ointment, (31:13)), and tells him to go back to his country.

In his prayers, before crossing the Jabbok, Jacob admits that God had fulfilled His part of the deal that he, Jacob, had set; he returns to Canaan prosperous and, with a substantial amount of irony, gives thanks to God for it (32:11):

קָטֹנְתִּי מִכֹּל הַחֲסָדִים וּמִכָּל־הָאֱמֶת אֲשֶׁר עָשִׂיתָ אֶת־עַבְדֶּךָ
כִּי בְמַקְלִי עָבַרְתִּי אֶת־הַיַּרְדֵּן הַזֶּה וְעַתָּה הָיִיתִי לִשְׁנֵי מַחֲנוֹת׃

I am unworthy of all the kindness and all the truth which you have bestowed, upon your servant;
because with my stick, I had crossed this Jordan and now I have become, two bands.

Although the cited verses are a prayer where due thanks and a token of humility "קָטֹנְתִּי - I am unworthy" are offered, still, ironical remarks are indirectly made about dangers which Jacob had to undergo: the stick which points to his wound, and the two camps that indicate a forthcoming danger. But Jacob retains his practical attitude to God and, in spite of the expressed modesty, appears before him as a claimant rather than as the servant he proposes to be (11a), because this sentence is placed between two statements which intend to remind God of his part. Thus, in the opening of his prayer Jacob turns to the family-God *whose command he followed because a reward has been promised* (32:10):

...אֱלֹהֵי אָבִי אַבְרָהָם וֵאלֹהֵי אָבִי יִצְחָק
יהוה הָאֹמֵר אֵלַי שׁוּב לְאַרְצְךָ וּלְמוֹלַדְתְּךָ וְאֵיטִיבָה עִמָּךְ

God of my father Abraham and God of my father, Isaac;
Yhwh who tells me, return to your country and birthplace, and I will reward you.

and in the closing of his prayer Jacob sets before God the forthcoming danger to his descendants by reminding God of the promise regarding them 32:13:

וְאַתָּה אָמַרְתָּ הֵיטֵב אֵיטִיב עִמָּךְ
וְשַׂמְתִּי אֶת־זַרְעֲךָ כְּחוֹל הַיָּם אֲשֶׁר לֹא־יִסָּפֵר מֵרֹב

And you have said I will reward you
and multiply your seed [to be] like the sea-sand which its abundance, cannot be counted.

Encounters A and B

Our conclusion that encounters with angels are indirect encounters and not necessarily relevant to the discussion on *direct* communication with God, implies that encounter A has no contribution to our discussion and that encounter B in the Jabbok is relevant only inasmuch as Jacob's new name "Israel" is concerned (32:29). A reference in retrospect to this encounter (35:9) and to the name Israel (35:10) is made in encounter 3, where God presents himself as El-Shadai and repeats his promises on descendants and the land (35:11-12).

4. God Encourages Jacob to Go to Egypt

Jacob's last encounter with God (46:1-4) resembles the first, only inasmuch as the same promise of God's accompanying him in his journey to and back from Haran is concerned. In the first instance it was to Padan-Aram (28:15), and in the last — to Egypt (46:3-4a), but no new facet of the relationship between the parties is exhibited.

5. Conclusion: The Relationships with the Forefathers

The main points of the above presentation of the relationship between God and the forefathers in the encounters between them do not conform to what is generally described as 'religion' (p. 00). It basically takes the form of a pact between two equal partners, and can be summarized by the following table:

Encounter	Initiator	Communication	Nature of Relationship	Notes
Abraham	God	1) speaks 2) seen 3) a vision	God asks something, and in return — promises a reward.	
	God?	4) a state of mind	God's request bears no reward.*	differs from all others.
Isaac	God	1) speaks 2) seen	God asks something, and grants rewards.	
Jacob	God	1) a vision	God offers rewards.	
	Jacob	2) conscious vow	Jacob states the terms of rewards	differs from all others.

* Moreover, if fulfilled, it will contradict all previously promised rewards.

The table highlights the relevant points which have been discussed:

a) The common denominator with regard to the form of communication is that of vision/dream, where God sometimes is seen, but always speaks. When the method is not specified, the communications, as suggested in the analysis, take place in a dream state.

b) The common denominator with regard to the nature of the relationships is that reward is promised if God's request is fulfilled. This is the pattern of all but two of the encounters between God and patriarchs.

c) Abraham's last encounter differs in every respect from all the previous ones, because the issue itself is exceptional issue; the meanings of the unit regarded as a state of mind will be discussed in the next chapter.

d) The outstanding feature in the columns marked "Initiator" and "Nature of Relationship" is Jacob's encounter which differs sharply from the typical ones (a, b). The difference is not as peculiar as the previous one (c); it just reverses the pattern of the regular encounters. This change, however, is important because it gives the relationship between God and the forefathers its direction which culminates in two characteristic concepts: the forefathers' voluntary acceptance of God as their God, and a shift of initiative from the Creator to his intended created entity — the nation. To state that "The patriarch's stories theme is explicit in the actual words of God which promises blessing, land increase and influence, while overcoming obstacles with his help"[69] is a simplification, probably influenced by the traditional attitude towards God's task of salvation; it seems to disregard the subtlety of the text in the various encounters between the patriarchs and their chosen God.

For the notion of 'acceptance of God' is common to all the forefathers, each in his own way: Abraham's response to God's call and Isaac's continuation of the pact are, first and foremost, in return for a reward [this, however, does not mean that a degree of belief does not exist; it simply puts it in its proper perspective as a secondary factor]. Theirs are silent manifestations of acceptance; Jacob's explicit demand for material rewards as a condition of acceptance, on the other hand, is vocal.

The shift of initiative is evident in the basis of recognition and in the terms set for the pact between the parties:

— Abraham and Isaac do not question God's existence; they take it for granted. This is indicated by the straightforward conversation God holds with them without introducing himself (12:1, 16:2). Jacob's case, as evident from the first encounter, is different: God finds it necessary to introduce himself to Jacob; it may indicate that He is not taken for granted by Jacob.

— Abraham and Isaac's relationship with God is based on adherence to His commands and a belief in His promises, but the text shows that it is not blind worship or submission: the pact is workable because *all* partners show good will. Abraham, however, is the one to demand from God proof (passing between the pieces), and to put him to the test (the binding of Isaac). Jacob seems to carry Abraham's scepticism a step further; it is Jacob who sets the terms. With the promise to Abraham in the second covenant — "to be your God" (17:7b) one has the feeling that God is somewhat imposing himself; with Jacob it is a vow voluntarily taken — "Yhwh will be my God" (28:21b). Hence — what was said to Abraham as God's will, is converted by Jacob to become his own choice. God wants to be Abraham's God; Jacob, on the other hand, offers Him to be such. It is no coincidence that his terms are patterned on the same literary structure as God's offers, although the roles are reversed; the initiative is held by Jacob.

E. Meanings in the Narrative

1. Introduction

The above discussion suggested many points that differ from the traditional view of the text, but most noticeable is the interpretation we have suggested for 'The Binding of Isaac', traditionally regarded as the epitome of "יראת־יהוה YIR'AT YHWH", of obedience to God.

On the face of it, Abraham's intentions of going through with the sacrifice can be interpreted as obedience, regardless of the driving force that made him do it — whether God's intention of 'testing' him, as it is presented in the text, or his own sense of guilt driving him to put himself and his belief to the test. Abraham's obedience in this case, unlike in previous encounters, does not depend on, and is not conditioned by a reward; on the contrary — if fulfilled, it would have contradicted all previous agreements between him and God. This face-value meaning is dubious, because if valid, then we are left with the question as to why the author has chosen to convey a zeal for God, commonly considered a positive value, by means of an act which contradicts natural justice as well as legal justice — the two notions which, although not always compatible, constitute the pillars of civilized society.

On the other hand, a careful reading of Abraham's words conveys the sense that ultimately it is Abraham, in his peculiar state of mind and driven by his sense of guilt, who is testing God's integrity.[71] This reading projects a sophisticated author who cleverly uses the statement 'God tested Abraham' as a literary device to question whether irrational zeal, even when excused as blind obedience, has a place in man's life side by side with civilized human notions.[72] The author's answer to this question, according to our new reading of the text, seems to be negative: not only because the text projects the occurrence as being the product of a disturbed state of mind, but also because, as a matter of fact, Abraham's act of human sacrifice — as an expression of a zeal for God — is exceptional and did not become a source of inspiration or accepted example in Biblical literature or Biblical life. The one and only other case mentioned in the Bible is that of Yephtah's daughter, and the text leaves a clear impression of a negative attitude toward Yephtah [and I have seen no commentary which regards this case as an example of YIR'AT YHWH]. Moreover — no book in the Bible stresses Abraham's act as a supreme manifestation of devotion to God, mainly because the Bible in general and the prophets in particular understood devotion to God through the negation of other deities ("do not have other gods") and stressed the importance of justice and human behaviour over ritual — the very notions contradicted by Abraham's act.

2. The Explicit Meaning

"Creation of a nation" has been regarded in this discussion as the acquisition of a spiritual national identity, 'a sense of purpose', developed in the course of a series of encounters between God and the protagonists. As was concluded in the discussion on God's relationships with the forefathers, the process culminated in two notions:

— the vocational and spiritual notion which is summed up by "he shall be our God", i.e., ***We chose Him as our God***;

— the shift of power of initiative, in the pact, from Creator to Created.

These notions, as the findings of our voyage tell us, sum up the meanings of the patriarch's stories. They constitute the spiritual backbone and the common denominator of the people (Am) of Israel and, to my mind, they manifest the state of mind which implies a peculiar Biblical cultural value: after Jacob, it is the new entity called "nation" (Goy) which, of its own volition, retains the alternative of continuing the special relationship with its creator. The book of Judges (e.g. 5:8a) and some of the prophets emphasize the point that the nation is responsible for the continuation of the relationship with God, depending on its adherence to Him and to His laws.

The issue of territory is an important factor for this new entity — the nation called Israel — and the road to it is told in the rest of the Pentateuch. The territory, as discussed in the chapter on word-analysis, is given several different borders; but, as explained, the area encompassed in each promise will suit Abraham's promised child. No conditions are attached to the possession of territory by all the other descendants; for Jacob's line, on the other hand, permanent hold of their land depends on their adherence to the pact made with the patriarchs.

Their territory, thus, is part of their national 'sense of purpose'.

3. The Implicit Meaning — The Mythic Motif

The explicit meanings underlined above suggest two corresponding implicit meanings for the narrative-body:

— Man's statement that 'this and that will be "my" God', in practice, means that ***man creates his own God***. Creation (in the Biblical sense of 'origination') of a personal God is a universal phenomenon,[73] and the author of Genesis is no exception in his 'creation'. Only his unique narrative and a correspondingly unique God, when combined with the concept discussed below, differs distinctively from other creations.

— The initiative for the relationship with God lies in one's own hand; in other words: ***the created is the one who has the power of volition — authority***. This notion is unique to the Genesis narrative, because all other myths stress the opposite view — Man's relations with the gods depend on, and they are a mere toy for, their satisfaction.

The common denominator of both mythic motifs is the consciously and subconsciously desired victory of the created over its creator — what was previously referred to as the "son-father" conflict [mentioned in the previous chapter (p. 141) and will be elaborated further on]. This motif culminates in the created "son" acquiring the freedom of choice of both his God and the terms to the pact between them. Once having the freedom of choice, the chosen concept narrated indicates, or points to, the nature of its beholder — as will be discussed in the next chapter.

Chapter V
CONCLUSIONS

A. Introduction

[Page numbers of issues elaborated upon, are given in brackets.]

As we stated in the introduction to this research, and have attempted to substantiate throughout the discussion, our approach to Genesis was to relate to the text "as it is" from a standpoint of literary analysis (28), and to leave aside disputes about author, authenticity and unity (13), superimposed religious connotations or liturgical uses made of it (22). The argument that literary appreciation may be occasional, whereas religious perceptions and the use made of the text in worship are regular and current,[1] is irrelevant for an objective literary approach because religion and ritual are subjective for the believer. Just as irrelevant, for the reasons of subjectivity, is the question of the implications on the text of whatever findings regarding its status as a holy book.[2]

In contrast to those subjective applications, the Genesis text as it stands (20) is an objective fact which requires investigation; first and foremost of what it says, even when it is found to be theologically neutral or secular in its cultural outlook (25). Therefore, freedom from prejudice and prejudgment prevailed throughout our interpretation, where conclusions had to be grounded on textual presentation and its facts.

Our discussion, through analysis of words related to the nature of 'creator-created relationships', presented the subtle richness of the language used, and disclosed the peculiar nature of the entity of the creator and of his created ones. This concluding chapter presents the common denominators of the two concepts, God and Blessings, discussed in all previous chapters, and its following paragraphs will attempt to find a coherent line of thought in the explicit and implicit meanings of the text. Let us sum up the findings of our journey.

B. Concepts

1. God

It was found that the creator's designations were also used as adjectival suffixes and in some cases as a synonym to 'awe' and 'dread' (166-167); in one place, it was suggested, also as an idiomatic phrase (167). I find the linguistic freedom in the text regarding the deity's designations unmatched in ancient literature.[3] Another peculiar facet — there is no distinction between the everyday and the sublime in Genesis because, fundamentally, the text does not relate to the sublime![4]

Although commentators are aware of these facets,[5] they refuse to acknowledge, even as a possibility, that when written and before its inclusion in the canon, Genesis was a secular book — insofar as stories about the deity could be secular. It is only in these secular terms, in my modest opinion, that our contemporary classification of Genesis as 'legend' has any validity; if the text is not 'holy' and is not part of ritual, then it is as secular as any other genre.

Eschewing the alternative of an exalted language, the secular and simple language of the text suggests a corresponding philosophical attitude regarding the perception of the deity: He is viewed as part of the secular life and moreover — He is called when needed and taken for granted.[6] Thus, unlike Egyptian and Mesopotamian mythologies which tell how Gods were created,[7] in Genesis God is a matter of fact; with the exception of Jacob, He does not bother to present himself to the protagonists — He talks with them and no one asks "who are you?".

The text states His acts of creation in an everyday-life prose which, although it has a poetic element to it, does not elevate itself above reality, as do the poetic incantations of other contemporary mythologies. His created ones, as we shall show, have their own 'raison d'être' and are not mere playthings at His service, as suggested in Mesopotamian mythologies.[8] On the other hand, and unlike these mythologies, no explanation is given for God's reason for creating a world; probably because this also was taken to be a matter of fact — the same lack of curiosity as manifested toward God himself: God and the world exist. This perhaps was reason enough for the author to go on attempting to explain the nature of what exists and to discuss the three main issues of the book:

a) The world. The secular and practical attitude, despite the fact that creation is attributed to God, is evident in the *scientific approach* to the world's creation. Whether this science does or does not correspond to our contemporary knowledge is irrelevant to the issue; and the issue is the approach as well as the created elements themselves. By turning his back on mythological notions such as 'sky created of a cut body of the Goddess'[9] and presenting the elements as resulting from a divine command and created in a logical order, the author conveys a sense of reality and of natural process (58); his is a world where each new element serves and correlates to a preceding one, and all elements are combined into *a logical whole.*

God leaves his mark during the process of creation, and He is the one who imposes order and logic, but after completion *God takes no part* in the functioning of creation. The function of 'ruling' has been transferred to man who purposely was created for this task.

b) Human beings. The same secular attitude is evident in the *attempt* to view the issue of human beings scientifically, in two stages (93): creation, and an essential phase of development where the created one separates himself from all other beings and establishes himself closer, in essence, to his creator. The narrative of creation of a world and the first stage of creation of human beings deals with natural phenomena and, as expressed above, presents no logical difficulties in understanding it as scientific data.

The second stage of the creation of human beings is concerned with abstract notions of spiritual development, which are more difficult to deal with; hence the above emphasized "attempt", because several unrealistic mythological elements are engaged in order to convey them. Our discussion of the second stage, however, had illuminated most of the legendary and irrational elements of the text through an attempt at logic [Adam's identification and the so-called 'second creation' (71-74), the special trees (95-97), the issue of the snake (105-106)], excluding the account of the separate creation of the woman. The latter has been regarded as expressing a mythic motif (139). The rest of the text, therefore, is a narrative which conforms to logic.[10]

The attempt to apply a logical explanation for the most crucial phase of human development, the gaining of consciousness (132), is not entirely free of legendary matter (eating a fruit, 136). Man's acquisition of consciousness culminates in God's abdication: if in the creation of the world it was God's will to abdicate authority, in the second phase of human existence God *is obliged to accept* man's acquisition of a divine faculty of moral autonomy as an irreversible fact. The state of affairs in human life as we know them, i.e., the fact that man *has* moral autonomy, apparently was perceived by the author; his narrative, therefore, is a reflection of reality upon a legendary matter.

c) The Nation. The secular attitude toward the process of creation of a nation, in all its complexity, is expressed by the literary treatment of the forefathers as complicated human beings with their vices and virtues rather than as demigods of Mesopotamian mythology.[11] Their human nature is characterized by a non-religious attitude to God which, although ultimately expressing faith, is interwoven with sceptical irony toward the nation's ceator (187, 189), putting him to test (208) and laying down the terms of relationship with Him (212).

2. Blessings

The creator's blessings have the common literary trait of stating first the purpose of creation for the created: the living elements of the world are created in order to occupy their designated spaces, and afterwards blessed — to increase and multiply; humans are created in order to rule over created creatures and blessed — to multiply and settle their designated place — earth; the forefathers are chosen in order to form a new nation and are blessed with territory and descendants. However, reality is not just blessings which, in the context of this research, were the issue discussed, but also obstacles which are outside the scope of this research. These common characteristics imply a thematic link common to all parts of the text — "creation, blessings, overcoming obstacles", where the first two serve as introduction or motto to the third which is the main narrative.* No conditions are attached to the blessings of the created species and humans, but for the nation — the blessings are conditioned on the fulfilment of specific demands, found in the formula "if... then...". Although the phrasing of some of the promises is distinctively poetic, the businesslike pattern of the above formula gives a secular aura to the direct encounters between God and the forefathers. In their case, therefore, the two concepts of God and the blessings are conveyed as secular

* D.Sutherland ("The Organization of the Abraham Narratives", 337-43) limits his thematic suggestion of "tension between promise and obstacle to promise" to the patriarch's narratives; within these limits, it is similar to this paper's suggestion.

practical issues and, as such, they compel a secular understanding of the explicit meanings of the text.

C. The Explicit Meanings

The conclusions from the explicit meanings of the three created objects are expressed in the table below which, when read horizontally, conveys the opinions expressed on each object (the relevant verse or pages in which issues were unconventionally treated are in brackets):

A created	B conceived	C creator	D creation	E authority
world	by God (3:b)	first omnipotent then mighty — his logical acts and limitations assume quasi-human qualities.	a process where each created element is a logical continuation of the previous one.	God is the one to act, up to the seventh period.
humans	by God (1:26)	God passes on his form and image to the created (1:27).	processed from earth and breath (2:7, discussed — 98).	God transfers his authority to the created.
Adam	by God (2:15)	God initiates the conditions for acquisition of autonomy (trees).	taken from existing stock (101).	a certain kind of authority is taken by the created.
nation I	by God (12:2) (26:3)	God lays down promises on land and descendants	a spiritual process, via two generations of forefathers.	a pact between partners.
nation II	by God (28:23)	God introduces himself, offering his blessings.	a vision which induces Jacob to make a pact with God.	Jacob sets the terms for the pact.

For the final conclusion, a vertical reading is required:

A. **The Created**. These were the subjects of this research, and in the process of their creation I have tried to draw out the explicit meanings of the relationships between creator and created. The original project, as indicated in the introduction, was to analyse *three* objects: a world, humankind and a nation (5); yet this table offers five. It seems that the chpater on the world presents no difficulties, whereas whatever concerns human beings is more complex: each object is divided into two stages, a fact which perhaps has not been so evident in the course of our discussion. The reasons for the sub-divisions are made clear when the other factors of the table are considered.

B. **The conceiving party**. In all cases it is God who conceives the intended object; but the creation of the nation, i.e., the spiritual process which forms its sense of identity, depends also on acceptance and agreement of the 'object'.

C. **The creator**. As no questions are asked about "who he is", the discussion throughout followed his acts and thereby deduced facets of his essence. Looking through the column in the table enables us to note a movement toward a notion which, albeit blasphemous, may be regarded as 'humility of the creator': from omnipotence to mightiness and then to contributing his form, image and volition. With the exclusion of the garden event, this tendency of humility continues by *offering* his pact to Abraham and Isaac and, at the last stage, his *unconditioned* blessings for Jacob (28:13-15).

D. **Creation**. The process of creation comprises two distinctive parts: physical phenomena and a spiritual one. Adam is the one who combines both elements, because although chosen from among the physical phenomena, the spiritual transformation he undergoes, the acquired power of volition, opens a new path of existence to his descendants. This power is manifested also in the choice placed before the forefathers — God suggests, but the option to accept or reject is theirs.

***E.* Authority**. The issue of authority expressed in the table corresponds to the direction discussed in column C and to the process of creation in column D — a transfer of volition from the creator to the created:

At first, 'dominion' is given to humankind; then Adam takes up a certain kind of authority. The forefathers, as Adam's descendants, inherit the same kind of authority and their pact with God is not that which exists between master and servant — both sides are committed. At the last stage, God expresses His unconditional blessings, and Jacob is the one to accept them as a precondition to a further bond between them.

For what clearly emerges from our presentation, the unifying core of the narratives and *their explicit meaning* suggested and stressed here, *is that of power/volition.*[12] All along our discussion on the relationships between creator and created (humans and nation) I elaborated on essence/nature of that power/volition rather than on the frequency of contact between them[13] or the amount of God's involvement in their affairs.[14] I may conclude, therefore, that the spiritual volition acquired by Adam results, in the case of the nation, in a relationship which is not that of creator-created but rather that of equal partners:

> E. Fromm suggests two kinds of relationship with authority: teacher-pupil and slave-master:[15] "The interests of the teacher and student, *in the ideal case*, lie in the same direction... of slave and master are antagonistic, because what is advantageous to the one is detrimental to the other". Fromm regards the Biblical attitude as that of

student-teacher, and thus the Bible for him is a liberated and liberating book.[16]

But the above words which I emphasized, leave room for a less ideal case. Furthermore, Fromm's understanding of the text, through justification of disobedience, goes along with the conventional notion of 'sin' and 'disobedience'. This may be the reason why the third possible kind of relationship with authority, that of equal partners (husband-wife; see p. 212), did not occur to him.

This possibility of equal partners taken up in our research leaves no room for ideal or less ideal cases — it sets the terms from start (as was the custom in marriage contract) and this, I suggest, is the only kind of relationship which, by the contract's limitations, allows to exercise both — power of volition and freedom of choice.

Does this explicit meaning of power/volition found in the text comply with the rest of the Bible? It does but, I suggest, only to the extent that the continuous relationship between God and the nation, the Abrahamic pact, is contingent on obligations of both parties to the pact. However, the sense of pride expressed by Jacob, the volition manifested by his choosing of God and laying down the terms to Him, is not repeated in the Biblical text and even contradicts the later concept of 'humility of the created' elaborated upon by the prophets. When and why was the transition?

The answer may be found in Exodus, the only place in the Pentateuch where 'creation of a world' is brought in as argumentation for a spiritual concept:

The first set of commandments brought down by Moses states a reason for keeping the Sabbath (Exodus, 20:11):

> For in six days Yhwh made the sky and earth, the sea and all that is in them
> and ceased on the seventh day;

Therefore Yhwh blessed the day of Sabbath and distinguished it.*

The reason for keeping the Sabbath, the verse suggests, is to follow God's attitude: He does not work on the seventh day, nor should His people.[17] The implication of "in god's image" assumes here, in addition to the corporeal similarity, also a spiritual one. But this perception of 'be like God' is not evident in the second version of the commandments, where the reason given for the Sabbath is one of social well-being (Deut., 5:15).[18] What happened in between the two versions was the affair with the Golden Calf, after which an individual leader in the text, Moses, might have realized that people, a collective nourished on the perception of "humility of the created", are slow or even incapable of grasping the opposite philosophical notion. To state that "while we [20th century people] are living technically in the Atom Age, the majority of men — including most of those who are in power — still live emotionally in the Stone Age"[19] is only partly correct. Humans are basically the same at any given time (as discussed on p. 8) and irrational or logical perceptions is an issue of quantity: we assume that the more technically advanced the period, the more rational perception prevails. It is a pleasant but an arguable fallacy. Logic, unfortunately, is the prerogative of relatively few; most of humanity, in all ages, tends to succumb to the irrational.

Therefore, Moses' need to apply to, or conform with, his non-abstract minded people (who needed a tangible object to stand for the abstract God "who took them out of Egypt") forced him to build a sanctuary and to establish clerical institutions in response to their mentality; a free mind does not require such institutions, and Moses' mistake was to misjudge his people. The Pentateuch tells us that the voice which expressed the uncommon perception to the people in Exodus, is the voice that denied it to them in Deut. From a literary point of view, therefore, the

* The translation follows what was suggested for 2:3a on p. 42.

protagonist Moses, characterized as a social and political superior leader of high values, shares the very perception and cultural attitude which prevails in the Genesis stories examined. This being said, however, does not involve an historical judgement as to the authorship of Genesis; it merely asserts the idea expressed here all along — that conceiving such an abstract notion has to be the rational product of an individual which, in the case of Genesis, has to be characterized as having a sophisticated philosophical perception. The basic assumption of this thesis, that Genesis may be regarded as a product of an individual mind (as discussed on p. 16), gains here a support *through literary analysis of its content and meanings*; a philosophical perception such as 'you are Godlike creatures; you should behave like God', as proven by the Israelite experience, is outside the scope of the collective mind.

The notion, or desire, to have godlike abilities is evident in tales of magic, magicians and in stories of the supernatural, which are usually limted to performances and, in most cases, have happy endings. But to aspire to the essence of God in matters of knowledge and stature — such a philosophical attitude is usually illustrated in literature as a farcical notion (e.g., Faust aspired to divine powers, and used them for foolish and superfluous ends). It is hardly ever stressed in literature, that when 'being like God' is achieved, man is left alone, burdened with responsibility on the top of his own mountain and, in general, is incapable of coping with absolute freedom and therefore evades it.[20]

D. The Implicit Meanings — The Mythic Motifs

The discussions on the implicit meanings of the three previous chapters are expressed in this table:

	object	the motifs found
A	world	1) longing for order; 2) desire for authority.
B	humanity	1) aspiring for the divine; 2) desire for authority.
C	Adam	1) womb-envy; 2) desire for authority.
D	nation	1) creating one's own God; 2) desire for authority.

The common denominator of all parts is obvious — the second motif of each case expresses the mythic desire to acquire power, a motif which was mentioned, in passing, in the discussion as the 'Father-Son Conflict'. The perception of this conflict which we regard as relevant to this discussion is that of Freud,[21] and a brief presentation is essential before applying it to the chapters of Genesis:

> Application of psychoanalysis to the concept of God reveals that God is nothing other than an exalted father. His first manifestation, the totem, acquired the form of object or animal; the God is a later manifestation in which the father has regained his human shape. Both manifestations are but a surrogate of the primordial, hated, feared and envied father killed by his sons. The transition from hate to worship is suggested as follows: after a lapse of time, the bitterness against the father decreased and the longing for him increased, and this resulted in the emergence of an ideal of the unlimited power of the primal father, as well as the readiness to submit to him. The religious covenant with the

totem, thus, was an attempt at atonement for the murdered father.

Freud relates to myths and societies which reflect the state of the "aborigine" — of "examplary history", as M. Eliade defines them;[22] Genesis' stories on the other hand reflect a much later period — "of corrupted myths". Totemistic perceptions as such, therefore, do not apply for Genesis. But the later perception of God, that of the exalted father and the covenant with him, may suggest for Genesis a far more serious attempt at atonement with the supposed primordial murder:

The "Father-Son Conflict" in almost all ancient mythologies ends with the rebel son being victorious and, thus, they conform to Freud's theory. In Genesis, on the other hand, a kind of compromise is achieved — a mutual understanding that the bond between "father" and "son" is maintained by the free will of two equally obligated partners. The primordial conflict, I suggest, exists only inasmuch as it forms the basis for the Genesis narrative.

The conscious author of Genesis, whose eclecticism and sophistication produced artificial versions of ancient myths, in practice corrupted those myths to suit his own ends — to explain and state his personal opinion on man's position and purpose of existence in one's own world. He left no room for the assumed original murder of the father.

The solution at which he arrived in his narratives was to make Man the most important object of creation by means of three factors: he has a divine form; God's authority was invested in his hands; and a divine prerogative made him also in essence similar to God. The mythic motif, which is usually hidden, seems by these three factors to acquire in Genesis a more explicit expression.[23] This can be done only by an individual and conscious mind — societies tend to keep the mythic motifs hidden in their collective unconsciousness.[24]

The first three different motifs in the table (marked 1) support the motif of "Father-Son Conflict" by expressing the facet of envy of different spheres of His powers: the longing for order set by authority, the aspiring to his divine form, his faculty of moral autonomy, and the womb-envy — the power of creation of life. These are all manifestations of the wish to acquire his creative capabilities.

The fourth motif in this category (D1) seems to be a natural result of this jealousy: by creating his own God, man gains a victory over his "father". Man creates Him in light of the qualities he envies and wishes to project upon himself. Contra opinions of later Jewish philosophy, laid down by Maimonides,[25] the God that the author created in Genesis is not a transcendental entity that goes beyond the sensual and comprehensional faculties of man, but rather a practical and useful God who relates to the existence of this world and serves the practical demand of the believer.

But the mythic motif, by virtue of presenting man's wish-fulfilment, does not necessarily find its true representation in the logical interpretation of a text. Insofar as people's needs are not answered by the narrative which aims at conveying a specific meaning, human imagination takes over the narrative and interprets it in a more accommodating light to serve its own needs.[26] Quite often different interpretations suggest contradictory meanings, and the wish-fulfilment factor, the mythic motif, is not the same; it varies according to interpreter and audience. The issue discussed in this book, "creator-created relationships", has given rise to several interpretations: the early Christian commentaries dwelt on "Original Sin"; Protestant opinions stressed "Crime and Punishment"; psychological notions suggest a fundamental "Sense of Guilt";[27] modern concepts suggest "Authority and Freedom" as part of the philosophy of "Humanistic Ethics".[28] To a large extent, and in spite of following the traditional reading of the text, the last perception advocated by E. Fromm shares the opinion expressed in this book regarding creator-created relationships:

> "The idea of the covenant constitutes indeed, one of the most decisive steps in the religious developments of Judaism, a step which prepares the way to *the concept of the complete freedom of man, even freedom from God*".[29]

Fromm's statement talks about "religious developments of Judaism", which reflect the Bible as a whole, whereas the words I emphasized project the philosophy that we found in our journey through the text of Genesis only. I claim, therefore, that "freedom" had already been suggested from the outset by the Genesis text, in which the factor of God's omnipotence has been consciously reduced, authority passed on to man, and a covenant between equally obliged partners suggested to the patriarchs of the nation. By this kind of reduction of God's authority, while still referring creation and mightiness to Him, the element of 'jealousy' seems to lose its sharp edge of hate.[30] Moreover — the reduction of God's omnipotence becomes not only the kind of unconscious atonement for the father, as suggested by Freud, but, I suggest, also a projection of a logical wish-fulfilment ***to become the father***.

'Becoming the father', or the prerogative of a total freedom, is thus suggested in *The Book of Genesis*. But every one who consciously aspires to maintain such a freedom has to ask himself the crucial question: "is my aspiration to a godlike total freedom accompanied by a simultaneous godlike sense of responsibility?"

Chapter VI
READING AIDS

A. Appendix

The term "Linguistic Problems" is used because of the tendency, expressed several times in this book, to prefer neutral ones. However, as clearing linguistic problems is the basis of all that has been done in this research, a further elaboration on method is imperative:

The analysis of words carried out is not on etymology (account of a word's formation and sense-development) or philology (science of the structure and development of language), or comparison with other languages. It is more on semantics (on usage and meanings derived from the Biblical text). This approach, to a large extent, corresponds to what P.J. Smith calls "Semotaxis", i.e., "a semantic evaluation of a given word or phrase in terms of specific sphere of meaning, by analyzing the content in which a relevant word or phrase is used" ("A Semotactical Approach to the Meaning of 'Rûah Elohim' in Genesis 1:2", 99).

As stated in the introduction, the possible meaning for a word has been chosen from Steinberg's The Bible Dictionary and compared with other commentaries; except a few cases elaborated upon, no further linguistic investigation is presented in the discussion. However, a process of thought and elimination of possibilities has been carried out all along, although it is not always fully expressed in the research or the footnotes, due to the fact that it is literary orientated. The following paragraphs are an example to the research's treatment of a linguistic problem in a chosen verse (1:2):

וְהָאָרֶץ הָיְתָה תֹהוּ וָבֹהוּ וְחֹשֶׁךְ עַל־פְּנֵי תְהוֹם
וְרוּחַ אֱלֹהִים מְרַחֶפֶת עַל־פְּנֵי הַמָּיִם

TOHU VAVOHU

The expression has aroused several interpretations: desert, waste, devastation, nothingness (Westermann, 103). Westermann concludes his survey with the suggestion that the expression means "God's creation from a 'before' which is *beyond words* and can only be described in *negative terms*". The underlined expressions point to the direction of my reservations, because they contradict each other: if there are "terms", they are expressed 'within words'. The author of the text, thus, narrates what can be described by words and, as it seems to me, there is no room to apply at this stage an assumed personal judgment of 'negative' or 'positive' to the state of affairs.

This state prior to creation is given in *physical factors*: wind, water, land, darkness, and TOHU VAVOHU which, therefore, should be regarded in the same light — as a physical factor — and not as an expression for non-existence (as suggested in T.L. Fenton, "Differing Approaches to the Theomachy Myth in Old Testament Writers", 377). Suggestions for TOHU as 'desert' (a geographical term commonly used for an arid and uninhabited land — O.E.D.) are implausible and even impossible as we are told that everything is covered with waters.

Before I draw my conclusion, I would like to address one of the latest researches on this expression: D.T. Tsumura (The Earth and Waters in Genesis 1-2: A Linguistic Investigation (Sheffield, 1989).

Tsumura looks for the meanings of the expression in other books of the bible and analyzes each of them separately by comparing their grammatical roots to other Middle Eastern languages.

His conclusion that TOHU is 'a desert' is argued in two stages:
a) a Biblical source cited — Deut. 32:10

יִמְצָאֵהוּ בְּאֶרֶץ מִדְבָּר וּבְתֹהוּ יְלֵל יְשִׁמֹן

thus, in this verse the term TOHU "*probably* means 'desert' or 'waste', where it appears in parallel with ERETZ MIDBAR — a desert land" (italics, mine).
b) the Hebrew root TOHU is an equivalent to the Ugaritic one, both meaning 'desert' (Ibid., 19); this allows Tsumura to omit 'waste' and leaves for TOHU the probability of 'desert'.

But his arguments, I suggest, are unsatisfactory:
a') the suggested analysis of the Deut. 32:10 verse's syntax seems to be faulty: the parallel words are the nouns 'ERETZ MIDBAR' and 'YESHIMON'; TOHU in its juxtaposition describes *the state of the cry* of the wilderness (of YESHIMON), and Leeser's rendering of the verse reflects this notion:

"He found him in a desert land and in the waste of the hollowing of the wilderness".

In order to make the distinction more acute, I would render the second part of the verse as: "amidst the chaos of the wilderness' cry". Tsumura's rendering of TOHU as 'desert' ignores the syntax of the verse by suggesting a triple use of synonyms.

b') comparative philology, as J. Barr suggests in his conclusion (Comparative Philology and the Text of the O.T., Oxford, 1986), might be useful "if it appears to fit the needs for the healing of a difficulty found in the O.T., and if no obstacle or impediment is at once obvious" (Ibid., 36), but he warns against the approach which "defines Hebrew word by thinking what 'it means' in another language", while the results to be reached are "*meanings in Hebrew*" (Ibid., 292). The value of the Ugaritic root could have been useful, had Tsumura presented it within an Ugaritic compound, because this is the meaning looked for in Hebrew. TOHU as a separate word in Hebrew, according to The Bible Dic., offers several meanings and nuances besides 'desert':

nothingness, Isa., 40:17 — כָּל־הַגּוֹיִם כְּאַיִן נֶגְדּוֹ מֵאֶפֶס וָתֹהוּ נֶחְשְׁבוּ־לוֹ
in vain, Isa., 45:19 — לֹא אָמַרְתִּי לְזֶרַע יַעֲקֹב תֹּהוּ בַקְּשׁוּנִי
and the problem which nuance to choose, I suggest, depends on the context rather than on comparative philology.

VOHU is a difficult term, and in Biblical language it is *always* attached to TOHU. Tsumura's investigation of it as an independent word is unsuccessfully carried into other languages, and the only affiliation found is with the Arabic, where BAHIYA is "to be empty" (Tsumura, Ibid., 21) in the concrete meaning of an empty house or tent rather than of vacuum. He regards the Hebrew word, in the Biblical context and as part of a compound, as expressing the same concrete meaning, "a state of unproductiveness and emptiness" (Ibid., 41). The compound, Tsumura suggests, is the direct translation of its components: "an unproductive and empty desert" [the "unproductive", as can be seen, has no connection with the Arabic root and seems to be his addition to justify the choice of 'desert']. He finds support to this interpretation by comparing the state of creation in chapter 1 to that in chapter 2, thus tacitly implying that he follows the school of thought which regards the two stories as describing the same event.

My reservations suggested for his interpretation of TOHU and VOHU, therefore, are extended also to Tsumura's attitude to the stories in chapters 1 and 2; in this research I argue for a different attitude toward the stories.

Linguistically, I agree with U. Cassuto (A Commentary on The Book of Genesis, Jerusalem 1978, 11) who states that, as in chemistry, a compound in a language may offer a taste which is not found in its original components. Cassuto suggests to find the unfamiliar taste in the verse as a whole, and his conclusion for TOHU VAVOHU is "a state of confused matter... with no differentiation or organisation" (Ibid., 12). Although avoiding the term 'chaos', this, in fact, is what Cassuto describes, and Speiser terms this chaos as "formless waste" (see also Skinner, 16-17).

Therefore, "formless waste" was the rendering chosen for TOHU VAVOHU in this research (p. 56). Whether 'chaos' may be applied to other places where the compound is mentioned, depends on analysis of the text's content in discussion.

RUAH ELOHIM

RUAH is both spirit and wind; Elohim, in this construct, may be the possessor of the spirit or an adjectival suffix which stresses an awesome nature or occurrence.*

The suggested translation "awesome wind" is by Speiser; it is supported by Skinner, 18 (citing the ancient Jewish scholar Ibn Ezra) and H.M. Orlinsky, "Enigmatic Bible Passages: The Plain Meaning of Genesis 1:1-3", 237.

TEHOM

Cassuto, Westermann and Speiser identify it with Mesopotamian TIHAMAT, thus — water as matter. This allusion raises two objections:

1) the compound מֵי־תְהוֹם MEY-TEHOM (the waters of TEHOM — Isaiah, 51:10) indicates that TEHOM is a different entity than the waters belonging to it; rendering it as 'water's water' makes no sense.

2) Genesis 1:2 is patterned as an account, *without repetitions*, of several elements; 'Tehom', therefore and in the light of what was said before, has to be something — be it slightly different —

* For discussion on Ruah=wind or spirit, see: T. Friedman, "And God's 'RU'ACH' Hovers Upon the Water", 309-312; Skinner, 17-18; Westermann 107-108; J.N.P. Smith, "The Use of Divine Names as Superlatives", 212-220; P.J. Smith, "A Semotactical Approach to the Meaning of the Term 'ruah elohim' in Genesis 1:2", 99-104.

from 'water'. Cassuto suggests 'ocean', but the geographical term (great body of water *surrounding the land* of the globe — O.E.D.) is not relevant in a text which points out that there is no land, that is — no geography. The suggested translation "Abyss" (or 'deep' in K.J. & Leeser) seems to correspond to the text because it is the confused element over which, above its watery surface, an awesome wind sweeps.

The suggested rendering of 1:2 on p. 56, thus, corresponds to the conclusions suggested above:

And earth, had been a formless waste	and darkness over the surface of the abyss
and an awesome wind	sweeping, over the water.

B. Notes

Technical Notes

a) Sources which do not appear in the bibliography list are indicated by [n.m. in bib.].
b) Hebrew books — title is given in italics; Hebrew articles — publications given in italics.
c) References to other chapters: the Roman sign and Arabic number, e.g.: I/34.

Chapter I: Introduction

1. e.g.: H.N. Wallace, The Eden Narrative (Atlanta, Georgia, 1985), 69-70. On "sagas" in the Bible, see: K. Koch, The Growth of Biblical Tradition, 148-158.

2. G.S. Kirk, The Nature of Greek Myths, 34,36.

3. H. Deutsch, A Psychoanalitical Study of the Myth of Dionysos and Apollo, 10.

4. T.H. Gaster, Myth, Legend and Custom in the Old Testament, xxxiv.

5. T. Reik, Myth and Guilt, 136.

6. G.S. Kirk, The Nature of Greek Myths, 38-91. I have consulted also H. & H.A. Frankfort, "Myth and Reality", in H. Frankfort & Others, The Intellectual Adventure of Ancient Man, 7-8; and J.W. Rogerson's Myth in Old Testament Interpretation, but especially the last one's list on myth's essence, in my opinion, is too long, 12 articles, and less convincingly grouped; Kirk's presentation on the other hand, supplied a better ground for my discussion.

   For types of myths in the ancient Near East, see: S.H. Hooke, Middle Eastern Mythology, 8-11.

7. G.S. Kirk, The Nature of Greek Myths, 69.

8. Ibid., 43.
See: E.E. Evans-Pritchard, Theories of Primitive Religion, New York [n.m. in bib.].

9. G.S. Kirk, The Nature of Greek Myths, 53.
See: A. Lang, Myth, Ritual and Religion, London, 1887.

10. G.S. Kirk, The Nature of Greek Myths, 59.
See: B. Malinowsky, "Myth in Primitive Psychology", Myth, Science and Religion, New York, 1954.

11. G.S. Kirk, The Nature of Greek Myths, 63.
See: M. Eliade, The Myth of the Eternal Return, New York, 1954.

12. G.S. Kirk, The Nature of Greek Myths, 66.
See: J. Fontenrose, The Ritual of Myth, Berkeley, 1955.

13. G.S. Kirk, The Nature of Greek Myths, 70.

14. Ibid., 70; 70-72.
See: S. Freud, Totem and Taboo, Vol. XIII of the standard edition of The Complete Psychological Work (eds. T. Strachey & A. Freud), London, 1955.

15. G.S. Kirk, The Nature of Greek Myths, 76-77.
See: C.G. Jung, The Archetypes and the Collective Unconscious, Vol. IX of the Collected Works, London, 1950.

16. S. Freud, "The Interest of Psychoanalysis From the Point of View of The History of Civilization", in S. Freud, Vol. XIII of The Standard Edition of the Complete Psychological Work, 184-187. On "the hidden meaning" — p. 185.

17. C.J. Jung, The Archetype and the Collective Unconscious, vol. IX of The Collected Works, 3.

18. C.L. Strauss, "Study of Myth", 85.

19. e.g.: There are several suggested meanings of the Oedipus myth: E. Fromm challenges Freud ("The Oedipus Myth", The Forgotten Language, 196-229). Another suggestion is made by C.L. Strauss ("The Structural Study of Myth", 80-86). For this particular subject, see:

L. Edmunds & A. Dunder (eds.) Oedipus: A Folklor Casebook, N.Y., 1981 [n.m. in bib.].

20. On interpretation-subjectivity, regarding the fathers of psychoanalysis Freud, Jung and Adler, see: O. Rank, Beyond Psychology, 29-30.

21. J.W. Rogerson, Old Testament Criticism in 19th Century England and Germany, London, 1984.

22. The second edition (Prolegomena zur Gesschichte Israels, 1883) was translated to English by J.S. Black & A. Manzies, Prolegomena to the History of Israel, London, 1885 (all the above sources, n.m. in bib.). For further developments, see: R.E. Clements, A Century of O.T. Study, London (revised ed.) 1983.

23. A. Lang, Myth, Ritual and Religion; J.G. Frazer, in two works: The Golden Bough [n.m. in bib.] and mainly in Folk-Lore in the Old Testament, London, 1906, 1918, respectively.

24. E. Kuhn, über die Herabkunst des Feurs und des Göttertranks (1886), as summarized in K. Abraham, Dream and Myths, 27-28.

25. C.G. Jung, Psychology of the Unconscious, [1912]; S. Freud, Totem and Taboo, [1913].

26. The articles were taken from the following Indexes:
P. Ackroyd, Bible Bibliography, (1963-73), Oxford, 1974;
G.W. Anderson, A Decade of Bible Bibliography, (1956-66), Oxford, 1967;
Old Testament Abstracts (The Catholic Biblical Ass. of America), Vols. 1-13, 1978-95;
Index of Articles on Jewish Studies, Jerusalem, 1970-95.

27. J. Skinner, Critical and Exegetical Commentary on Genesis, Edinburgh, 1930. This is the revised edition with updated bibliography, and is the same in the 1980 ed. used in this research. Indicated hereafter as Skinner.

28. C. Westermann, Genesis 1-11 & Genesis 12-36, London, 1984 [hereafter: Westermann and a proper indication (1-11 or 12-36)].

As my knowledge of German does not suffice to cope with the original book, or with lengthy articles in German, I have availed myself of English translations.

29. E.A. Speiser, Genesis [The Anchor Bible], New York, 1964. Hereafter: Speiser.

30. "The Documentary sources", Ibid., xxii-xxxvii; U.D. Cassuto, *The Documentary Hypothesis and the Composition of the Pentateuch*, Jerusalem, 1965.

31. I. Engnell, "The Pentateuch", Critical Essays on the Old Testament, trans. by J.T. Willis, London, 1970, 50-67.

32. I. Pardes, Countertraditions in the Bible (A Feminist Approach), Cambridge, Mass., 1990.

33. U.D. Cassuto, *The Book of Genesis (A commentary on)*, Jerusalem, [1944]. I have used the 1978 edition. Hereafter: *Cassuto.*

34. Y.M. Emmanueli, *The Book of Genesis*, Tel-Aviv, [1978] 1984. Hereafter: *Emmanueli.*

35. For different divisions of schools, see: D.W. Barrick, "Current Trends and Tensions in O.T. Textual Criticism", 301-308.

36. It is the outcome of H. Gunkel's 1901 monumental commentary on Genesis, especially its introduction (available as a separate book — The Legends of Genesis, N.Y., 1964). His followers developed the Form-Criticism method of Biblical analysis.

37. Speiser, XXII-XXXVII; A. Bar-Tana, *Genesis of Jewish Thought*, 55-6.

38. M. Buber, *The Way of The Bible*, Jerusalem, 1968.

39. e.g.: Sir F. Kenyon, The Bible and Archaeology, London, 1940.
W. Keller, The Bible as History [first English and Hebrew editions — 1956].

40. e.g.: H.B. Bonsal, Bible: Fact or Fiction, Birmingham, 1979 [n.m. in bib.]. The main problem which scientists tackle is the creation story. More on this scientific approach, see also I. Asimov, In The Beginning, London, 1981; J. Gribbin, Genesis: The Origins of Man and Universe, Oxford, 1982; P. Newman & H.J. Eckelman Genesis One and the Origin of Earth, Dawners Grove, Ill., 1977 [all — n.m. in bib.].

41. D.A. Robertson, Linguistic Evidence in Dating Hebrew Poetry; W.B.

Hallo, "Biblical History in its Near Eastern Setting: The Contextual Approach", 1-27.

Agreeing that the patriarchal narratives should be placed within the 21st-19th century B.C. are J.J. Binson, "Archaeological Data and the Dating of the Patriarchs"; Y. Grintz, The Book of Genesis: Its Uniqueness and Antiquity (Jerusalem, 1983); M.J. Selman, "Comparative Customs and the Patriarchal Age", in A.R. Millard & D.J. Wiseman, Essays on the Patriarchal Narratives, 85, 128 [n.m. in bib.].

42. *Emmanueli*, 30-33.

43. Y.M. Grintz, The Book of Genesis (Its Uniqueness and Antiquity), Jerusalem, 1983.

44. Additional sources consulted:
E.A.W. Budge, The Teachings of Amen-Em-Apt, Son of Kenekht, London, 1924.
—, The Book of the Dead, London, 1898.
S.N. Kramer, Enki and Ninhursag New Haven, 1945 [n.m. in bib.].
—, Gilgamesh and the Huluppu Tree, Chicago, 1938 [n.m. in bib.].

45. W.G. Lambert & A.R. Millard, Atra-Hasis: The Babylonian Story of the Flood. For a comparison with the Bible, see: T. Freymer-Kensky, "The Atrahasis Epic and its Significance for Our Understanding of Genesis 1-9", 447-455.

46. W.B. Hallo, "Biblical History in the Near Eastern Setting", 3.

47. See: 1 Kings, 5:1, 9:18,20; Y. Aharoni, *Carta's Atlas of the Bible* 74, map 115.

48. R.A. Kitchen, Ancient Orient and Old Testament, 18.

49. F.M. Cross Jr., Canaanite Myth and Hebrew Epic; E. Dambin, *Creation Stories in The Bible and in External Sources*, 46; Z. Rin, *The Acts of the Gods; The Ugaritic Epic Poetry*.

50. A recent opinion which *recognizes the unity of the text*, although regards it as a late composition of the sixth century, is expressed by N. Whybry, The Making of the Pentateuch: A Methodological Study, 232-5.

51. On him and on the MASSORA tradition, see: M.H. Goshen-Gottstein, "The

Rise of the Tiberian Bible Text", in A. Altman, Biblical and Other Studies, 79-123.

52. J.P. Fokkelman, "Genesis", 36 (emphasis, mine). On similar lines, although using different terms: Y. Amit, The Book of Judges, 11.

53. A.S. Geller, "Literary Approach to Biblical Narratives", 408-415.

54. A.R. Millard, "Methods of Studying the Patriarchal Narratives as Ancient Text", 47.

55. I. Epstein, Judaism, 196.

56. W.F. Albright, New Horizons in Biblical Research, 8.

57. Another manuscript (The Aleppo Bible) is lately in the process of exposition but, while this book was under preparation, only Joshua and Judges had been published.

Other translations that commonly lend support to the Biblical text but will not be regarded here: The Greek translation, the Septuagint, 1st century B.C.; the Latin translation — the Vulgate, 1st century A.D.; the Aramaic, of Onkelos, 2nd century. These are translations and, as such, will always be interpretations. On this subject, see: Speiser, lxxi-lxxiii.

The Qumran Texts in Hebrew (1st Century B.C.) vary very little from the Massoretic text but, being unvocalized, they do not provide the kind of information that the Massoretic text does, suggests J. Barr, Comparative Philology and the Text of the Old Testament, 1.

The Samaritan Hebrew version (11th century A.D., also unvocalized) has certain differences with the Massoretic text (see: Genesis, Jewish and Samaritan Versions, eds. A. & R. Sadaqa, Tel-Aviv, 1962) but, as I observed, they do not influence the issues raised in this research.

58. Isaac Leeser, The Twenty-four Books of the Holy Bible, Hebrew Publishing Co., N.Y.

59. Contra Speiser's approach: "On Translating Genesis", Speiser, xii-xix.

60. For recent outlines, see: R.A. Spencer, ed., (Orientation and Disorientation in Literary Criticism, Pittsburgh, 1980; C.E. Armerding, The Old Testament Criticism, Grand Rapids, 1983; J. Barton, Reading the Old Testament: Method in Biblical Study, London, 1984; D.M. Gunn, "New Directions in the study of Biblical Hebrew Narrative", JSOT, XXXIX, 1987, 65-75.

A brief reference [n.m. in bib.] to popular methods, however, seems to be in order:
Historical-Critical: E. Krentz, The Historical-Critical Method, London, 1975.
Form-Criticism: K. Koch, The Growth of Biblical Tradition, London, 1969.
Rhetorical Criticism: J. Muilenburgh, "Form Criticism and Beyond", JBL, LXXXVIII, 1969, 1-18.
Structuralism: C. Lévi-Strauss, "The Structural Study of Myth", in T. Sebeok Myth: A Symposium, London, 1955, 80-106.
Patternism: I. Engnell, Methodological Aspects of Old Testament Studies (Supp. VT, VII, 7), Leiden, 1960, 13-30.

61. e.g.: G.V. Smith, "Structure and Purpose in Genesis 1-11: Source and Form Criticism v. Rhetorical Criticism", JETS, XX, 1977, 307-319; D.W. Barrick, "Current Trends and Tensions in Old Testament Textual Criticism", 301-8.

62. M. Weiss, The Bible From Within, 1-46.

63. Recommended also by J. Barton, "Classifying Biblical Criticism", 30.

64. R. Alter, Art of Biblical Narrative, 202.

65. H. Creager, "The Divine Image", 105.

66. N. Kravitz, Genesis: An Interpretation of the First Three Chapters, 14.

67. N. Leibowitz, "How to read a Chapter in the Bible", 130. Unfortunately, Nehama Leibowitz passed away while this book was in printing-preparations.

68. Ezekiel — *Cassuto*, 30; M. Weinfeld, "God the Creator, in Genesis 1 and in Isaia's prophecies", 105-132.
G.M. Landes, "Creation Tradition in Proverbs 8:22-31 and Genesis 1", 279-293; F. Landy, Paradoxes in Paradise which compares Genesis and Song of Songs.

69. e.g.: The Yehwist or Priestly codes, as elaborated in G. Vin-Radd's work, The Problem of the Hexateuch and Other Essays, 1-78.

70. G.E. Mendelhall ("The Shady Side of Wisdom: The Date and Purpose of Genesis 3") examines several words, finds them also in later books

(Ezekiel, Psalms, Proverbs) and concludes that Genesis is a "parade example of exilic imitation of archaic language". Mendelhall is aware that such a method for dating passages is met with scepticism (Ibid.).

His conclusion seems to me to emanate from an assumed known date of the later books and thereby to reflect on Genesis. The possibility that Genesis is the original source for linguistic use made by the later books seems to be ignored.

71. M. Weiss, The Bible From Within, 54-62.

72. G.W. Coats, Genesis, 4.

73. G.W. Coats, Saga, Legend, Tale, Novella, Fable: Narrative Forms in O.T. Literature, 7-16.

74. N. Frye, Fables of Identity: Studies in Poetic Mythology, 11.

75. H. Gunkel, The Legends of Israel.

76. J.W. Rogerson (Anthropology and Old Testament), regards the book as "folklore", and the era as "primitive".

For a brief conclusive refutation, see: M. Warner, "Primitive Saga Man", 325-335; also: P.G. Kirckpatrick, The Old Testament and Folklore Study, 115-117.

77. D. Jobling, "The Myth Semantics of Genesis 2:4b-3:24", 42, sec. 1, 2.

78. S. Bar Efrat, *The Art of Narration in the Bible*, Tel-Aviv, 1979. Works in English consulted: Z. Adar, The Biblical Narrative, Jerusalem, 1971; R. Alter, The Art of Biblical Narrative, New York, 1968; M. Sternberg, The Poetics of Biblical Narrative, Bloomington, 1985.

A recent book highly recommended by M. Weiss (which I could not attain) is L.A. Schökel, A Manual of Hebrew Poetics (English transl. by A. Graffy), Rome, 1988.

79. Y. Steinberg, *The Bible Dictionary* — "DAT".

80. Westermann 12-36, 106 (emphasis added).

81. R. Otto, The Idea of the Holy, 6.

82. H.H. Hirshberg, Hebrew Humanism, 90; I. Epstein, Judaism, 23-28; S. Bakon, "Kedusha-Holiness", 5.

83. B. Spinoza, *Tractatus Theologico Politicus*, Chapter III, 134-5.

84. For a different opinion, see: J.C. McConville, Interpreting Genesis 1-11, 6.

85. Westermann 1-11, 60, point 1. This being said, however, theologian Westermann cannot avoid stating that "Israel [which one?] does see a divine activity behind... human achievement" (Ibid., point 4).

The anti-theological stand suggested here is contra J. Barr who does not accept that objectivity in Biblical study can be attained through the exclusion of theological interest because, in his view, it makes room for secular or pseudo-theological ideology which is equally destructive of objectivity (J. Barr, Does Biblical Study Still Belong to Theology, 11). While agreeing that any presupposed ideology is destructive of objectivity, I fail to see why theology is superior to secularity. Saying, as Barr does, that a scholar has to be prepared, even if only as an hypothesis for the sake of argument, to ask "how would it be if this were really true to God?" is stating that, outside and regardless of what is written in the text, there is a priori a code or perception which is "true to God". This, I suggest, is a prejudice which aspires to some kind of objectivity.

86. I am indebted to R.H. Wilensky for, what I regard as, the most appropriate and *condensed* definition of 'Culture'. The Meaning of Modern Sculpture, 5.

87. A.L. Kroeber & C. Kluckholm, Culture: A Critical Review of Concepts and Definitions, New York, 1952 [n.m. in bib.]. The authors present 164; since then probably some more were added.

88. E.B. Taylor, Primitive Culture, London, 1871, p. 1 (first paragraph); termed as "the classical definition" and cited in "Civilization and Cultural Evolution", Britanica (Macropedia, 15th ed., 1974), 657.

89. "Human Culture", Ibid., 1151.

90. F. Boas, The Mind of Primitive Man, 149.

91. J.W. Rogerson, Anthropology and the Old Testament, 10, 19.

92. Ruth Benedict, Patterns of Culture, 11.

93. F. Boas, The Mind of Primitive Man, 149.

94. e.g.: J.B. Bury, The Idea of Progress: An Inquiry into its Origin and Growth (London, 1920). F. Boas is less categorical about this common

notion: "It is often assumed that because modern cultures are complex... the chronological history had been from the simple to the complex (The Mind of Primitive Man, p. 159)... In reality, the course of history may have been quite different" (p. 161).

95. In art, see: T.E. Hulme, Speculations, 34, 75-10;
Sociology: J. Ortega Y Gasset, Man in Crisis, 97-99;
Anthropology: F. Boas, The Mind of the Primitive Man, 106;
Religion: A. Lang, The Making of Religion, 281-2, who claims that a phase of Monotheism preceded that of paganism, after which comes the Hebrew monotheistic one.

96. As notes J.W. Rogerson (Anthropology and the Old Testament, 46): "The use of theories of primitive mentality has continued in Old Testament studies to the present day".

97. e.g.: *Emmanueli*, 11.

98. J. Ortega y Gasset, Man in Crisis, 97-99.

99. The Mind of Primitive Man, 201.

100. E. Fromm, You Shall Be As Gods, 7.

101. W.A. Irwin, "The Hebrews", 224.

102. A similar opinion, "the witness of the text itself should take pride of place until unassailable cases are made against it", is expressed by A.R. Millard ("Methods of Studying the Patriarchal Narratives as Ancient Text", 48).
For an earlier source of the same approach, see: B. Spinoza, "On Bible Interpretation", *Tractatus Theologico-Politicus*, 80.

103. S. Mandelkern, *Veteris Testamenti Concordantiae: Hebraicae Atque Chaldaicae*, 12th imprint which includes additions by M. Goshen-Gotshtein and P. Margolin (Jerusalem, 1986).

104. F. Broun, S.R. Driver & C.A. Briggs, Hebrew and English Lexicon of the Old Testament seems to be the most popular and handy dictionary for the English reader.

105. G. Bergsträsser, *Hebräische Grammatik* (mit Benutzung der von E. Kautzsh bearbeiteten 28. Auflage von W. Gesenius' Hebräische Grammatik; mit beiträgen von M. Lidzbarski), Jerusalem, [1926] 1972; hereafter — Bergsträsser.

Chapter II: Creation of a World

Unless otherwise stated, Westermann in this chapter is 1-11.

1. E.K.V. Pearce, Who Was Adam?, 17.
For interesting attempts to find scientific correlations to Genesis, see: S.M. Coder & G.F. Howe, The Bible, Science and Creation. For bibliography, see: Westermann, 79.

2. For a brief account of Mesopotamian scientific achievements which preceded the Biblical narratives, see: W. Todd, New Light On Genesis, 16.

3. Skinner, 5; B. Vawter, On Genesis: A New Reading, 30; G.W. Coats, Genesis, 47; C.P. Scaer, "The Problems of Inerrancy and Historicity in Connection With Genesis 1-3", 5-12.
Opposed to this approach is E. Hill ("How Historical is Genesis 1-11?", 400-407) who believes that the authors imposed an historical form upon a non-historical content.

4. Skinner, xiv-xx.

5. H. Gunkel, The Legends of Genesis, 37.
An elaborate discussion — in Westermann, 90: "Genesis 1 — Poetry or Prose".

6. W.F. Albright, New Horizons in Biblical Research, 8.

7. Cassuto's presentation of the verses conveys a more recognizable form of poetry than that of the method of presentation in this paper. However, his imposed structure sometimes results in an imposed meaning, and I will point to such occurrences in due course.

8. Biblical poetry does not correspond to defined systems (Skinner, xviii-xix); the rhythm is accentual but the number of stresses in each verse is not fixed or permanent (on principles of Biblical verse, see: Encyclopedia Judaica, 1200-1203).

9. E. Dambin, *Creation Stories in the Bible and in External Sources*, 19-47; H. Gunkel, "The Influence of Babylonian Mythology upon the Biblical

Creation Story", in B. Anderson (ed.), Creation in the Old Testament, 47; G.H. Livingston, The Pentateuch in Its Cultural Environment, 141; B. Vawter, On Genesis: A New Reading, 31.

10. See: A. Tweig, "Genesis 1 and the Sabbath", 288; Skinner, 11; Westermann, 90.

11. On the number seven and the problematic correlation between the periods and tasks, see: Skinner, 8-10; Westermann, 88-90; *Cassuto*, 5-7.

12. Westermann says: "The process of creation has not been and cannot be established definitely; each age can only express it in a way intelligible to itself" (Creation, 5); and Albright states that "the extraordinary thing is that it is more evolutionary in some respects than anything published before early 19th Century Europe" (W.F. Albright, New Horizons in Biblical Research, 8).

13. Skinner, 9; *Cassuto*, 7.

14. On literary equivalents in Near Eastern poetry, see: T. Gaster, Myth Legend and Custom in the Old Testament, 6.

15. Fokkelman, "Genesis", 44.

16. For an extensive discussion of the subject, see: Bergsträsser, 366-381.

17. Several uses as prepositions are suggested in Speiser, lxvi-lvii. To state, from this apparent alliteration, that the Waw is THE factor which creates the characteristic Biblical rhythm (G. Josipovici, The Book of God, 60) is to say everything and, at the same time, nothing. A similar use of Waw is equally evident in spoken Literary-Arabic, and ancient spoken Hebrew — being a sister-language — probably had it too. The Waw, thus, appears to be a general characteristic of some semitic languages, whereas the rhythm of Biblical literature is determined by the inner divisions of punctuation (TE'AMIM, see: *on p. 35) which are ignored in Josipovici's analysis.

18. For recent works on the subject, see: M.H. Silberman, "Syntactic Notes on the Waw Consecutive", 167-75; E. Rubinstein, "The Tense in the Biblical Narrative", 20-26.

19. See: J.W. Rogerson, Anthropology and the Old Testament, 62; U. Simon, *Time and Space in Biblical Thinking* (English summary of a Ph.D. Diss. for the Hebrew University of Jerusalem, Jerusalem 1961), m.

20. In all the English versions mentioned in this research (excluding Speiser in The Anchor Bible who avoids the word 'beginning') and many others. It causes G.J. Wenham to say: "Hebrew lacks the definite article but 'in the beginning' is an acceptable translation" (Genesis 1-15 (World Biblical Commentary), 2-3). This research, however, follows the exact Hebrew presentation.

21. See p. 19. Contra Skinner, 13, where the problem is resolved as "a matter of pointing", i.e., as a mistake of the voweller. Skinner compares it to the Greek translation and suggests that "in ancient times the first word was *sometimes* read as 'BAreshit' (emphasis added)". "Sometimes", I suggest, is not a valid argument. Also Rashi's reading of the first two words, and in Westermann, 90, ultimately point to a vowelling mistake.

22. A similar conclusion seems to be expressed by E. Jenni ("Ewägungen Zu Gen 1.1 'am Anfang"', ZAH 2, 1989, 121-127) in an English abstract, saying: "Since the Hebrew for "Beginning" and "end" do not distinguish between extreme and non-extreme meanings, BERESHIT may best be rendered "in primeval time" (O.T.A., XIV, 1991, 2, 167).

23. *Cassuto*, 17.

24. A similar opinion: "The constantly recurring sentence which concludes the work of each day plots the regular rhythm of the passage of time and gives [the] account of creation the character of an event in linear time which links it with history" Westermann, 88.

25. 'Aeon', being an unconcrete concept, has no Hebrew equivalent. "The length of days is not stated. What is important is that each of the "days" is a period of time which may be legitimately determined Yom", says E.J. Young (Studies in Genesis 1, 103 [citing (p. 41-7) Swedish works inaccessible to me]. For U. Simon, Yom is a "beat" — where the well defined rhythm of the seven days serves as one of the means for expressing creation's harmony (*Time and Space In Biblical Thinking*, j.).

Skinner, 21, on the other hand, objects to the interpretation of day-aeon because "if the writer had had aeons in his mind, he would hardly have missed the opportunity of stating how many millennia each embraced". But, I suggest, stating the span of each period is something that even with our technical advantages is, at best, defined as "God knows"; the author, as it seems to me, purposely "missed the opportunity" of stating something he did not know.

26. "ארץ - ERETZ" (*Concordancia*, 144) indicates, mainly, "under" (similar to Aramaic), and it is "opposite to sky" (sky's Arabic verb indicating heights). For a similar distinction, see: "ארץ", *The Bible Dic.* alternative 1; Eng. Dic., 1b.

"Sky" seems to me to be a more appropriate expression, since "heaven" is commonly used as "the abode of God, usually placed beyond sky" (O.E.D.).

27. Later medieval interpretations regard "Earth and Sky" as implying the universe (Radak, in "ארץ" *The Bible Dic.*), but it may not necessarily be the *Biblical* meaning.

Words that in modern Hebrew connote 'universe', have different meanings in Biblical Hebrew (all in *The Bible Dic.*):

"Heled חלד": connotes life of this world; "Olam עולם": Time as a whole — past and present; "Tevel תבל": a fertile peopled land; "Yekum יקום": the living world — humans and animals.

28. The possibility of other worlds is found already in old Jewish sources and legends. As we today understand it, they are mentioned in the fourth day.

29. (Skinner, 14); because of this uniqueness, Skinner suspects the validity of linguistic comparisons with other languages. To suggest that this uniqueness indicates that the verb belonged to a sacred vocabulary (J. Daniélou, In The Beginning: Genesis 1-11, 33), seems to take the issue too far.

30. See "ברא", *The Bible Dic.*, 120:2; Eng. Dic.: 3, 4. A. Funkelstein (*Styles in Medieval Biblical Exegesis*, 32) cites Ibn Ezra who says that the verb has also other meanings.

31. Verse 3b is a problematic one for Bergsträsser's classification of the infinitive (*Bergsträsser*, 410) and he regards it as connoting two acts simultaneously performed, adding the comment: "if the text is properly transmitted". The nature of the acts, however, is not solved by stating that they are simultaneous; BARA La'ASOT might be two simultaneous acts, as Bergsträsser suggests, but if one is definitely physical (La'ASOT) the other (BARA), according to the grammatical explanation in * above — *has to be a conceptual one.*

The same applies to Leeser's rendering "created in making it" and

B. Jacob (Genesis, 12) "created to make"; both make a perfect sense if 'created' is taken as 'accomplished' and 'intended', respectively.

32. Contra Cassuto (*Cassuto*, 43-44).
Tur-Sinai (*Pshuto Shel Mikra*, 6) offers the Arabic verb בדא — BADA instead of ברא — BARA, thus pointing to a textual mistake; he explains BARA La'ASOT as "thought and conspired", a non-physical act. The correct meaning, I suggest, is the outcome of Hebrew syntax rather than comparison with a slightly different verb in Arabic.

33. Speiser employs synonyms for the verses (1:1 — to set about; 2:26 — undertaken), both are notions — not physical actions. In my suggested translation I preferred a more acute notion of creativity for 1:1, and in 2:26 I added "to make" in order to retain the Hebrew pattern of conjugated verb + infinitive.

34. In the Akkadian Creation Epic (ANET, 63-67); see also Z. Rin, *Acts of the Gods*, 58; T.L. Fenton, "Differing Approaches to the Theomachy Myth in Old Testament Writers", 337-381.

35. "Omnipotence", O.E.D.: "infinite power". This, to some extent, is also the monotheistic perception of the totality of the creator (see: B. Spinoza, *Ethics*, Book one sentence 16; Y. Kaufmann, *The History of the Israeli Religion*, vol. II, book 2, 221.

36. To a certain extent, Z. Adar's statement (*God in the Bible*, 12) that there is no 'one and only' perception of God in the Bible justifies my point of view that God is perceived as He is exposed in the text (for the same opinion, see: H.H. Hirshberg, Hebrew Humanism, 84). Contra M. Eliade (Patterns in Comparative Religion, 9), who claims for Him, among other things, "infinitive goodness".

37. The citations, as said before, are spaced according to the suggested treatment of TE'AMIM (p. 35), and in the first verse already there is a slight difference from the way in which Cassuto presents his version (*Cassuto*, 10):

בראשית ברא אלהים   את השמים ואת הארץ

as opposed to this paper's presentation:

בראשית, ברא אלהים
את השמים, ואת הארץ

The difference is mainly the poetic rhythm: longer v. shorter spans of words, and differentiation between the elements (by the comma).

Arguments which favour my suggested interpretation: *Emmanueli*, 43; M. Naor, "Bereshit BARA or Bereshit BRO" *Beit Mikra*, XVI, 1981, 11; Westermann, 97; E.J. Young, Studies in Genesis One, 7.

38. Although Cassuto gives the verse a poetic form (see above, note 36), still, he presents one sentence; his basic approach to the verse is similar to that of K.J.'s version — as an opening general statement after which details are to follow. This is an example, how a meaning emanates from presentation.

39. Rashi claims that there is no RESHIT in the Bible which is not attached to the following word, thus forming a *status constractus*. But in all Biblical cases the *nomen rectum* of RESHIT are clear-cut case of nouns and pronouns (see: Concordancia, 1065), whereas in Genesis 1:1 there is a clear-cut case of a verb. Rashi seems to be aware of the usual pattern, because he points to the one exception in the whole Bible where there may be a verb in a similar situation: Hoshea, 1:2 and thereby regards the two verses as having the same grammatical pattern:

בְּרֵאשִׁית בָּרָא אלהים......... ויאמר אלהים (3)

תְּחִילַּת דִּבֶּר־יהוה ויאמר יהוה

This comparison may be questionable because דִּבֶּר, syntactically, has two forms: a noun (a shortened form of דִּבְּרָה — a say, a command) and the finite form of the verb .ד.ב.ר. This ambiguity allows to regard in Hoshea as a constract where דִּבֶּר־יהוה is a noun. Such is not the case with the conjugated form BARA, *where no form of it as a noun appears in the Bible*; it is strictly a verb, unless the "ת" is added in order to form a noun and this is what Rashi has done (as Hoshea's תחילת).

40. The English rendering is cited from Cassuto's English version, A Commentary on the Book of Genesis (Jerusalem, 1961), 19.

41. Arguing for this interpretation: H.M. Orlinsky, "Enigmatic Bible Passages: The Plain Meaning of Genesis 1:1-3", 203-7. Skinner, 12-13; Speiser, 12-13. Speiser's translation avoids 'beginning', and his "when" seems to me less appropriate because it implies 'at the same time' and not 'beforehand' (which in my rendering is expressed by "had been").

42. See: J. Blau, A Grammar of Biblical Hebrew, artic. 119-121 & Remark pp. 114-115.

43. As suggested in Cassuto, 10.

44. See: J. Blau, A Grammar of Biblical Hebrew, artic. 105, p. 106.

45. E. Rubinstein, Contemporary Hebrew and Ancient Hebrew, 23-4; this is Rashi's approach, and he systematically interprets such grammatical occurrences as past perfect (mentioned as alt. 2, p. 45).

46. Rashi's approach makes sense in such a case as 31:33-34: ויבא... (33) באהל (34) ורחל לקחה. The forms of the verbs, VeYQTL is in accordance with the pattern which indicates successive actions: "and he went out of... and he came into... but Rachel had previously hidden the amulets"; this is an intrusion of past events into the fluency of the current story.

But such is not the case in 37:11 — "ויקנאו בו אחיו, ואביו שמר את...". According to Rashi's system the verse says that the second act preceded the first — Jacob kept in his heart Joseph's dream *before* the jealousy of his brothers roused; the narrative, however, points to those actions as happening simultaneously or in the order of their presentation. The change of the regular rhythm (waw+verb... waw+verb... waw+noun) seems to me to be a literary device, similar to the last two lines in a Shakespearean sonnet — stating a point. Therefore, in this verse, and as it well may be in others, the 'Waw' of the noun followed by a verb conjugated in the regular past tense does not necessarily indicate the past perfect but rather serves as "and".

47. See elaboration in Westermann, 26-47.

48. (Skinner, 13). On the same trend, also Speiser, 13. Contra Skinner and Speiser's hesitations on the subject, Naor ("Bereshit BARA or Bereshit BRO?", 9) does not regard it as a stumbling block; as he understands it — chaos, darkness and Tehom, were created before light.

49. ANET, 5; fully discussed in: Westermann, 70.

50. ANET, 60. For a bibl. on Mesopotamian texts: Westermann, 70-71.

51. (W. Eichrodt, "In the beginning: A Contribution to the Interpretation of the First Word of the Bible", 72-3).

52. Westermann (Westermann, 99) and T.H. Gaster (Myth Legend and Custom in the Old Testament, 232), regard BARA as a physical act, equal to ASA and YATZAR.

53. The distinction and the following clarification is influenced by Steinberg's analysis; *The Bible Dic.*: "ASA", p. 670; "BARA", p. 120.

54. e.g.: *Cassuto*, 6; Westermann, 88-9.

55. Emmanueli, as I understand, narrowly refers the verb 'to create' only to the TANINIM (and humans) but not to other creatures mentioned in verse 21 (*Emmanueli*, 39).

56. Speiser suggests that the intransitive verb "teem" is restored from LXX (Speiser, 4). The conjugated verb in Hebrew, however, points clearly to this direction.

57. (E.A.W. Budge, The Book of the Dead, cixxxiii).
A.W. Ultredt ("Genesis 1 og Literaere Beilder" NNT, LXXXI, 1980, 37-54) finds similar elements in other Egyptian writings and points to the possibility that the author of Genesis has built (directly or indirectly) upon the Egyptian cosmogony rather than upon Mesopotamian traditions [as I do not read Swedish, the above note was cited from A.W. Ultredt's abstract in Old Testament Abstracts, III, 1980, a.667].

58. ANET, 100.

59. The history of Mesopotamian religion (i.e., what the author understands about their religion as interpreted from myths) is titled by T. Jacobsen as The Treasures of Darkness, and this epithet conveys what has been suggested in this paper. For a recent comparison of creation stories, see: J.A. Jackson, "Creation Stories of the Ancient East", 20-25.

60. Westermann, 78, and Speiser, 5, respectively.
"ceased" — practically implies a rest, as it emerges from a comparison with its meaning in Exodus 23:11 and Deut. 15:12-15. Speiser states that ש.ב.ת. carries more particular shades of meanings (Speiser, 7); the parallel Akkadian verb has the sense of "inspect and approve"; this is applied to the work of the craftsman, and even to the birth of the God Marduk (ANET, 62, line 9).

61. The Samaritan version solves this problem by stating in 1b "the sixth day"; this is a rare and meaningful departure, relevant to our discussion, from the Massoretic version. For a discussion on the subject, see: V. Hurowitz, "When did God Finish Creation?" Biblical Review, IV, 1987, 12-14).

62. N.H. Tur-Sinai, *Pshuto Shel Mikra*, 5-6.

63. Kaufmann emphasizes this point as a Biblical characteristic feature: belief in a transcendental God is transmitted via physical references; the Biblical authors did not regard it as a contradiction (*The History of the Israeli Religion*, 221).

64. This conclusion contradicts Westermann's opinion which suggests that "all the narrative passages of Genesis 1-11 are concerned in some way with crime and punishment" (Westermann, 47). As the first chapter demonstrates the characteristics presented in our discussion, and it is devoid of the element of 'crime', Westermann's conception as a whole is questionable.

65. C. Lévi-Strauss, The Savage Mind, 268, 415.

66. "Instinct to Master (or Mastery)", in J. Laplanche & J.B. Pontalis, The Language of Psycho-Analysis, 217-219.

67. Freud's somewhat undeveloped definition, as interpreted and furthered by I. Hendrick (Ibid., 219).

Chapter III: Creation of Humans

Unless otherwise stated, Westermann in this chapter is 1-11.

1. For an extensive bibliography, see: Westermann, 178-181. The theories will be presented in the relevant parts of the discussion.

2. e.g., J.L. McKenzie, "The Literary Characteristics of Genesis 2-3", 541-72; A.J. Hauser, "Linguistic and Thematic Links Between Genesis 4:1-6 and 2-3", 297-305; J.B. Doukham, The Literary Structure of Genesis Creation Story (Ph.D. Diss., Andrews University), 1978); various authors in Semeia, XVIII, 1980.

3. e.g., E. Dambin, *Creation Stories in the Bible and in External Sources*, 14-18.

4. e.g.: Cassuto, 54-55; J.F.A. Sawyer, "The Image of God, The Wisdom of Serpents and the Knowledge of Good and Evil", p. 66.

5. This claim is made by Cassuto of the Jerusalem School (*Cassuto*, 55) but it is supported also by commentators of the European School.

R. Alter describes the first record as a coherent process and the second — as a complicated web of relations, among them moral and psychological (The Art of Biblical Narrative, 164-5), relating them to different authors; their inclusion in one volume he regards as the redactor's intention to present two perspectives of Creation, and of God as being both transcendental and immanent (167).

6. *Cassuto*, 10 (on 1:1), 64 (on 2:4).

7. J.P. Fokkelman, "Genesis", 44.

8. e.g., E. Dambin, *Creation Stories in the Bible and in External Sources*, 13;
Y.T. Radday, "The Four Rivers of Paradise", 23-31.

9. Emmanueli's suggestion for the differences between the accounts avoids Cassuto's philosophical speculation and is similar to what has been suggested in our discussion (*Emmanueli*, 66); S. Breitbart ("Adam I and Adam II", 191-6) accentuates the same differences presented in my discussion about their different functions but does not go far enough to separate, completely, the two Adams.

10. Speiser, LXVI.

11. D.J. Wiseman, Clues to Creation (London, 1977), 41-42.

12. e.g.: J. Barr, Comparative Philology and the Text of the Old Testament.

13. e.g.: W. Todd, New Light on Genesis, 22.

14. S.N. Kramer, Enki and Ninhursag.

15. A parallel analysis is made by R.H. Hess, "splitting the Adam: The Usage of Adam in Genesis 1-5", 1-15. His distinctions, however, do not correspond to all my conclusions on the subject.

16. P. Trible's linguistic suggestion, "Let us make *humankind*..." (God and the Rhetoric of Sexuality, 13), seems to me to contradict her following preposition of "and let *them* have..." (emphasis added); if 'humankind' is understood, then 'it' should follow — as suggested in this paper. Although disagreeing with her on this point, I am greatly indebted to her for drawing my attention to the complexity of the verse.

17. In Speiser (4), it is: "man" and continued by "let him have"; Westermann's translation of 26b is missing (Westermann, 77); however, his text in the same place implies "Adam" as plural human beings. On the other hand, on p. 143 he uses the singular "humankind", and "human race".

    Skinner agrees that "Adam" is here a generic name and not the proper name of an individual (Skinner, 33).

18. e.g.: *Cassuto*, 32; Westermann, 143; P. Trible, God and the Rhetoric of Sexuality, 14.

19. Skinner, 33.
    For a recent bibliography, see: P. Bird, "Male and Female He Created Them": Genesis 1:27b in the Context of the Priestly Account of Creation", 129, note 2.

20. D.J. Wiseman, Clues to Creation, 41.

21. Y. Zakowitz, "On the Anticipatory Clue in Biblical literature", 85; N. Tocker, "The Voice of the Narrator in Genesis", 33.

22. Westermann, 159-160.

23. e.g.: D.T. Asselin, "The Notion of Dominion in Genesis 1-3", 277-294.

24. *Cassuto*, 36; emphasis added. Also *Emmanueli*, 59.

25. e.g.: R.J. Clifford, "Genesis 1-3: Permission to Exploit Nature?", 133-137.

26. K.W. Butzer, Environment and Archaeology: on hunting — p. 148; on agriculture — 553; on shepherding — 555, tab. 23.

27. This anthropological data corresponds to E.K.V. Pearce's speculation on the identity of Biblical Adam as a late Stone Age creature (Who Was Adam).

28. Luc De Ves ["Entwürfe von Universumssystemen. Entstehungsmythen und Ideologie", LB, L, 1982, 41-411; the quotation is from the author's published abstract in OTA, V, 244].

29. M. Rosenbaum & A.N. Silberman, Pentateuch, 17/4.

30. E.A.W. Budge, "The Teachings of King Khati", paragraph xxviii, The Teachings of Amen-Em-Apt, Son of Kenekht, 22.

31. For a general bibliography, see: Westermann, 142, 147-148.
For discussions, see: *Cassuto*, 34-36; *Emmanueli*, 56-58; Skinner, 30; Westermann, 148-158; P.A. Bird, "Male and Female He Created Them", Genesis 1:27 in the Context of the Priestly Account of Creation", 129-159.
P.D. Miller, Genesis 1-11: Studies in Structure and Theme, 9-20.

32. Skinner holds to the pagan court, citing Jewish sources leaning on legends, such as Philo, Rashi and Ibn-Ezra (Skinner, 31); also argued by B. Jacob (Genesis, 9). An interesting suggestion is made by Ramban: as Man was formed from the earth, the plural must refer to the originator God and to the element earth (cited in Y. Koler's discussion, "Creation of Man", 223).
Miller (Genesis 1-11: Studies in Structure and Theme, 25) gives a different emphasis to this interpretation: not a pagan court but "rather as dealing with the divine world as such and not simply with Yahweh".

33. For a comprehensive discussion on this issue, see: R. Gilboa, "Cherubim: An Inquiry into an Enigma", BN, 82, 1996, 59-75.

34. See: Skinner, 146; Westermann, 494-7; for various contemporary commentators, see the special issue of JSOT (XIII, 1979), dedicated solely to this subject.

35 *Cassuto*, 34; an equivalent rendering of one pushing oneself is "self-deliberation" (Westermann, 145; also W. Harrington, In The Beginning God, 30).
A Jewish religious interpretation claims that God was in a hurry to finish his tasks before the coming of the Sabbath. Such an argument is homiletic and elegant but, here, is out of place.

36. Westermann, 36.

37. For a general bibliography: Westermann, 147-8; and discussions: Ibid., 145-7, 148-158; *Cassuto*, 34-5; J.F.A. Sawyer, "The Meaning of 'God's Image' in Genesis 1-11", JTS, XXV, 1974, 418-26. A recent study on the subject, is G.A. Jónsson, The Image of God: Genesis 1:26-28 in a Century of Old Testament Research (trans. by L. Svendsen & H.S. Cheney, Stockholm, 1988).

38. My approach is as follows: 'בְּ — in' and 'כְּ — as' have a different meaning in spoken language: 'in our house' and 'as our house' are two different

sentences. But when the prepositions are combined with synonyms A and B to create compounds which project the same idea, the equilibrium acquires a mathematical logic:

in our house, as our home;   in our home, as our house

if   [in A + as B] conveys the same idea as [as A + in B], then —

[in A = as A] and [in B = as B];   hence, in = as.

The same conclusions about these linguistic aspects, although on different grounds: *Emmanueli*, 55; J.F. Sawyer, "The Meaning of 'God's Image' in Genesis 1-11", 421.

39. Westermann, 150.

40. M. Nadel, *The Bible and Cultures of the Ancient World*, 213.

41. R. Hirshberger, "Image et ressemblance dans la tradition sacredotale Gen 1:26-28, 5:1-3, 9:6b", 185-99.

42. A. Ahuvya, "In the Image of God Created He Him", 367.

43. Y. Koler, "Creation of Man", 227. A similar opinion: N. Kravitz, Genesis. A New Interpretation of the First Three Chapters, 45.

44. *Emmanueli*, 15.

45. M. Weinfeld, "In the Image of God", 113-16.

46. On God's androgyny in Jewish sources — *The Talmud, Eruvin 8:71*; *Bereshit Raba*, 8:1.

P. Trible (God and the Rhetoric of Sexuality, 80) suggests that Adam was an earth creature sexually undifferentiated, and only after the operation gained his sexual identity. This is a plausible suggestion which covers verse 1:27 but only if the chapters are referred to "sources". It does not answer the problem if, as done here, we claim for the unity of the text.

The primordial gods-creators of Memphis are perceived by commentators as bisexuals (M. Nadel, *The Bible and Cultures of the Ancient World*, 25). If such is the case, then Nun and Naunet of the ANET manuscript (above, p. 56) are male and female entities of the God Ptah. On similar perceptions in other mythologies: M. Nadel, "Male and Female", 80-85.

47. This is a controversial claim, as generations of interpretations have

elaborated on the distinctions between humans and other creatures (Skinner, 56-7). Westermann, on the other hand, agrees that the expression נפש חיה — NEFESH-HAYA "can describe the animals in general; animals and humans together, as living beings".

48. Contra N. Wyatt ("Where Adam Dwelt: The Meaning of Genesis 3:23", 117-22), who renders the verse as: "Yahweh God expelled him from the garden of Eden (and) *from tilling* the land from which he had been taken", meaning — from Eden. He bases his assumption on Ugaritic, where the preposition as prefix to the infinitive means 'from' — from work. Whatever the Ugaritic usage, the Hebrew infinitive לַעֲבֹד — La'AVOD indicates an intention to work and not its prevention; there is not even one mention in the Bible of this form of the verb where it means 'prevention of work' (*Concordancia*, 809).

49. ANET, 99: lines 20-26; 100. Also in W.G. Lambert & A.R. Millard, Atra-Hasis: The Babylonian Story of the Flood, 21: 210-213.

50. The Biblical אֵת — ET has several roles [see: R. Sivan, "אֵת", *Leshonenu* XXXIX, 1988, 30-34; S. Izrael, "אֵת = אֶל in Biblical Hebrew", *Shnaton*, III, 1978, 204-12; both n.m. in bib.], but in this verse usually two are given: "with" — [R.V.]; Westermann, 170; Speiser, 29, "from"— [K.J.]; [L]; L.M. Hopfe, A History of Interpretation of Genesis 4:1-16 and Its Relevance for Biblical Hermeneutics, 155. Interpreting ET as 'from', therefore, is acceptable.

51. The letters 'א' and 'י' belong to a group called AHOY (אהו"י) and they interchange with each other in the conjugation of verbs. The method of changing letters is usually employed by Tur-Sinai (*Psuhuto Shel Mikra*), but the tendency to rewrite the Bible does not appeal to me. In this case, however, an exchange of a letter in affiliated verbs is *only an added support* and not the main argument.

52. A theory of the creation of humans by stages, i.e., Adam was another stage added to existing humans, is made by M. Freilich ("Myth, Method and Madness", 214-15). Although the creation of Eve out of Adam can be regarded as 'a further stage', my interpretation differs from Freilich's theory.

For a similar understanding to what I present, of the 'taken Adam', see W. Todd, New Light on Genesis, 34. Another, based on scientific grounds, is E.K.V. Pearce, Who Was Adam, 22-51. Pearce's anthropological approach places Adam in the New Stone Age (10,000 B.C. onwards).

53. "The importance that irrigation can, and should have made to exegesis is ignored — although irrigation was the first applied science in history of backgrounds of the world" says W. Todd (New Light on Genesis, 11). Irrigation in its metaphorical disguise is expressed in the old Sumerian legend of Enki and Ninhursag (ANET, 38 - line 55; 39 — lines 65-75).

54. A.R. Millard points out that in Akkadian (borrowed from the Sumerian) עֶדֶנוּ — EDENU denotes 'steppe, plain' ("The Etymology of Eden", 103-106) cf. whereas the Semitic verb denotes 'abundant, lush'; Millard favours the Semitic one, and hence his epithet 'the garden of delights'. The former possibility is preferred here and supported by Speiser and Skinner who point out that the text relates to Eden *as a geographical place* distinguished from the garden (Speiser, 16; Skinner, 57).

55. H.N. Wallace, The Eden Narrative, 80; 83-6.

56. An interesting speculation of a possible locality: D. Ashbel, "Four Rivers Come from Eden", 100-104. For refutation of such attempts — T.Y. Radday ("The Four Rivers of Paradise", 23-31), who suggests that "if data found in reality conform to the general aim of scripture, there is no reason why they should not be accepted on face value; if not, they must be taken *cum grano* and as being presented as reality adapted and moulded in order to agree with that aim. After the story of the Four Rivers, there can be no clash between Science and Religion" (Ibid., 31).

57. Westermann, 211-216; M. Eliade, Patterns in Comparative Religion, 287; J.G. Frazer, Folk-Lore in the Old Testament, 76.

58. I was drawn to this conclusion, in spite of differences of opinions, by a paragraph in M. Marzel "Tree of Knowing Good and Evil — Comprehension of Life and Death", 359.

59. Cassuto's explanation of "work" and "guard" as referring to עבודת יהוה ושמירת מצוותיו — worship god and following his instructions (*Cassuto*, 80) is based both on Jewish traditional interpretation and comparison with the Mesopotamian concept where humankind was created in order to worship the Gods (ANET, 68). But Genesis, as Cassuto points out more than once, often uses mythological elements in a contradictory sense, and

'worshipping' is out of place in a text where all its elements are physical and geographical, and where MITZVOT, in the orthodox sense, are not stated in the text.

F. Landy (Paradoxes of Paradise, 169), avoids the possible implication of 'guarding' by suggesting that "the garden is essentially private, protected against the elements, weeds and wildness". The last two items, I suggest, address the requirements of the work; the word 'private', on the other hand, may be implied only when there is someone else to intrude.

60. e.g.: F. Landy (Ibid., 169) talks of the garden being "cultivated aesthetically... a place of passive harmony... of essentially imaginative activity"; P. Trible (God and the Rhetoric of Sexuality, 85-6) suggests that "to serve and to keep the garden is to live in harmony and pleasure". E. Fromm (The Forgotten Language, 245-7) talks of "peace and rest".

61. For a similar opinion, see: *Cassuto*, 84.
A demeaning attitude is expressed by R. Sacks ("The Lion and the Ass", 55) who says: "God's first attempt to find a helper for Man led Him to make the beasts". God's 'failure' is also in A.J. Hauser, "Genesis 2-3: The Theme of Intimacy and Alienation", 20-36, and in a recent research: J. Magonel, "The Themes of Genesis 2-3", p. 41. M. Jastrow's century-old suggestion and several followers carried the issue too far: naming the animals does not imply having sexual intercourse with them ("Adam and Eve in Babylonian Literature", AJSL, XV/4, 1899, 202).

62. See also: R.D. Freedman, "Woman, A Power Equal to Man", 56-8.

63. E. Cassirer, Language and Myth, 28.

64. *Cassuto*, 90; Skinner, 70; Westermann, 233; a recent research: A. Tosato, "On Genesis 2:24", 394.

65. R.B. Lawton, "Genesis 2:24: Tribe or Tragic", 97-8; Westermann, 233.

66. Contra W. Brueggemann ("Of the same flesh and bone' (Genesis, 2:23)" and *Cassuto*, 90.
Westermann regards the Hebrew בָּשָׂר as describing the human existence as a whole under the aspect of corporality (Westermann, 23), but had the author wanted to express that wholeness he could have said:
"ויהיו לאחד — and they will become one" instead of "לבשר אחד — become one flesh".

A narrow perception of "flesh" as a legal term for clan membership is suggested by A.F.L. Beeston ("One Flesh", 117), who thereby attempts to resolve the contradiction between ancient Near Eastern customs and the Biblical verse (2:24). The term BASAR cannot have this meaning in the preceeding verse (23), where it clearly indicates an individual's flesh. The same meaning has to apply to both verses, and Beeston does not solve this point.

Emmanueli separates the two expressions: 'cleave' is suggested as a spiritual union and 'one flesh' as a physical one (*Emmanueli*, 78). Of the quotations brought to support this distinction (Gen., 34:3; Ruth, 1:14; Deut., 4:4, 11:22; Kings, 18:6) only the first stands clearly as spiritual relationship: "and his *soul cleaved* unto Dina..." (emphasis added); the addition of "soul" seems to me to indicate that 'cleave' by itself has a physical aspect. Indeed, the other citations indicate 'following', which has also the physical aspect of 'joining a party' and not necessarily of a spiritual union only.

67. J.M. Sasson, "Welo Yitbosaso (Genesis 2:25) and Its Implications", 419) sees the word as having ambiguous meaning, resulting from the Hitpael form of the verb: to feel shame — intransitive, and to relate to each other — the distributive and the reciprocal (also H.N. Wallace, The Eden Narrative, 173). Sasson prefers the reciprocal meaning, probably because Adam and Eve are alone; God's clothing, therefore, is "temporarily halting their propensity to embarrass each other" (Ibid., 421). But the notion that nakedness causes embarrassment is a social one (to be discussed below).

68. e.g., P. Trible (God and the Rhetoric of Sexuality, 74) describes the state prior to the act of disobedience as "the development of Eros (where 'Eros' means "Life-unity, fulfilment, harmony and delight").

69. Contra J. Magonet, "The Theme of Genesis 2-3", p. 43.

70. A similar opinion: J.M. Higgins, "The Myth of Eve: The Temptress", 645-47. Westermann suggests that "if he was with her, listening to her conversation, no second temptation took place" (Westermann, 185, note 6[c]).

71. (Skinner, 72).
A common perception, deriving from the notion of 'documents', is that the serpent is an incorporated motif from a story where he was God's

messenger sent to "bear the glad tidings of immortality to Man" but he perverted the message (J.G. Frazer, Folk-Lore in Old Testament, 51; for a similar argument, M. Eliade, Patterns in Comparative Religion, 288).

72. K.R. Joines ("The Serpent in Genesis 3") mentions: YOUTHFULNESS, WISDOM, LIFE, CHAOS. A.J. Williams ("The Relationship of Genesis 3:20 to the Serpent") gives Rabbinical sources, and regards him as a metaphor for : IMMORTALITY, WISDOM, CHAOS. F. Landy (Paradoxes in Paradise, 207) regards the serpent as a metaphor for NAKEDNESS.

'Wisdom', at any rate, is not 'cunning', and no one of the above metaphors seems to correspond to the actual happenings in the Genesis text.

73. D.E. Burns, "Dream and Form in Genesis 2:4b-3:24: A Sleep in the Garden", p. 9. Another suggestion, that the serpent, of all beasts of the fields, is the best equipped for survival thanks to his skills and power (J.F.A. Sawyer, "The Image of God, The Wisdom of Serpents and the Knowledge of Good and Evil", p. 67) is arguable because one can argue in favour of every creature's means of survival.

74. M. Nadel, *The Bible and the Cultures of the Ancient World*, 131.

75. See: H.H. Hirshberg, Hebrew Humanism, 65.

76. *Cassuto*, 94. Contra: Westermann, 238.

77. On similar line: P. Lapid, "Illustration: Touching the Forbidden Fruit", 13-16.

78. Also Freilich, "Myth, Method and Madness", 213, point 6.
O. Davidson's perception of the story as a debate between two alternatives, is correct only to the extent that the tree represented temptation; the alternatives are either to eat or not ("The Mythical Foundation of History: A Religio-Semiotic Analysis of the Story of the Fall", 23-36; cited from the author's abstract in O.A.T., VI, 1982, No. 169). But Davidson, influenced by the notion of the 'Fall', describes them as "*a progressive* move toward 'having eternal life rightfully' and a *digressive* move toward 'having knowledge unlawfully'" (Ibid., emphasis added), and thus he adds a moral judgement which is not stated in the text.

79. J.M. Higgins, "The Myth of Eve: The Temptress", 646-7, note 58.

80. Contra Westermann, who finds only three: the opening of their eyes, the awareness, the covering (Westermann, 250).

81. See: Rashi, and compare with Genesis, 21:19.

82. e.g., *Cassuto*, 74: "out of his fatherly love, God prohibited Adam of eating the fruit". On the same speculative line is Abarbanel's interpretation cited in N. Leibovitz, *Thesis On Genesis*, 16.

83. e.g.: Y. Marzel, "The Tree of Knowing Good and Evil", 352-60.

84. Westermann suggests seven categories, but as he joins 6 and 7, he ultimately offers six (Westermann, 241-51). The suggested categories of this book are similar to those of Westermann; the differences are a matter of definition rather than essence.

85. Westermann, 243/3, and 247; *Cassuto*, 72-4; T.H. Gaster, Myth, Legend and Custom in the Old Testament, 34; N.H. Wallace, The Eden Narrative, 128; Von Rad, Genesis, 79.

86. e.g.: *Cassuto*, 72, citing Ibn Ezra.

87. An observation suggested by W. Todd, New Light on Genesis, 41 and B. Jacob, Genesis, 31. Regarding 'clothing' as a barrier or zone where one must not look (F. Landy, Paradoxes of Paradise, 228) is a social/psychological attitude.

88. E. Dambin, *Creation Story in the Bible and External Sources*, 6; W.M. Clark, "A Legal Background to the Yahwist's Use of 'Good and Evil' in Genesis 2-3", 277; R. de-Jules, "On Freilich's Interpretation of Genesis 1-3", 140/10.

89. Also P. Lapid, "Illustration: Touching the Forbidden Fruit", 42-3.

90. Skinner, 96. F. Landy (Paradoxes of Paradise, 189) expands the scope of this notion by suggesting that "it is awareness of a universe divided into good and bad... hence the first knowledge is that of nakedness, of the disturbing duality of gender". One is left to wonder why nakedness or, more so, duality of gender is disturbing, i.e., bad.

91. In his discussion, Skinner mentions also an element of magic (Skinner, 96); both he and Westermann (Westermann, 243/2) reject these interpretations.

An interesting interpretation of the useful and harmful aspects of the story, related to the Mesopotamian geographical and anthropological background, is suggested by W. Todd (New Light on Genesis, 41-44); but he deals with what the story *originally* was about, and this — as we stressed in our introduction (pp. 20-21) — was of no interest to the later author who must have had a different aim.

92. e.g.: A.J. Hauser, "Genesis 2-3: The Theme of Intimacy and Alienation"; Skinner, 51; J. Armstrong, The Myth of Paradise, 3; *Cassuto*, 44; J.G. Frazer, Folk-Lore in the Old Testament, 45.

93. J. Pedersen, "Wisdom and Immortality", 238-246.

94. Westermann, 301. For a discussion: 299-301. See also: L.M. Hopfe, A History of Interpretation of Genesis 4:1-16 and Its Relevance for Biblical Hermeneutics.

95. S.N. Lambden compares their inadequate fig-leaves cover with God's skins garments ("From Fig Leaves to Fingernails", p. 76), but his comparison cannot diminish the creative nature of their act; it simply dismisses the quality of the product.

96. See: M.P. Carroll, "Genesis Reconstructed" in B. Lang, Anthropological Approaches to the Old Testament, 129; see also the discussion in J.M. Higgins, "The Myth of Eve: The Temptress", 639-644; L.A. Beily, "Initiation and the Primal Woman in Gilgamesh and Genesis 2-3", 137-150.

97. Contra Skinner, Speiser, Westermann, Cassuto (for a bibliography on the notion of 'sin', see: Westermann, 256). A Modern Israeli scholar, Z. Adar (*Introduction to the Biblical World*, 21) adopts the Christian notion of regarding the act as "not a sin of the individual but of the first human being, and therefore the punishment is not on just the individual but on humanity as a whole".

H.H. Hirshberg (Hebrew Humanism, 65), on the other hand, points out that this is not a Biblical perception but a later interpretation of Paul and some Jewish apocryphal authors of his age who derived from the story the doctrine of 'Original Sin'. Against this interpretation, Hirshberg argues that had this been the basic theme of the book, the author would not have attached it to an obscure myth and, of all places, to its prologue.

The same perception of the notion as being completely alien to the spirit and content of the O.T. is expressed by M. Freilich ("Myth, Method and Madness", 212), who answers the claim that "the absence of Sin makes a farce out of the Garden of Eden story" (by Dr. Raedt, CA, XVII, 139-141), with: "it makes the story very un-Christian, but hardly farcical" (Ibid., 141).

98. On this issue: M. Sternberg, The Poetics of Biblical Narrative, 89.

99. e.g.: Skinner, 77-8. Westermann points to a possible blaming of God by Adam (Westermann, 255).

100. On the etymology of what is regarded as a curse 'א.ר.ר.' and on its interpretation as 'ban', see H.C. Brichto, The Problem of 'Curse' in Hebrew Bible, 83-86. Hence the suggested "condemnation" instead of 'curse'.

101. For bibliography: Westermann, 267; discussion: 268. For a discussion of the name and comparison with Mami of the Atra-Hasis legend, in I. Kikawada, "Two Notes on Eve", 33-37.

102. Westermann, 263.

103. N.H. Tur-Sinai, "Sin Lies at Your Door", 75.

104. Ibid., 10. Also: C. Gilead, "The Plain Meaning of the Cain and Abel Story", 14-28. The same conclusion on different grounds: K.A. Derulo, "תְּשׁוּקָה > dependence <, Gen 4,7", 405-6.

105. E. Leach, "Genesis as Myth" (J. Middleton, ed., Myth and Cosmos), 7; A.J. Hauser, "Linguistic and Thematic Links Between Genesis 4:1-16 and Genesis 2-3", 297-8; J.B. Doukham, The Literary Structure of Genesis Creation Story, 36-42; J.T. Walsh, "Genesis 2:4b-3:24: A Synchronic Approach", 170; P. Trible, God and the Rhetoric of Sexuality, 106; A special issue of Semeia (XVIII, 1980) with articles by T. Boomershine, R.C. Culley, D. Jobling, D. Pate & F. Parker.

106. P. Trible, God and the Rhetoric of Sexuality, chapter 4.

107. Westermann, 281; Speiser, 30; L.M. Hopfe, A History of Interpretation of 4:1-16, 159; I. Kikawada, "Two Notes on Eve", 37.

To this category of dependence on God, belongs also M. Caspi's interpretation of the phrase as "I have cultivated (ק.נ.ה.) this man with the help of God" ("Kaniti Ish et Yhwh", 32).

108. Skinner, 102-3; Cassuto does not relate to the crucial 'את' but stresses Eve's *pride and comparison to God* rather than her dependence on him: "I stand with him in the line of creators" (*Cassuto*, 135); thus he may be included in this category, in spite of the 'with' in his interpretation.

109. E.M. Good, Irony in the Old Testament, 14.

110. See: J. H. S. Armstrong, The Paradise Myth, 14.

111. B.D. Naidorff, "A Man to Work the Soil: A New Look of Genesis 2-3", 2-14. A summary of all three opinions mentioned in the discussion can be found in D. Jobling, "Myth and its Limits in Genesis 2:4a-3:24" The Sense of Biblical Narrative, 17-43.

112. Any structural division depends on the interpreter's point of view and on the reading of the text. As the reading of the text in this research differs from the conventional reading on so many issues, there is little chance that our suggested division will correspond to others which, on their part and in spite of responding to the conventional reading, suggest several structures and thematic links for the different parts of the text as a whole. Presenting, discussing or comparing other suggestions is not within the scope of this research; some, for the interested reader, are mentioned in the bibiliography of note 105.

113. On the principles of Biblical verse, see: Encyclopedia Judaica, 1200-1203.

114. A similar opinion is suggested by D.P. Scaer ("The Problems of Inerrancy and Historicity in Connection With Genesis 1-3", 5-21) who says: "Using the usual literary yardsticks to distinguish history from illustrative stories, there is absolutely nothing [in Genesis 1-3] to suggest that we are dealing with anything else than a purely historical account".

115. Likewise, the first chapter of Genesis which is regarded by some commentators as a possible incantation for a religious ritual, similar to what existed in the Mesopotamian culture (H. Gunkel, The Legends of Genesis, 30-34), there is nothing in the Bible to indicate such a use in the Israelite tradition; the reading of the Torah in synagogues is a much later practice.

116. For a similar observation, but only regarding the correspondence between limits, see: J.B. Doukhan, The Literary Structure of Genesis Creation Story, 54.

117. N. Spiegel, *A History of Ancient Ethics*, 13.

118. F. Boas did (The Mind of the Primitive Man, 152) but he is an anthropologist. Philosophers usually regard ethics as a social "necessity,

because man's desires conflict" (B. Russell, History of Western Philosophy, 745). A similar opinion on social grounds is expressed by E. Fromm: "Since man *cannot* live without values and norms" (Man for Himself, 5).

119. To this perception, as well as other observations in the following presentation, I am greatly indebted to A. Rand "The Objectivist Ethics" (a paper delivered at the University of Wisconsin Symposium on "Ethics in Our Time", 9/2/1960), in The Virtue of Selfishness, 13-35). Unfortunately, although using the Biblical connotation of "good and evil" and arguing for it as 'a matter of must' fŏr Life, no comment is made on, what I believe to be, the reasonable source for this perception — the Eden story.

120. The author's psychological understanding differs in this point from E. Fromm, who suggests that "the sources of norms for ethical conduct are to be found in man's *nature* itself" (Man For Himself, 39).

121. A. Lang (Myth Ritual and Religion, 33). It seems that in the Genesis saga, the alternative of the author borrowing a legendary element is at work.

122. T. Reick, Myth and Guilt, 119.

123. To describe events in the garden, between Adam's sleep (2:21) and until his eyes "are opened" (3:7), as a narrative which "may be read as if it were Adam's dream" (D.E. Burns, "Dream Form in Genesis 2:4b-3:24", 5) is an attempt to apply our logic into the text. It solves the legendary issues of the peculiar creation of Eve, the talking serpent and the special trees; 'dream', thus, may be applied as an excuse to problematic legendary elements. In the case of Genesis, however, this approach has two pitfalls: the text states the legendary nature of the trees *before Adam's sleep*; 'dream' does not explain the appearance of the woman in reality [Adam's awakening stage] and thus the narrative has a lacuna in its report of events.

124. I find T. Reik's suggestions for the 'ratio' as being connected with primitive primordial rituals, unconvincing:

a) Of Adam's deep sleep and the taking of a bone out of him, he says that it resembles "the ritual of death and rebirth which we trace in the puberty ceremonies of pre-literate people" (The Creation of Woman, 98). This seems to me too far-fetched: whoever wrote Genesis was not pre-literate but influenced by data that long beforehand had been recorded *in writing*. Physical puberty ceremonies were never part of Hebraic life (circumcision has nothing to do with puberty as the object of the ceremony is a baby; the Bar-Mitzva, a much later practice, introduces a youngster to manly *spiritual* obligations — nothing to do with puberty).

b) A comparison between 'bringing forth the boys' in puberty rituals [or, for that matter, in Bar-Mitzva] (Ibid., 118) and the father figure Adam who 'brings forth' the woman, is not a convincing argument because a paternal social obligation and a natural phenomenon are two issues apart.

125. "Idealization", J. Laplanche & J-B. Pontalis, The Language of Psycho-Analysis, 202.

126. "Ego-Ideal", Ibid., 144.

127. A similar observation: "for the Hebrew thinker, the appeal of wisdom... is the bridge between the human and the divine; by this means God and man have come into relationship...", is expressed by W.A. Irwin ("The Hebrews", 292).

128. E. Fromm, The Forgotten Language, 233.
T. Reick elaborates and suggests that the two sexes deriving from one creature is "a variation of the original situation in which the couple have melted into one body by means of sexual intercourse" (The Creation of the Woman, 30); he concludes that the Genesis narrative does not present the story of Eve's birth, but a distorted tradition of Adam's rebirth (Ibid., 83).

129. K. Abraham, Dream and Myths: A Study in Race Psychology, 62.
The thesis' suggested notion of "womb envy" for this particular narrative differs from A. Cunningham's interpretation titled as "incent", which he regards as an attempt to regain order in a state of chaotic social relationships — a notion founded on viewing the Eden story as that of the first and only human couple ("Psychoanalitic Approaches to Biblical Narrative (Genesis 1-4)", 113-132).

130. On this conflict, see: S. Freud, Totem and Taboo, 146-153. A detailed discussion will be in the concluding chapter V.

131. See: E. Fromm, The Forgotten Language, 202-5.

Chapter IV: Creation of a Nation

Unless otherwise stated, Westermann in this chapter is 12-3b.

1. e.g.: Y. Leibowitz, *Judaism, Jewish People and the Israeli State*, Jerusalem, 1979.

2. For the same opinion, see: W.A. Irwin, "The Hebrews", 326, 331.

3. E.A. Speiser, "'People' and 'Nation' of Israel", in J.J. Finkelstein & M. Greenberg, ed., Oriental and Biblical Studies (Collected writings of E.A. Speiser), 169. For a recent discussion of the topic but on different lines, see: L. Kutler, "Structural Semantic Approach to Israelite Communal Terminology", 69-77.

4. W.F. Albright, Yahweh and the Gods of Canaan, 56.

5. D.L. Mattson, The Blessing Themes in the Abraham Story and the Implications for the Date and Purpose of the Story, who discusses (Ibid., 5-34) opinions by: M. Noth (A History of Patriarchal Traditions [n.m. in bib.], H. Gunkel (The Legends of Genesis), T.L. Thompson (The Historicity of the Patriarchal Narratives: The Quest for the Historical Abraham), and J. van Setters (Abraham in History and Tradition).

6. Z. Weisman, "National Consciousness in the Patriarchal Promises", 56 (italics, mine).

7. Ibid., 68-9.

8. The literature on the patriarchs is abundant (for a bibliography, see in note 5, and: Westermann, 87-104 and J.J. Scullion, "Some Reflections on the State of the Patriarchal Studies", 50-65. The interpretations of the whole cycle of each patriarch's life and historical background are not the concern of this research.

9. A lengthy explanation is needed here, to explain calculations:

   The place is stated in 18:1; the time is estimated as the same as in encounter 6 because in both encounters Sarah's son is mentioned as due next year (17:21; 18:9, 14).

   The text does not specify either when in Abraham's life the event occurred or Isaac's age. Isaac's title נַעַר — NA'AR does not clarify the issue because it indicates an emotional connection between the protagonists rather than an age [this will be explained in the due discussion of the issue, p. 198]. As for Isaac's age, the issue remains unsolved. *Bereshit Rabah*, 58:5 deduces, from the juxtaposition of Sarah's death immediately after the event, that her death occurred by a stroke after she heard of Isaac's tribulations. This is an implausible suggestion, as Sarah died at the age of 127 (23:1) and she gave birth at the age of 90; Isaac was 37 when she died and, thus — according to *Bereshit Rabah*, the same age at The Binding. It is hard to accept that a 37-year-old man, silently and without comment, would let himself be tied to an altar by an elderly father, 137 years old.

10. This is the general concept of the designations; U. Cassuto adds other philosophical implications (*The Documentary Hypothesis and the Composition of the Pentateuch*, 19-38) which do not concern this discussion (see also Cassuto, 56).

11. Ellen Van Wolde, Words Become Worlds, p. 46.

12. See: N.E. Wagner, A Literary Analysis of Genesis 12-36, 13. On 'EL', see: M.H. Pope, "The Word El as Appellative and as a Proper Name", El in the Ugaritic Texts, 1-15.

13. See: F.N. Cross, "Yahweh and the Gods of the Patriarchs", 225-259.

14. J.A. Motyer, The Revelation of the Divine Name, 12; K. Joines, "God Almighty", 17. For a discussion on this issue, and citations from Cassuto, B. Jacob, Segal and Jewish sources: N. Leibowitz *Thesis on Exodus*, 97-103 [n.m. in bib.].

15. This research's literary approach follows C.H. Gordon (Ugaritic Literature, 6) who finds in Ugaritic tablets a similar vacillation of the designations of the deity. Similar vacillation is found also in tablets from Ebla, where the deity is both El and Ya (Is-ra-Il/Is-ra-Ya; see: G. Pettinato, "The Royal Archives of Tell-Mardikh — Ebla", 50). In both cultures — Ebla and Ugarit, of the early and late Bronze Age, respectively — the designations have no bearing on meaning, that is: they refer to the same deity and *do not imply a different religion.*

16. Cassuto, although attempting to give a literary answer, leans heavily on his interpretation which imposes transcendental notions (*Cassuto*, 56); the results are arguable.

17. See M. Nadel, *The Bible and Cultures of the Ancient World*, 126.

18. On 'vision', see: Skinner, 278; on the nature of Abraham's vision: M. Anbar, *Genesis Stories on Abraham*, 24-38. The problematic issue of the time factor in this chapter is discussed further on; at this stage only the aspects of the nature of the communication are dealt with.

19. In a recent paper, L.K. Handy suggests that the Biblical concept of "messengers" derives from a four-tiered divine hierarchy that constituted the Syria-Palestina regional religion: Highest authority, Major (active) Gods, Craft-Gods, Messenger-deities ("Dissenting Deities or Obedient Angels: Divine Hierarchies in Ugarit and the Bible", 18-35).

20. Rofé, *The Belief in Angels in the Bible and in Early Israel* 3-4; W. Eichrodt, Theology of the Old Testament, vol. I, 23-29. Skinner calls it 'theophany' (Skinner, 286-7).

21. Rodin-Oberski, *The Patriarchs in Hebron and Sodom*, 35.

22. Rodin-Oberski acknowledges their over-anthropomorphism, but regards it as a projection of the earliest foundations of the stories whic are extra Biblical; this ultimately supports her basic 'documents' theory and makes the application of theological reasoning for the redactor possible (Ibid., 89).

23. On the designation 'THE God': Y. Koler, "HaElohim — a definite particle or Enlonged Name of God", 447-82. On the grammatical use and syntactical juxtaposition: Y. Lerner, "The forms HaElohim and Elohim in the Pentateuch and Prophets", 195-8. For our discussion — it is another designation of the same deity, that has no bearing on meaning or His entity.

24. The following sources are but a selected survey [n.m. in bib.]: A. Murtonen, A Philological and Literary Treatise on the Old Testament Divine Names 'L, 'Lwh, 'Lhym, and Yhwh, Helsinki, 1952; M.H. Segal, "El, Elohim and Yahwe in the Bible", JQR, XLVI, 1955, 89-115; M. Reisel, The Mysterious Name YHWH, Assen, 1957; R. Abba, "The Divine Name Yahweh", JBL, LXXX, 1961, 320-328.

25. Westermann suggests the option that the different expressions are alternatives of an author who was not tied down to any particular designation of God (Westermann, 361); such a claim undermines the

foundation of the 'documents' notion to which Westermann, in his next remark (Ibid.) adheres.

S. Breitbart ("The Akeda — A test of God", 19-28) regards the linguistic change as a development of the concept of the deity: what started as just another God, became Yhwh, a mature concept (Ibid., 27). As at the end it is not Yhwh but his angel who intervenes, the transformation does not justify Breitbart's argument suggested above.

26. J.C. Coleman, Abnormal Psychology and Modern Life, 271.

27. Westermann, 552; Skinner, 424; Speiser, 244, note 13.

28. "פגע" basically indicates a clash of elements (The Bible Dic., 678) and the meanings of the three categories have an added, somewhat violent, stress: 1) meet, touch, find; 2) ask, insist, press; 3) to cause physical damage.

32:2 "וַיִּפְגְּעוּ־בוֹ" is rendered in Westermann 502, as "met him", thus softening the nature of the event; in Speiser 252, it is rendered as "encountered him" which retains the violent element (the same approach in Skinner 405).

29. Skinner, in spite his notion of 'spirit' (see: *, p. 169) realizes that the struggle is a physical one (Skinner, 411); Westermann, as well, is aware of the physical implications (Westermann, 256), but in spite of his awareness he regards the struggle as a "frightening *spiritual* experience" (Ibid., 255; emphasis added). Neither of these commentators suggests a plausible explanation for a spiritual experience which causes a physical wound which, in all probability, could only have been caused by physical means.

30. Such is not the case with F. Brossier's analysis, "Jacob at Penuel", 39-40), who gives the event a theological emphasis stating that it is not Jacob who encounters God, but God who lets him grapple with death and ultimately corrects [?] him. In Brossier's analysis, God is the prime actor of the episode, and neither the "man" in the text nor the physical wound are taken in their proper perspective.

31. Identification of the attacker as Esau's messenger can be found in Jewish traditional sources (*Bereshit Rabah*, 77, 3, and Rashi). For a discussion of the spiritual implications of this identification, see: N. Leibowitz, *Thesis on Genesis*, 255-258.

32. e.g.: Fokkelman, "Genesis", 50, and in his perception of the whole event in Narrative Art in Genesis, chapter V.

33. See: S.A. Geller, "The Struggle at the Yabbok: The Uses of Enigma in Biblical Narrative", 37-60.

34. Speiser, "'people' and 'nation' of Israel", 163.

35. M. Anbar, "Abrahamic Covenant — Genesis 15", 49.

36. For the same observation, see W. Todd, New Light on Genesis, 97.

37. Westermann, 105-6.

38. W. McKane, Studies in the Patriarchal Narratives, 195-225; G.J. Wenham, "The Religion of the Patriarchs", 157-188.

39. Westermann regards the structure as typical of the narrative of Genesis and compares it with 26:1-3, 31:3, 32:10, 46:1-5. More comparisons will follow.

40. The first correlation is similar to the one suggested by P. Auffert, ("Essai sur la structure littéraire du Gn. 12:1-4a", 243), but the second (Ibid., 244) differs. My approach is based on subject matter embodied by expressions and not, as it seems to be in Auffert's essay, by breaking sentences into words (Ibid., 244-5).

41. On 'covenant' in general, see: M. McCarthy, Old Testament Covenant; H. Tadmor, "Treaty and Oath in the Ancient Near East: An Historian Approach", 149-173.

42. On the legal aspects of the inheritance, see: Speiser, 112.

43. Skinner, 280.

44. J.P. Fokkelman, "Genesis", 49; M. Anbar, "Genesis 15", 35.

45. "צדקה — ZeDAKA", The Bible Dic., 713; 1st meaning. Arguing for this notion while discussing Ramban's suggestion (below) is R.L.W. Moberly in "Abraham's Righteousness (Gen. 13:6)", 108.

46. "צדקה — ZeDAKA", The Bible Dic., 713, 3rd meaning.

47. Y. Elitzur, "The Covenant", 39. Elitzur shares the sceptical attitude presented in this paper, which contradicts the conventional attitude (e.g.:

Westermann, 222-3). E.M. Good regards Abraham's response as ironical (Irony in the Old Testament, 91).

48. For a similar opinion: M. Weinfeld, "B^{e}rith — Covenant v. Obligation", 48-9.

49. Skinner, 290-1; Westermann, 257-259; Speiser, 124, who concludes that a satisfactory explanation of this term is yet to be proposed.

50. e.g.: Speiser, 125 and Westermann, 268.

51. "אמה — AMA", The Bible Dic., 51; see: 2 Samuel, 25:41; linguistically cognate with 'mother — EM' or to part of the AMA — arm. The same order prevails for N. Avigad (Bullae and Seals from a Post-Exilic Judean Archive, 1976, 12 [n.m. in bib.]), who says that Amah outranks Shif'hah; he suggests the terms 'maidservant' and 'bondmaid' respectively and, as N. Abraham adds, neither rivals the status of the wife ("Notes on the Status of Ama in Exodus 21:7-11", p. 300).

This order is challenged by C. Cohen ("Studies in Extra-Biblical Hebrew Inscriptions, I.: The Semantic Range and Usage of the Terms Amah and Shif'hah") who regards them as equal. With respect to Hagar, he points to the title Shif'hah in 16:5, where she has already been given to Abraham (Ibid., xxxiv). This argument overlooks the *literary narrative* and use of vocabulary as I presented above, in which there is a distinct move away from the status of Shif'hah: *only after the child is born* does Hagar receive her title AMAH from the same Sarah who called her Shif'hah, even during the pregnancy.

52. P. Trible, Texts of Terror, 9.

53. J.C. Coleman, Abnormal Psychology and Modern Life, 7.

54. A similar opinion — M. Nadel (*The Bible and Cultures of the Ancient World*, 203. Nadel presents Abraham's state of mind as a case that the Ancient author could resolve only through divine intervention.

55. Z. Gitay ("Hagar's Expulsion — A Tale Twice Told in Genesis") follows the 'documents' theory and therefore overlooks the crucial difference between the stories: one is a real occurrence whereas the other is a state of mind; they are not 'a tale told twice' but rather a development of a literary issue in a similar pattern.

56. See: S. Ben-Reuben, "Boy v. Son in the Bible", 148-9.

57. Skinner, 321: "The age of weaning in modern Palestine is said to be 2-3 years; in ancient Israel also, it must often have been late". Speiser, 155: "at least fifteen years old"; *Emmanueli*, 248 — sixteen-seventeen.

58. 'לְצַחֵק — LeTZAHEK' *is not* 'to play' as suggested in Skinner, 322 and Speiser, 155, note 9; Westermann, 421.

The reason for the different attitude toward the same word is not clear to me. Obviously, the king of Gerar could deduce that Isaac and Rebekah are husband and wife only if the 'play' had in it some sexual element; the same connotation for the expression applies regarding Joseph's affair with Potiphar's wife. The same has to apply to Ishmael's case, the more so when the text *does not specify with whom Ishmael was 'playing'* because the partner, for the author and his story, is irrelevant — the mere act is what counts. The supposition that the object for Ishmael's play was Isaac and that he was mocking, abusing, or that they were "peacefully... playing with each other" (discussion in Westermann, 337) is not grounded in the text, because had it been Isaac, he would have been very relevant for the author to mention him.

59. As suggested by Y. Mazor ("Genesis 22: The Ideological Rhetoric and the Psychological Composition", 82). I agree with this literary approach, but have arrived to different conclusions on the message.

The point of 'test' is discussed by N. Leibowitz, Thesis on Genesis, 133-137, where the leading message is that of 'belief'; this is the central line of almost all interpretations, and more sources will be mentioned in due course. One provocative commentary, however, based on linguistic interpretation of an unusual nature, is by H. Patcas ("Akeda: The Binding of Isaac", Dor Le-Dor, XIV, 1985/6, 112-14 [n.m. in bib.]), who suggests the whole incident as a linguistic misunderstanding of Abraham, from which God had to save him by a miracle; Patcas' interpretation imputes senility to Abraham. This research, as will be seen, treats the event as an inner experience of Abraham's psyche (for a similar opinion which describes it as a state of mind, see: H.H. Hirshberg, Hebrew Humanism, 94).

60. P. Tribel, Texts of Terror, 30, note 9.

61. The same opinion is argued by B. Jacob (Genesis, 164).

62. J.C. Coleman, Abnormal Psychology and Modern Life, 170.

63. E. Auerbach, Mimesis, 5-10.

64. For the same opinion, see: Westermann, 359: "he throws the ball back into God's court"; also S. Breitbart, "The Akeda — A Test of God", 26.
J. Moster ("The Testing of Abraham", 241) regards Abraham's phrase (22:18) as "A Freudian slip, revealing Abraham's true inner belief that under the circumstances it was God's obligation to supply a substitute to Isaac".

65. A point noted by Skinner, 330; Speiser, 165/8; Westermann, 362; and with a different emphasis, also A. Savir, "God Will See — The Place He Will Choose", *Beit Mikra*, 26, 1980, 279-281 [n.m. in bib.].

66. Also noted by Westermann, 362.

67. The angel who praises Abraham, calls him "יְרֵא אֱלֹהִים — God Fearing" and this is rendered as "moral disposition" (Skinner, 330), "dedicated to God" (Speiser, 163/12), "Abraham's perfect obedience" (Westermann, 361).

68. M. Weinfeld, "B^{e}rith — Covenant v. Obligation", 125.

69. J. Goldingay, "The Patriarchs in Scripture and History", 22-24.

70. e.g.: Skinner, 331-2; Speiser, 166; *Emmanueli*, 291.

71. Although the notion of inner conflict is suggested also by Y. Zmudi ("The Inner Struggle in the story of The Binding", 382-87), his argument points to it as the *result* of Abraham's sense of obedience; our argument is that the inner conflict *created* the situation which raises the question of obedience.

72. A similar understanding of the text can be observed in A. Adar, The Biblical Narrative, 37-8; our approach, however, stresses this as the author's view of a zeal for God carried to an extreme, which practically negates the Biblical idea of that God.

73. T. Jacobsen, "The Rise of Personal Religion", The Treasures of Darkness, 145-146.

Chapter V: Conclusions

1. J. Barr, The Bible as Literature, 66.

2. Ibid., 64-65. These two remarks are a prime example of a legitimate, but utterly subjective, approach.

3. I reached this conclusion after reading literature of the ancient Middle East. For some references, see note I/44.

4. Westermann 12-36, 14. C. Tresmontant (A study of Hebrew Thought, 46-7) tries to find a synthesis for the dichotomy commonly suggested between the secular and the sublime, by pointing to the concrete nature of the language (Ibid., 46) and then by incorporating them into synthesis expressed by words *to what exists*; the synthesis at which he arrives defines Hebrew thought as "poetic materialism or a carnal idealism".

5. Westermann 12-36, 14; E. Auerbach, Mimesis, 19.

6. Westermann points out that God, in the Israeli tradition, is called when needed; it is a useful God (Westermann 12-36, 14).

7. ANET, 4, 61.

8. Ibid., 68.

9. Ibid., 69.

10. For a similar observation, applied to the whole Bible: B. Spinoza, "Introduction", *Tractatus Theologico-Politicus*, 6.

11. "Gilgamesh", ANET, 73.

12. A similar opinion, although with different distinction of power, seems to be expressed by A. Patric & A. Scull: "We conclude that Genesis 1-3... is less about creation as such than about the dimensions of power." (Rhetoric and Biblical Interpretation, 119).

13. E. Fox, "Can Genesis Be Read As a Book?", 33.

14. R.L. Cohn, ("Narrative Structure and Canonical Perspective in Genesis", 14), who states that, in regard with the amount of God's involvement in Genesis as a whole, God appears less and less, and at the end of the

book "human actions become more independent of divine control, more autonomous".

15. E. Fromm, "Disobedience as a Psychological and Moral Problem", 5.

16. E. Fromm, You Shall Be as Gods (London, 1967), 6-7.

17. For a discussion on the subject, see: N. Leibowitz, Thesis on Exodus, 389-393; Rabbi Kook (cited Ibid., 393) stresses the nation's tendency to a non-secular life on the Sabbath.

18. The difference is obvious to all commentators, but in most cases the attempt to resolve it is by reconciliation (e.g., S. Albeck, "The Ten Commandments and the Principle of Faith", 206-7). My approach, on the other hand, accentuates the difference and justifies it by a social-philosophical setting.

19. E. Fromm, "Disobedience as a Psychological and Moral Problem", 3.

20. E. Fromm, The Fear of Freedom, ix-x.

21. S. Freud, "Totem and Taboo", 146-153.

22. M. Eliade, Patterns in Comparative Religion, 429.

23. Contra J.G. Frazer, Folk-Lore in the Old Testament, vii.

24. C.G. Jung, The Archetypes of the Collective Unconscious.

25. See: Y. Leibowitz, *The Faith of Maimonides* (Tel-Aviv, 1980), 31.

26. H. Deutsch, A Psychoanalitical Study of the Myth of Dionysos and Apollo, 10; discussed on p. 4.

27. T. Reick, Myth and Guilt.

28. Mainly in the writings of E. Fromm: "Epilogue", You Shall Be as Gods. Regarding the Bible, see: Man For Himself, 12.

29. E. Fromm, You Shall Be as Gods, 23, (emphasis, mine).

30. I was happy to read a similar conclusion, published shortly after I handed my thesis for examination, expressed by A. Cunningham: "Intra-Biblically, the growth of human consciousness may be traced in the psychodynamics of its leading personalities, the development of a collective super ego... It may be claimed that unlike the hero of other

mythologies, gratifying intellectual wishes of *overcoming* the father, the story of the Biblical hero is one of *identifying* with the father and his commandments" ("Psychoanalitic Approaches to Biblical Narrative (Genesis 1-4)", 128).

C. Bibliography

Technical Notes

1. The bibliography list includes only the books relevant to the discussion; other sources are mentioned in the notes, indicated by [n.m. in bib.].
2. Books from which articles were taken are not mentioned separately.
3. Dates of first editions are given between square parentheses.
4. Hebrew books: titles are underlined and given in italics; Hebrew articles: Publications are underlined and given in italics.

Abraham, K., Dream and Myths: A Study in Race Psychology (trans. W.A. White), New York, 1913.

Abraham, N., "Notes on the Status of Ama (Exodus 212:7-11)", *Beit Mikra*, XXXVII, 1992, 289-301.

Ackroyd, P., Bible Bibliography, Oxford, 1974.

Adar, Z., *God in the Bible*, Tel-Aviv, 1984.

—, *Introduction to the Biblical World*, Tel-Aviv, 1977.

—, The Biblical Narrative, Jerusalem, 1971.

Aharoni, Y., *Atlas Carta of the Bible*, Jerusalem, 1970.

Ahuvia, A., "In The Shape of God Created Him", *Beit Mikra*, XXX, 1985, 361-9.

Albeck, S., "The Ten Commandments and the Principles of Faith", in B-Z. Segal (ed.), *The Ten Commandments*, Jerusalem, 1985, 199-221.

Albright, W.F., New Horizons in Biblical Research, London, Oxford, 1966.

—, YHWH And The Gods of Canaan, London, 1968.

Alter, R., The Art of Biblical Narrative, New York, 1968 [Heb. ed. 1981].

Amit, Y., *The Book of Judges*, Tel-Aviv, 1992.

Anbar, M., "Abrahamic Covenant — Genesis 15", *Shnaton*, III, 1978, 34-52. ["Genesis 15", JBL, CI, 1982, 39-55].

—, *Genesis Stories on Abraham* (M.A. Thesis, Tel-Aviv University), Tel-Aviv, 1964.

Anderson, B.W., Creation in Old Testament, London, 1984.

Anderson, G., "The Interpretation of Genesis 1:1 in the Targums", CBQ, LII, 1990, 21-29.

Andersen, G.W., A Decade of Bible Bibliography, Oxford, 1967.

Armerding, C.E., The Old Testament and Criticism, Grand Rapids, 1983.

Armstrong, J.H.S., The Myth of Paradise, London, 1969.

Ashbel, D., "Four Rivers Come From Eden", *Beit Mikra*, XV, 100-4.

Asselin, D.T., "The Notions of Dominion in Genesis", CBQ, XVI, 1954, 227-94.

Auerbach, E., Mimesis, Princeton, 1984 [1953].

Auffert, D., "Essai sur la structure litteraire de Gn. 12:1-4a", Bz, XXVI, 1982, 243-48.

Baker, D.W., "Diversity and Unity in The Literary Structure of Genesis", in Millard, A.R. & D.J. Wiseman, Essays on the Patriarchal Narratives, Leicester, 1980, 189-205.

Bakon, S., "Kedusha-Holiness", Dor LeDor, XVI, 1987, 2-9.

Bar-Efrat, S., *The Art of Narration in the Bible*, Tel-Aviv, 1979. [English: JSOT, series, LXX, Sheffield, 1989].

Barr, J., Comparative Philology and the Text of the Old Testament, Oxford, 1986.

—, Does Biblical Study Still Belong to Theology?, Birmingham, 1979.

—, The Bible as Literature, London, 1973.

—, "The Meaning of Mythology in Relation to the Old Testament", VT, IX, 1959, 1-10.

Barrick, D.W., "Current Trends and Tensions in Old Testament Textual Criticism",

BT, XXXV, 1984, 301-8.

Bar-Tana, A., *Genesis of Jewish Thought*, Tel-Aviv, 1973.

Barton, J., "Classifying Biblical Criticism", JSOT, XXIX, 1984, 19-35.

—, Reading the Old Testament: Method in Biblical Study, London, 1984.

Batto, B.F., "The Sleeping God: An Ancient Near Eastern Motif of Divine Sovereignty", Biblica, LXVIII, 1987, 153-177.

Beeston, A.F.L., "One Flesh", VT, XXXVI, 1986, 115-117.

Beily, J.A., "Initiation and the Primal Woman in Gilgamesh and Genesis 2-3", JBL, 1970, LXXXIX, 137-150.

Benedict, R., Patterns of Culture, London, [1935] 1961.

Ben-Reuven, S., "Son v. Boy and Child in The Bible", *Beit Mikra*, XXVIII, 1983, 147-49.

Bereshit Rabah, Jerusalem, 1971.

Bergsträsser, G., *Grammar of the Hebrew Language*, Jerusalem, 1972. [Hebräische Grammatik, Mit Benutzung der von E. Kautzch bearbeiteten 28. Auflage von W. Gesenius 'Hebräische Grammatik'), übersetzt ins Hebräische von M. ben-Asher].

Binson, J.J., "Archaeological Data and the Dating of the Patriarchs", in A.R. Millard & D.J. Wiseman, Essays on the Patriarchal Narratives, Leicester, 1980, 59-92.

Bird, P.A., "Male and Female Created He Them: Genesis 1:27 in the Content of the Priestly Account of Creation", Harvard Theological Review, LXXIV, 1981, 129-154.

Blau, J., A Grammar of Biblical Hebrew, Wiesbaden, 1976.

Boas, F., The Mind of The Primitive Man, London, 1963.

Breitbart, S., "Adam I and Adam II", Dor LeDor, XVI, 1988, 191-196.

—, "The Akeda — A Text of God", Dor LeDor, XII, 1986-7, 19-28.

Brichto, H.C., The Problem of 'Curse' in The Hebrew Bible (JBL Monograph, Series), Philadelphia, 1963.

Brossier, F., "Jacob at Penuel", La Monde de la Bible, XLVI, 1986, 39-40.

Brueggermann, W., "Of the Same Flesh and Bone (Genesis 2:23)", CBQ, XXXII, 1970, 532-40.

Buber, M., *The Way of The Bible*, Jerusalem, 1978.

Burns, D.E., "Dream Form in Genesis 2:4b-3:24: A Sleep in the Garden", JSOT, XXXVII, 1987, 3-14.

Budge, E.A.W., The Teachings of Amen-Em-Apt, Son of Kenekht, London, 1924.

—, Book Of The Dead, London, 1898.

Bury, J.B., The Idea of Progress: An Inquiry Into Its Origins and Growth, London, 1920.

Butzer, K.W., Environment and Archaeology, London, 1972.

Cameron, N.M., In The Beginning, Glasgow, 1980.

Carroll, M.P., "Genesis Reconstructed", in B. Lang, Anthropological Approaches to the Old Testament, London, 1985, 127-135.

Caspi, M., "Kaniti Ish et Yhwh", *Beit-Mikra*, XXXIII, 1988, 29-35.

Cassirer, E., Language and Myth, New York, 1964.

Cassuto, U.D., *A Commentary on The Book of Genesis*, Jerusalem, 1978.

—, *The Documentary Hypothesis and the Composition of the Pentateuch*, Jerusalem, 1965.

Childs, B.C., A Study of Myth in Genesis 1-11, Plymouth, 1955.

Clark, W.M., "A Legal Background to The Yahawist's Use of 'Good and Evil' in Genesis 2-3", JBL, XXXVIII, 1969, 266-78.
Clements, R.E., A Century of Old Testament Study, London, [1976,] 1983.
Clifford, R.J., "Genesis 1-3, Permission to Exploit Nature?", TBT, XXVI, 1988, 133-37.
Clines, D.J.A. et al., Art and Meaning: Rhetoric in Biblical Literature, Sheffield, 1984.
Clines, D.J.A., "Theme in Genesis 1-11", CBQ, XXXVIII, 1976, 483-501.
Coats, G.W., Genesis, Grand Rapids, 1983.
—, Saga, Tale, Novella, Fable, Sheffield, 1985.
Coder, S.M. & G.F. Howe, The Bible in Science and Creation, Chicago, 1966.
Cohen, C., "Studies in Extra-Biblical Inscriptions, I: The Semantic Range and Usage of the Terms AMA and SHIFHA", *Shnaton*, V-VI, 1982, xxv-xxxiii.
Cohn, R.L., "Narrative Structure and Canonical Perspective in Genesis", JSOT, XXV, 1983, 3-16.
Coleman, J.C., Abnormal Psychology and Modern Life (4th ed.), London, 1972.
Creager, H., "The Divine Image", in Bream, H.N. & others, Light Unto My Path, Philadelphia, 1974, 103-118.
Cross, F.M. Jr., Canaanite Myth And Hebrew Epic, Cambridge, Mass., 1973, 3-75.
—, "Yahweh and the Gods of the Patriarchs", Har. Th. Rev., LV, 1962, 225-259.
Cunningham, A., "Psychoanalitic Approaches to Biblical Narrative", in ed. D. Cohn-Sherbok, A Traditional Quest (JSOT series, CXIV), Sheffield, 1990, 113-132.
Dahan, H., *The Paths of Language*, Jerusalem, 1979.
Dambin, E., *Creation Story in The Bible And In Other Sources* (M.A. Diss., Tel-Aviv University), Tel-Aviv, 1974.
Daniélou, J., In The Beginning, Genesis 1-11, Baltimore, 1965.
Davidson, O., "The Mythical Foundation of History: A Religio-Semiotic Analysis of the Story of the Fall", LB, LI, 1982, 23-36.
Deurloo, K.A., "Te'shuka > Dependency <, Gen 4,7", ZAW, XCIX, 1987, 405-6.
Deutsch, H., A Psychoanalitical Study of the Myth of Dionysos & Apollo, New York, 1969.
Doukhan, J.B., The Literary Structure of Genesis Creation Story, (Ph.D. Diss., Andrews University), 1978.
Eichrodt, W., Theology of Old Testament, vol. I, Philadelphia, 1983.
—, "In the Beginning: A Contribution to the Interpretation of the First Word

of the Bible", in B.W. Anderson (ed.), Creation in Old Testament, London, 1984, 53-73.

Eliade, M., Patterns In Comparative Religion, London, 1958.

—, The Myth of the Eternal Return, New York, 1954.

Elitzur, Y., "The Covenant", *Hagut Bamikra*, IV, 1983, 34-45.

Emmanueli, Y.M., *The Book of Genesis*, Tel-Aviv, 1984.

Emerton, J.A., "The Origin of The Promises To The Patriarchs In The Older Sources of The Book of Genesis", VT, XXXII, 1982, 14-32.

Engnell, I., "'Knowledge' and 'Life' in the Creation Story", Supp. to VT, III, 1955, 103-119.

—, "The Pentateuch", Critical Essays on the Old Testament (trans. by J.T. Willis), London, 1970.

Epstein, I., Judaism, Harmondsworth, 1964.

Fenton, T.L., "Differing Approaches to the Theomachy Myth in Old Testament Writers", Studies in Bible and The Ancient Near East, Jerusalem, 1978, 337-381.

Fokkelman, J.P., Narrative Art in Genesis, Assen, 1975.

—, "Genesis", in R. Alter & F. Kermode, The Literary Guide to the Bible, London, 1987, 36-55.

Fox, E., "Can Genesis be Read as a Book?", Semeia, XLXI, 1989, 31-40.

Frankfort, H., The Birth of Civilization in the Near East, London, 1951.

Frankforth, H. & H.A., "Myth and reality", in Frankfort, H. et al., Before Philosophy: The Intellectual Adventure of Ancient Man: an Essay on Speculative Thought in the Ancient Near East, Chicago, 1946, 3-27.

Frazer, J.G., Folk-Lore in The Old Testament, London, 1918.

Freedman, R.D., "Woman, a Power Equal to Man", BAR, IXII, 1983, 56-58.

Freilich, M., "Myth, Method and Madness", CA, XVI, 1973, 207-26 [respond and comments: CA XVII, 1976, 137-141].

Freud, S., "Totem and Taboo" in Vol. XIII of the standard edition of The Complete Psychological Work (eds. T. Strachey & A. Freud), London, 1955, 1-162.

—, "The Interest of Psychoanalysis From the Point of View of the History of Civilization", in Vol. XIII of the standard edition of The Complete Psychological Work (eds. T. Strachey & A. Freud), London, 1955, 184-187.

Friedman, T., "And God's 'RU'ACH' Hovers Upon the Water", *Beit Mikra*, XXV, 1982, 309-12.

Fromm, E., Escape From Freedom, New York, 1941.

—, Man for Himself, London, 1949.

—, "On Obedience As a Psychological and Moral Problem", On Obedience and Other Essays, London, 1984, 1-8.

—, The Forgotten Language, New York, 1957.

—, You Shall Be As Gods, Greenwich, Conn., 1966.

Frye, N., Fables of Identity: Studies In Poetic Mythology, New York, 1963.

Frymer-Kensky, T., "The Atra-Hasis Epic and Its Significance For Our Understanding of Genesis 1-9", BA, XL(4), 1977, 147-55.

Funkenstein, A. *Studies in Medieval Biblical Exegesis (An Introduction)*, Tel-Aviv, 1990.

Garr, W.R., "The Grammar and Interpretation of Exodus 6:13", JBL, CXI, 3, 1992, 385-408.

Gaster, T.H., Myth Legend and Custom in the Old Testament, New York, 1969.

Geller, S.A., "Literary Approach to a Biblical Narrative", JQR, LXXIV, 1984, 408-415.

—, "Struggle At The Yabbok", JANES, XIV, 1982, 37-60.

Gianotti, C.R., "The Meaning of the Divine Name YHWH", BSa, CXLII, 1985, 38-51.

Gilead, Ch., "The Plain Meaning of the Cain And Abel Story", *Beit Mikra*, XXIX, 1984, 14-28.

Gitay, Z., "Hagar's Expulsion — A Tale Twice Told in Genesis", BR, II, 1986, 26-32.

Goedicke, H., "Adam's Rib", in A. Kort & S. Morschauser (ed.), Biblical and Related Studies Presented to Samuel Ywry, Winona Lake, 1985, 73-76.

Goldingay, J., "The Patriarchs in Scripture and History", in A.R. Millard & D.J. Wiseman, Essays on the Patriarchal Narratives, Leicester, 1980, 11-42.

Good, E.M., Irony in the Old Testament, London, 1965.

Gordon, C.H., Ugaritic Literature, Roma, 1949.

Goshen-Gotshtein, M.H., "The Rise of The Tiberian Bible Text", in A. Altman (ed.), Biblical And Other Studies, Cambridge, Mass., 1963, 79-123.

Granot, M., "Thou are Dust... (Genesis 3:19)", *Beit Mikra*, XVII, 1972, 310-319.

Grintz, Y.M., *The Book of Genesis: Its Authenticity and Antiquity*, Jerusalem, 1983.

Gruber, M.I., "Fear Anxiety and Reverence in Akkadian, Biblical Hebrew and Other North-West Semitic Languages", VT, XL, 1990, 441-422.

Gunn, D.M., "New Directions in the Study of Biblical Hebrew Narrative", JSOT, XXXIX, 1987, 65-75.

Gunkel, H., The Legends of Genesis, New York, 1964.

Hallo, W.B., "Biblical History in Near Eastern Setting: The Contextual Approach", in C.D. Evans, W.W. Hallo & J.B. White, Scripture In Context: Essays On The Comparative Method, Pittsburg, 1980, 1-27.

Handy, L.K., "Dissenting Deities or Obedient Angels: Divine Hierarchies in Ugarit and the Bible", Biblical Research, XXXV, 1990, 18-35.

Harrington, W., In The Beginning God..., Manchester, 1976.

Hauser, A.J., "Linguistic and Thematic Links Between Genesis 4:1-6 and 2-3", JETS, XXIII, 1980, 297-305.

—, "Genesis 2-3: The Theme of Intimacy and Alienation", in D.J. Clines et al., Art and Meaning: Rhetoric in Biblical Literature, Sheffield, 1982, 20-36.

Hess, R.S., "Splitting the Adam: The Usage of ADAM in Genesis 1-5", Studies in the Pentateuch (Supp. to VT, XLI), Leiden, 1990, 1-15.

Higgins, J.M., "The Myth of Eve The Temptress", JAAR, XLIV, 1976, 639-44.

Hill, E., "How Historical is Genesis 1-11?", TNB, LVIII, 1976, 400-407.

Hirshberg, H.H., Hebrew Humanism, Los Angeles, 1964.

Hirshberger, R., "Image et resemblance dans la tradition sacredotale Gen 1:26-28", Revieu Sacredotale Religieuse, LIX, 1985, 185-99.

Hoffmeier, J.K., "Some Thoughts on Genesis 1 & 2 and Egyptian Cosmology", JANES, XV, 1983, 39-49.

Hooke, S.H., Middle Eastern Mythology, Harmondsworth, 1963.

Hopfe, L.M., A History of the Interpretation of Genesis 4:1-16 and Its Relations for Biblical Hermeneutics (Ph.D. Diss.), Boston, 1965.

Hulme, T.E., Speculations, London, 1960.

Hurowitz, V., "When Did God Finish Creation?", BR, IV, 1987, 12-14.

Index of Articles on Jewish Studies, Jerusalem, 1970-89.

Irwin, W.A., "The Hebrews", in H. Frankfort et al., The Intellectual Adventure of Ancient Man: an Essay on Speculative Thought in Ancient Near East, Chicago, 1946, 223-260.

Jackson, T.A., "Creation Stories of the Ancient Near East", Biblica, XV, 1983, 39-49.

Jacob, B., Genesis (trans. from German by E.I. Jacob & W. Jacob), New York, 1974.

Jacobsen, T., The Treasures of Darkness: a History of Mesopotamian Religion, London, 1976.

Jobling, D., "The Myth Semantics of Genesis 2:46-3:24", SEMEIA, XVIII, 1980, 41-49 [a further elaboration of this article in: "Myth and its Limits in

Genesis 2:4b-3:24", The Sense of Biblical Narratives (JSOT supp. series), Sheffield, 1986, 17-43].

Joins, K., "God Almighty", Bib. Ill., xII, 1986, 17-18.

Joines, K.R., "The Serpent in Genesis 3", ZAW, LXXXVII, 1975, 1-11.

Jonson, B., "Who Reckoned Righteousness to Whom", Svensk Exegeticsk, Arsbok, LI-LII, 1986-7, 108-115.

Jónsson, G.A., The Image of God: Genesis 1:26-28 in a Century of Old Testament Research (trans. by L. Svendsen & H.S. Cheney), Stockholm, 1988.

Josipovici, G., The Book of God, London, 1988.

de-Jules, R., "On Freilich's Interpretation of Genesis 1-3", CA, XVII, 1976, 139-42.

Jung, C.G., The Archetypes and the Collective Unconscious, vol. IX of the Collected Works, London, 1950.

Kaufmann, Y., *The History of the Israelite Religion*, Tel-Aviv, 1973.

Keller, W., The Bible as History, New York, 1974.

Kenyon, F., The Bible and Archaeology, London, 1940.

Kikawada, I.M., "Two Notes on Eve", JBL, XCI, 1972, 33-37.

Kirk, G.S., The Nature of Greek Myths, New York, 1975.

Kirkpatrick, P.G., The Old Testament and Folklore Study (JSOT supp. 62), Sheffield, 1988.

Kitchen, K.A., Ancient Orient and Old Testament, Tyndale Press, 1966.

Koch, K. The Growth of Biblical Tradition, London, 1966.

Kogut, S., "'To this ISHA will be called, because from ISH this one was taken' (Genesis 2:23): A Folk Etymology?", *Tarbitz*, LI, 1981-2, 293-98.

Kodell, J., "Jacob Wrestles with Esau (Gen. 32:23-32)", Biblical Theology Bulletin, X, 1980, 65-70.

Koler, Y., "Creation of Man", *Beit Mikra*, XXVIII, 1983, 223-29.

Koler, Y., "HA'Elohim — a Definite Article or Enlonged Name of God", *Beit Mikra*, XXII, 1977, 477-82.

Kramer, S.N., Enki and Ninhursag, New Haven, 1945.

—, Gilgamesh and The Huluppu Tree, Chicago, 1938.

Kravitz, N., Genesis: A New Interpretation of The First Three Chapters, New York, 1967.

Kutler, L., "Structural Semantics Approach to Israelite Communal Terminology", JANES, XVI, 1982, 69-77.

Lambden, S.N., "From Fig Leaves to Fingernails: Some Notes on the Garments of Adam and Eve in the Hebrew Bible and Select Early Post Biblical Jewish Writing" in P. Morris & D. Sawyer, A Walk in the Garden (JSOT sup. No. 136), Sheffield, 1992, 74-90.

Lambert, W.G. & A.R. Millard, Atra-Hasis: The Babylonian Story Of The Flood, Oxford, 1969.

Landes, G.M., "Creation Tradition in Proverbs 8:22-31 and Genesis 1", in H.N. Bream & others, A Light Unto My Path (Old Testament Studies in honour of M. Meyers), Philadelphia, 1974, 279-93.

Landy, F., Paradoxes in Paradise (Ph.D. Diss. for Sussex University), Lewis, 1983 [published as a book: Sheffield, 1983].

Lang, A., Myth Ritual and Religion, London, 1887.

Lang, A., The Making of Religion, London, 1985.

Lang, B., Anthropological Approaches to the Old Testament, London, 1985.

Lapid, P., "Illumination: Touching the Forbidden Fruit", BR, IV, 1989, 42-43.

Laplanché, J. & J-B. Pontalis, The Language of Psychoanalysis, London, 1985.

Lawton, R.B., "Genesis 2:24: Trite or Tragic?", JBL, LV, 1986, 97-8.

Leach, E.R., "Genesis as Myth", in J. Middleton, ed., Myth and Cosmos, London, 1967, 1-13.

Leeser, I., The Holy Bible (The Twenty-four Books of), Hebrew Pub. Co., New York.

Leibowitz, N., "How To Read a Chapter in the Bible", *Hagut Bamikra*, I, 129-138.

—, *Thesis on Genesis*, Jerusalem, 1983.

Leibowitz, Y., *Judaism, Jewish People and the State of Israel*, Jerusalem, 1979.

—, *The Faith of Maimonides*, Tel-Aviv, 1980.

Lerner, Y., "The Forms 'Ha'Elohim' and 'Elohim' in the Pentateuch and Prophets", *Leshonenu*, XLVIII-IX, 1985, 195-8.

Lévi-Strauss, C., "The Structural Study of Myth", in T.A. Sebeok, Myth: A Symposium, London, 1955, 80-106.

—, The Savage Mind, London, 1966.

Livingston, G.H., The Pentateuch In Its Cultural Environment, Grand Rapids, 1965.

Magonet, J., "The Themes of Genesis 2-3", in M. Morris & D. Sawyer A Walk in the Garden (JSOT sup. No. 136), Sheffield, 1992, 39-46.

Malinowsky, Myth, Science and Religion, New York, 1954.

Mandelkern, S., Vetris Testamenti Concurdancia: Hebraicue Atque Chaladicae, 12th imprint with adaptations by M. Goshen-Gotshtein & P. Margolin, Tel-Aviv, 1986.

Mattson, D.L., The Blessings Themes In The Abraham Story And Their Implications for the Date and Purpose of the Story. Ph.D. Diss. for the University of Michigan, 1983.

Marzel, Y., "Tree of Knowing Good and Evil — Comprehension of Life And

Death", *Beit Mikra*, XXIX, 1984, 352-60.

Mazor, Y., "Genesis 22. The Ideological Rhetoric and the Psychological Composition", Biblica, LXVII, 1986, 81-88.

McCarthy, D.J., O.T. Covenant, Oxford, 1972.

McConville, J.C., "Interpreting Genesis 1-11", in N.M. Cameron (ed.), In the Beginning, Glasgow, 1980, 6-19.

Mckay, H.A., "Jacob Makes it Across the Yabbok", JSOT, XXXVII, 1987, 3-13.

McKane, W., Studies In Patriarchal Narratives, Edinburgh, 1979.

McKenzie, J.L., "The Literary Characteristics of Genesis 2-3", Theological Studies, XV, 1954, 541-72.

Mendenhall, G.E., "The Shady Side of Wisdom: The Date and Purpose of Genesis 3", in N.D. Bream (ed.), A Light Unto My Path, Philadelphia, 1974, 319-333.

Millard, A.R., "Methods of Studying the Patriarchal Narratives as Ancient Texts", in Millard, A.R. & D.J. Wiseman, Essays On The Patriarchal Narratives, Leicester, 1980, 43-58.

—, "The Etymology of Eden", VT, XXXIV (1), 1984, 103-106.

Millard, A.R. & D.J. Wiseman, Essays On The Patriarchal Narratives, Leicester, 1980.

Miller, P.D., Genesis 1-11: Studies in Structure And Theme, Sheffield, 1978.

Milward, P., The Bible as Literature, Tokyo, 1983.

Moberly, R.W.L., "Abraham's Righteousness", Studies in the Pentateuch (Supp. to VT, XLI), 1990, 103-130.

Mosten, J., "The Testing of Abraham", Dor LeDor, XVII, 1989, 237-242.

Motyer, J.A., The Revelation of The Divine Name, London, 1959.

Naidorff, B.O., "A Man to Work the Soil (Genesis 2-3)", JSOT, V, 1978, 2-14.

Nadel, M., "Male and Female", *Beit Mikra*, XXIII, 1977, 80-85.

—, *The Bible and Cultures of The Ancient World*, Tel-Aviv, 1962.

Naor, M., "Bereshit Bara — Bereshit Bro: Comments to Genesis 1:1", *Beit Mikra*, XVI, 1971, 306-11.

Oden, R.A. Jr., "Transformations in Near Eastern Myths: Genesis 1-11 and the Old Babylonian Epic of Atrahasis", Religion, 1981, 21-37.

Old Testament Abstracts, The Catholic Association of America, Washington, D.C., Vols: I-X.

Orlinsky, H.M., "Enigmatic Bible Passages: The Plain Meaning of Genesis 1:1-3", Biblical Archaeologist, XLVI, 1983, 203-7.

Ortega Y Gaset, J., Man in Crisis, London, 1959.

Otto, R., The Idea of the Holy (trans. by J.W. Harvey), London, 1957.

Ovid, Metamorphoses (trans. by M.M. Innes), Harmondsworth, 1978.

Patric, A. & A. Scull, Rhetoric and Biblical Interpretation (JSOT series, LXXXII), Sheffield, 1990.

Pardes, I., Countertraditions in the Bible (A Feminist Approach), Cambridge, Mass, 1992.

Parsons, T., "The Father Symbol: An Appraisal in the Light of Psychoanalitic and Sociological Theory", in L. Bryson, ed., Symbols and Values: An Initial Study, N.Y., 1954, 523-544.

Pearce, E.K.V., Who Was Adam, Exeter, 1976.

Pedersen, J., "Wisdom and Immortality", Supp. VT, III, 1955, 238-46.

Pettinato, G., "The Royal Archives of Tel Mardikh — Ebla", BA, XXXIX/2, 1976, 44-52.

Pope, M.H., El in the Ugaritic Texts, Supp. VT, II, 1955, 1-15.

Portnoy, S.L. & D.L. Peterson, "Genesis Wellhausen And The Computer", ZAW, 1984, 421-25.

Pritchard, J.B., Ancient Near Eastern Texts Relating to The Old Testament (ANET), New Jersey, 1969.

Rad, G. von, The Problem of the Hexateuch and Other Essays, London, 1965.

Radday, Y., "Genesis, Wellhausen and The Computer", ZAW, XCIV, 1982, 467-81. This is an abridged abstract of Y. Radday, H. Shore, M.A. Pollatchek & D. Wickmann, Genesis: An Authorship Study In Computer-Assisted Statistical Linguistics, Rome, 1985.

—, "The Four Rivers of Paradise", Hebrew Studies, XXIII, 1982, 23-31.

Rand, A., "The Objectivist Ethics", in The Virtue of Selfishness, New York, 1964, 13-35.

Reick, T., Myth and Guilt, London, 1958.

—, The Creation of Woman, New York, 1960.

Reicke, B., "The Knowledge Hidden in The Tree of Paradise", JSS, I, 1956, 193-201.

Rin, Z., *Acts of The Gods: The Ugaritic Epic Poetry*, Jerusalem, 1968.

Robertson, D.A., Linguistic Evidence in Dating Hebrew Poetry (Ph.D. Diss. for Yale University), California, 1966.

Rodin-Oberski, T., *The Patriarchs in Hebron And Sodom; Genesis 19-19*, Jerusalem, 1982.

Rofé, A., *The Belief In Angels In The Bible And In Early Israel* (Ph.D. Diss., The University of Jerusalem), Jerusalem, 1969.

Rogerson, J.W., Anthropology and Old Testament, Sheffield, 1984.

—, Myth in Old Testament Interpretation, New York, 1974.

—, Old Testament Criticism in the 19th Century England and Germany, London, 1984.

Rosenbaum, M. & A.N. Silberman, Pentateuch (with Rashi comm.), London, 1929.

Rosenberg, J.W., "The Garden Story Forward and Backward: The Non-narrative Dimension of Genesis 2-3", Prooftexts, I, 1981, 1-27.

Rubinstein, E., *Contemporary Hebrew and Ancient Hebrew*, Tel-Aviv, 1980.

Ruprecht, E., "Vorgegebene Tradition und Theologische Gestellung in Gen. xii:1-2", VT, XXIX/2, 1979, 171-188.

Russell, B., History of Western Philosophy, London, [1946] 1962.

Sacks, R., "The Lion and the Ass: A Commentary on the Book of Genesis", Interpretation, VIII 2/3, 1980, 29-101.

Sarna, N.H., "An Anticipatory Use of Information As a Literary Feature of the Genesis Narratives", in R.E. Friedman (ed.), The Creation of Sacred Literature: Composition and Redaction of the Biblical Test [New Eastern Studies, XXII], 77-82].

Sasson, L.M., "'W^{e}lo Yitbosasu' (Genesis 2:25) and its Implications", Biblica, LXVI, 1985, 418-421.

Sawyer, J.F.A., "The meaning of 'God's Image' in Genesis 1-11", JTS, XXV, 1974, 418-26.

—, "The Image of God, The Wisdom of Serpents and the Knowledge of Good and Evil", in P. Morris & D. Sawyer, A Walk in the Garden (JSOT sup. No. 136), Sheffield, 1992, 64-73.

Scaer, D.P., "The Problems of Inerrancy and Historicity In Connection With Genesis 1-3", CTQ, XLI/1, 1977, 5-21.

Scullion, J.J., "Some Reflection on the State of the Patriarchal Studies", Abr-Nahrain, XXI, 1983, 50-65.

Selman, M.J., "Comparative Customs and The Patriarchal Age", A.R. Millard & D.J. Wiseman, Essays On The Patriarch Narratives, Leicester, 1980, 93-138.

Silberman, M.H., "Syntactic Notes On the Waw Consecutive", AOAT, XXII, 1973, 167-175.

Simon, A., "Notes on The Binding of Isaac", *Hagut Bamikra*, I, 1973, 163-70.

Simon, U., Time And Space In Biblical Thinking (Ph.D. Diss., University of Jerusalem), Jerusalem, 1961.

Skinner, J., Critical Commentary on Genesis, Edinburgh, 1980 [1910].

Smith, G.V. "Structure and Purpose in Genesis 1-11: Sources and Form-Criticism v. Rhetorical Criticism", JETS, XXII, 1977, 307-319.

Smith, J.N.P., "The Use of Divine Names as Superlatives", AJSL, XLV, 1928, 212-220.

Smith, P.J., "A Semotactical Approach to the Meaning of the Term 'rûah elohim' in Genesis 1:2", JNSL, VIII, 1980, 99-104.

Speiser, E.A., Genesis (The Anchor Bible), New York, 1964.

—, "'people' and 'nation' of Israel", Oriental and Biblical Studies (by E.A. Speiser), ed. J.J. Finkelstein & M. Greenberg, Philadelphia, 1967, 160-170.

Spencer, R.A., ed., Orientation and Disorientation: Studies in Literary Criticism and Biblical Literary Criticism, Pittsburg, 1980.

Spiegel, N., *A History of Ancient Ethics*, Jerusalem, 1985.

Spinoza, B. de, *Tractatus Theologico-Politicus* (Hebraice raddidit et pauca adnotavi — Ch. Wirszubski), Jerusalem, 1983.

—, *Ethics* (trans. J. Klatzkin), Jerusalem, 1967.

Steinberg, Y., *The Bible Dictionary*, Tel-Aviv, 1977.

Sternberg, M., The Poetics of Biblical Narrative, Bloomington, 1985.

Sutherland, O., "The Organization of the Abraham Promise Narratives", ZAW, XCII, 1983, 337-43.

Tadmor, H., "Treaty and Oath in the Ancient Near East: An Historian Approach", *Shnaton*, V-VI, 1982, 149-173.

Talstra, E., "Genesis Bit by Bit", Biblica, LXVII, 1986, 557-564.

Thompson, T.L., The Historicity of the Patriarchal Narratives, New York, 1974.

Todd, W., New Light on Genesis, London, 1978.

Tocker, N., "The Voice of the Narrator in Genesis", *Criticism and Interpretation*, XVI, 1981, 33-69.

Tosato, A., "On Genesis 2:24", CBQ, 1990, 389-409.

Tresmontant, C., A Study of Hebrew Thought, New York, 1960.

Trible, P., God and the Rhetoric of Sexuality, Philadelphia, 1978.

—, Texts of Terror, Philadelphia, 1984.

Tsumura, D.T., The Earth and Waters in Genesis 1-2, (A Linguistic Investigation), Sheffield, 1989.

Tur-Sinai, N.H., *Pshuto Shel Mikra*, Jerusalem, 1962.

—, (Turtshiner), "Sin Lies at Your Door", *Tarbitz*, XVI, 1971, 22-26.

Tweig, A., "Genesis 1 and the Sabbath", *Beit Mikra*, XVII, 1972.

Tzevat, M., "Two Old Testament Stories and Their Hittite Analogies", JAOS, CIII, 1983, 321-26.

Ultredt, A.W., "Genesis 1 og Literaere Beider", NTT, LXXXI, 1980, 37-54.

Van Seters, J., Abraham in History and Tradition, New Haven, 1975.

Van Wolde, E., Words Become Worlds: Semantic Studies of Gen.1-11, Leiden, 1994.

Vawter, B., On Genesis: A New Reading, London, 1977.

Wagner, N.E., A Literary Analysis of Genesis 12-36 (Ph.D. Diss. for the University of Toronto), Toronto, 1965.

Wallace, N.H., The Eden Narrative (Harvard Semitic Monographs), Atlanta, 1985.

Walsh, J.T., "Genesis 2:4-3:24, Synchronic Approach", JBL, XCVI, 1977, 161-177.

Warner, S.M., "Primitive Saga Man", VT, XXIX, 1979, 325-35.

Weil, D. & D. Cohen, "Progress in Deductive Research on the Original Performance of Tiberian Accents", *Leshonenu*, LXXX, 1989, 7-30.

Weinfeld, M., "B^{e}rith — Covenant v. Obligation", Biblica, LVI, 1975, 120-128.

—, "God The Creator in Genesis 1 and in Isaia B's Prophecy", *Tarbitz*, XXXVII, 1968, 105-32.

—, "In the Image of God", *TArbitz*, XXXVII, 1968, 113-116.

Weisman, Z., "National Consciousness in the Patriarchal Promises", JSOT, XXXI, 1985, 55-73.

Weiss, M., The Bible From Within, Jerusalem, 1984.

Wenham, G.J., "Genesis: An Authorship Study and Current Pentateuchal Criticism", JSOT, XLII, 1988, 3-18.

—, "The Religion of The Patriarchs", in A.R. Millard & D.J. Wiseman, Essays On The Patriarchal Narratives, Leicester, 1980, 157-188.

Westermann, C., Creation, London, 1971.

—, Genesis 1-11, London, 1984.

—, Genesis 12-36, London, 1984.

—, The Promises to the Fathers, Philadelphia, 1980.

White, H.C., "Structural Analysis of the Narrative", in J. Buss (ed.), Encounter With the Text, Philadelphia, 1979, 45-66.

White, J.B., Scripture in Context: Essays on the Comparative Method, Pittsburg, 1980.

Whybray, R.N., The Making of the Pentateuch: A Methodological Study, (JSOT supp. 53), Sheffield, 1987.

Wilenski, R.H., The Meaning of Modern Sculpture, London, 1932.

Williams, A.J., "The Relationship of Genesis 3:20 to the Serpent", ZAW, LXXXIX, 1977, 357-74.

Wiseman, D.J., Clues to Creation, London, 1977.

Wyat, N., "Where Adam Dwelt: The Meaning of Genesis 3:23", VT, XXXVII, 1988, 117-22.

Young, E., Studies in Genesis 1, Grand Rapids, 1976.

Zakowitz, Y., "On the Anticipatory Clue in Biblical Narrative", *Beer-Sheba*, II, 1985, 85-105.

—, "The Woman in Biblical Narrative", *Beit Mikra*, XXXII, 1987, 14-32.

Zmudi, Y., "The Inner Struggle in The Binding Story", *Beit Mikra*, XXX, 1985, 382-87.

Collingwood College
South Road
Durham DH1 3LT
Tel. 0191 374 4500